2nd Edition

Learning

BASIC

for

TANDY®

Computers

by

David A. Lien

COMPUSOFT®
PUBLISHING

International Standard Book Number: 0-932760-43-0

Library of Congress Catalog Card Number: 86-71471

10 9 8 7 6 5 4 3 2 1

Printed in the United States of America

Table of Contents

Acknowledgments

The following played key roles in the creation of this book:

Project Coordinator: Jackie Bohan
Technical Researchers:
Dan Gookin
Jody Bailey
Editorial Director: Inez Goldberg
Production Coordinator: Janice Scanlan
Cartoonist: Bob Stevens
Cover Design: Masar/Johnston Advertising and Design
Cover Photo: Charles Smith

A Personal Note from the Author

Expansion of the Tandy MS-DOS computer line is an exciting development in the growth of personal computing. These powerful but modestly priced computers will bring knowledge and prosperity to countless new users. It's again an honor and a pleasure to write the official BASIC language tutorial for new Tandy computers.

The best of my earlier writings on the BASIC language is included, customized for these latest versions of BASIC -- plus much more. The style is light and non-threatening since I have no insecurities to pass along. There is no reason why learning should be intimidating.

So, sit back, relax, read slowly as though savoring a good novel, and above all, let your imagination wander. I'll supply all the routine facts and techniques. The real enjoyment begins when *your* imagination starts the creative juices flowing and the Computer becomes a tool in *your* hands. *You* become the master -- not the other way around. At that time, it will evolve from just a pretty box of parts into an extension of your own personality.

Enjoy your new Tandy Computer!

Dr. David A. Lien
San Diego -- 1986

Introduction

Learning BASIC for Tandy Computers is organized into 5 major sections.

A. The TUTORIAL is divided into 9 parts:

Part 1 -- Getting Started
Teaches how to set the realtime clock and calendar, FORMAT and **backup** disks, load BASIC, and enter and RUN a program. Also teaches use of the EDITor, the special keys and automatic line numbering.

Part 2 -- BASIC Fundamentals
Teaches beginning BASIC. Covers math operators, using the Computer as a calculator and SAVEing and LOADing files with disk. Also teaches looping, formatting with TAB, INTeger functions, RaNDom numbers, and READing DATA.

Part 3 -- Strings
Begins intermediate BASIC with a miscellany of BASIC "odds and ends" and a comprehensive look at Strings.

Part 4 -- Variable Precision and Math
Teaches the use of SiNGle and DouBLe precision numbers and intrinsic, trigonometric and DEFined FuNctions.

Part 5 -- Display Formatting
Teaches the use of LOCATE, the power of INKEY$, INPUT$, and PRINT USING, COLORing in the text mode, and using a printer.

Part 6 -- Arrays
Teaches how to create and use single and multi-DIMension arrays and to use search/sort techniques.

Part 7 -- Sound
Teaches how to use the SOUND feature.

Part 8 -- Miscellaneous
Introduces data processing. Teaches advanced features of BASIC including methods for SAVEing, MERGEing and CHAINing, PEEK and POKE, and logical operators. Concludes with some of BASIC's more "obscure" features.

Part 9 -- Program Control
Teaches flowcharting and debugging techniques.

B. ANSWERS TO THE EXERCISES found in the chapters.

C. USER PROGRAMS--examples of interesting and practical programs ready to type in and use. (Some are for business, some for education, some for fun.)

D. APPENDICES which provide useful reference tables and charts.

E. The INDEX, for easy reference after you've learned it all but forgotten where you learned it.

SECTION A

BASIC TUTORIAL

PART 1

GETTING STARTED

The Premise

Learning BASIC for Tandy Computers teaches Elementary and Intermediate BASIC and includes a brief introduction to Sequential File handling.

We wrote this book to be used with all the Tandy MS-DOS computers. Since our aim was to make it equally applicable to each computer, we've made certain assumptions.

We assume:

1. You are using Microsoft MS-DOS (version 2.11 or 3.2, depending upon which computer you have).

2. Your computer has a minimum of 256K of memory and one floppy disk drive.

3. You have a recommended monitor.

4. All the setup procedures outlined in the manual that came with your computer have been followed.

NOTE: At the time this book was written, the most current releases of BASIC and Disk Operating System (DOS) were:

Tandy 1000 and 1000 EX
BIOS ROM version 01.01.00
Microsoft MS-DOS version 2.11
Tandy version 02.11.22
GW-BASIC 2.02
TANDY 1000 GWBASIC 2.02
Tandy version 01.01.00

Tandy 2000
MS-DOS version 02.11.03
BIOS version 02.02.00
GW-BASIC 2.02
TANDY 2000 GWBASIC 2.02
Tandy version 01.01.00

Tandy 1000 SX
BIOS ROM version 01.01.00
Microsoft MS-DOS version 3.20
Tandy version 03.20.00
GW-BASIC 3.20
TANDY 1000 GWBASIC 3.20
Tandy version 03.20.00

Tandy 3000 and 3000 HL
BIOS ROM version 01.01.00
Microsoft MS-DOS version 3.20
Tandy version 03.20.00
GW-BASIC 3.20
Tandy version 03.20.00

Chapter 1

Getting Ready

A Real Turn On

Locate the power switch, and turn the Computer ON. Place the MS-DOS SYSTEM diskette with its label up in Drive **A** and close the door.

> On one-drive machines, **A** is the only drive. On the two-drive machines, except the 3000s, **A** is the **bottom** drive. On the 3000s, **A** is the **top** drive.

The Computer gives itself a perfunctory check up, the disk drive(s) whirs, and the screen displays copyright information then asks for the date:

```
Enter new date: _
```

Type in today's date using either format:

`12-1-87` or `12/1/87`

and press the **ENTER** key.

The screen then displays a time, such as:

```
Current time is  0:01:30.00
```

The "current time" is how long the Computer has been ON, or how long it's been since the time was last set. Computers keep track of time in the 24 hour system, so 2:15 in the afternoon would be written as:

```
14:15:00.00
```

accurate to 1/100 of a second.

Computers with a built-in "real time" clock (the 3000s) and those with optional clock boards will show the "real time," instead of the elapsed time.

My wristwatch says 1:26 (afternoon) so I'll type:

`13:26` and press **ENTER**.

You type in your own time.

The colon (:) that separates the hour and minute is found on the same key as the semicolon (;) and, as on an ordinary typewriter keyboard, requires that we press a **SHIFT** key to type it.

Computers remember the time only as accurately as we enter it, but *hour* and *minute* are usually close enough for government work. The date and time are stored in memory for future reference but have little value in our early study of BASIC.

Now that we've done it and know how to do it, we can reveal this little secret: it's not mandatory to enter **either** the date or time. To bypass them in the future, just respond to both opportunities by pressing **ENTER**. (Computers with real time clocks will thereby insert the correct date and time.)

Assuming all is well, the bottom Line will say:

```
A>
```

which tells us that we are at the SYSTEM, or COMMAND, level of computer control and that Drive A is "logged on" ready for action. From this Disk Operating System (DOS) control level, we can do all sorts of things. Our mission in this book, however, is **Learning BASIC**. To learn to do those other things, see my other books.

Start with **MS-DOS Volume 1, The Basics**, (Radio Shack Cat. No. 25-1506) available through your Radio Shack dealer, followed by **MS-DOS Volume 2, Advanced Applications**, (Radio Shack Cat. No. 25-1507).

Computers don't usually care if we use lower case or capital letters, but since beginning programmers traditionally use UPPER case, we will use only UPPER case throughout this book. To LOCK into the upper case mode, press the key marked **CAPS** or **CAPS LOCK**. When the caps lock light comes on, the keyboard is in UPPER CASE mode and we need not use the **SHIFT** keys for capital letters -- only for characters **above** the numbers and other special keys.

What's on the Disk?

Let's look at the list of programs that came on the SYSTEM diskette that's in Drive A. This activity is called "pulling a DIRectory." Type:

`DIR` and press **ENTER**

Few of the 2 dozen file names are of concern to us in this book, but look for the one named **BASIC**. It can program the Computer to speak BASIC, and that is what this book is all about.

Find the **CTRL** key to the left of the **A** key. Type DIR again and while the listing is scrolling by, press **CTRL** and tap the **S** key. This freezes the display so we can study it. To restart the listing, tap any key.

If your computer has a **HOLD** key, you can use it to freeze displays. To "unfreeze," press **HOLD** a second time.

Type:

`DIR` **ENTER**

again; this time freeze the display near its beginning. Look for a program named:

```
FORMAT
```

Then "unfreeze" the display.

FORMATting a Diskette

We need some diskettes to store our programs and assignments on. However, if we try to save them on a blank diskette, they won't stick. The FORMAT program writes special magnetic tracks on a diskette so it can remember.

A large amount of space on the SYSTEM disk is needed for SYSTEM, or DOS, information. This SYSTEM information is not needed on other diskettes, which leaves much more room on them for program and data storage. We will call a diskette containing the entire Disk Operating System, a **SYSTEM** diskette. One that contains only the information recorded by the FORMAT process will be called a **DATA** diskette.

Standard 360K drives (1000, 1000 EX, 1000 SX, and 3000 HL) take double-sided, double-density, 40-track diskettes (Radio Shack Cat. No. 26-412), and 1.2M drives take double-sided, *high*-density diskettes (Radio Shack Cat. No. 26-422). The Tandy 2000 can use double-sided, double-density diskettes in either 40 or 80-track format (Radio Shack Cat. No. 26-410).

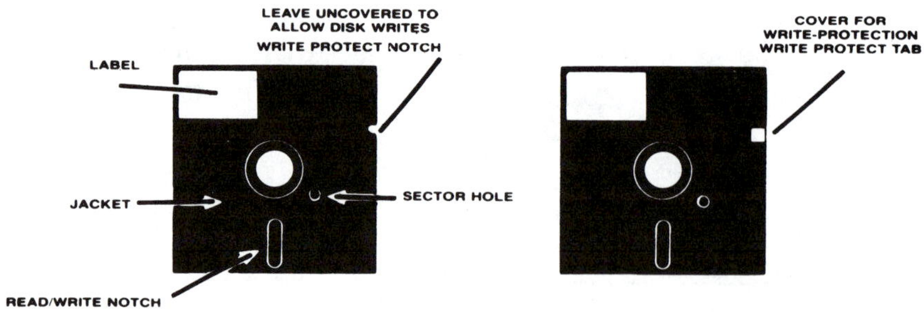

Check to be sure the original SYSTEM diskette is protected by a write tab (or has no notch), then put it back in Drive A.

Before FORMATting a diskette, it should be erased with an inexpensive "bulk eraser" of the type commonly used to erase cassette tapes. This process ensures that any information previously saved is removed, and it thoroughly "agitates" the iron oxide particles making sure they are awake. The result is a better quality recording. If you don't have a bulk eraser handy, buy one as soon as possible (Radio Shack Cat. No. 44-232).

To FORMAT a DATA diskette, type:

`FORMAT A:` **ENTER**

On a 2-drive system, you can avoid having to swap diskettes. With your SYSTEM disk is Drive A, insert a blank disk in Drive B and type:

`FORMAT B:` **ENTER**

and follow the instructions on the screen.

Be sure the blank diskette you insert does **not** have a write-protect tab.

Listen to the disk drive noises, and watch the display. They give a good hint of what's happening.

When the process is done, the screen will say:

`Format complete`

and will display the total bytes of storage space available on the just-formatted disk.

A byte is approximately the amount of space required to store one keystroke.

Type Y **ENTER** in answer to the question, `Format another (Y/N)?` Remove the FORMATted diskette, and FORMAT a second one.

Backup

Our next task is to make a complete *backup* (safety copy) of the original SYSTEM diskette. We'll use that *backup* copy as our *working master* and store the *original* away for safe keeping. This precaution may save a trip to the computer store to exchange a damaged original diskette. As the owner, you are allowed to make as many copies of the SYSTEM diskette as needed for your personal use, subject to any provisions stated in the factory notice.

Check again to be sure the *original* SYSTEM diskette is protected by a write tab, then insert it in Drive A. To make a the *backup* copy, type:

```
DISKCOPY        ENTER
```

and follow the instructions on the screen.

2000 users, make sure you DISKCOPY onto a diskette that is FORMATted.

If you have a 2-drive system, it's easier to place the blank diskette in Drive B, the SYSTEM master in Drive A, and type:

```
DISKCOPY A: B:        ENTER
```

Remember: On most 2-drive computers, A is the bottom drive and B is the top. On the 3000s it's just the opposite.

When the DISKCOPY program is complete, it will say so.

The diskette created by DISKCOPY is identical to the *original* SYSTEM disk. Hide the original away in a safe location, and write-protect the new *working master* before placing it back in Drive A.

Getting Down to BASIC

The SYSTEM disk contains that program named BASIC which can program the Computer to speak BASIC. To pour these instructions inside the Computer's "head," type:

```
BASIC        ENTER
```

which means, "Load in the program named BASIC from the diskette found in Drive A."

1. SIT DOWN
2. ....
THIS IS PRETTY BASIC...

The 1000/3000 SYSTEM disks contain a second program named BASICA. It is included to maintain compatibility with the IBM version of BASIC, which is called BASICA. Because BASIC and BASICA produce identical results, using either one is OK.

The Computer responds with:

```
OK
```

which means, "OK, I'm ready to speak BASIC." We begin learning BASIC in the next chapter.

Turning the Disk System Off

It's a good idea to exit BASIC and return to the SYSTEM, or DOS, level **first** before turning the Computer OFF. The command is very simple. Just type:

```
SYSTEM        ENTER
```

This is our way of telling BASIC, "I'm done!"

Once BASIC has escorted us back to MS-DOS's A> prompt, remove **all** diskettes before turning the system OFF. Punishment for failure to do so may be a "zapped" disk, one with some of its information accidentally erased or scrambled.

Learned in Chapter 1

Commands	Miscellaneous
DIR	Turning the Computer ON and OFF
FORMAT.	Setting the TIME
DISKCOPY	Setting the DATE
SYSTEM	How to load in BASIC
	Returning to SYSTEM level
	CTRL S (HOLD)

Chapter 2

Computer Etiquette

From the moment we turn them on, Tandy MS-DOS Computers follow a well-defined set of rules for coping with us, the "master." This makes them easy to use. To a large extent, all we have to do is say the right thing (via the keyboard) at the right time. Of course, there are lots of "right things" to say; putting them together for a purpose is called *programming*.

In this Chapter we'll start a conversation with our Computer and teach it some simple social graces. At the same time, you'll learn the fundamentals of computer etiquette. You'll even write your first computer program!

Getting READY

If you turned the Computer OFF, turn it back ON as described in Chapter 1. After entering the date and time, type:

```
BASIC        ENTER
```

to enter BASIC. (Remember, 1000 and 3000 users can also type BASICA.)

When:

```
Ok

_
```

appears, we're set to "go" again. The blinking line is called the *cursor*. The Computer is saying:

"I'm ready -- it's your turn!"

To make sure we start off with a clean slate -- erasing all traces of prior programs or tests -- type NEW and press ENTER. The Computer responds with:

```
OK

_
```

What Is a Computer Program?

A program is a sequence of instructions the Computer stores until we command it to follow (or "execute") them. Many programs for the Tandy Computers are written in this language called BASIC. The very name BASIC tells how easy it is to learn!

Let's write a simple one-Line program to let the Computer meet us.

Don't bother to use the SHIFT key; letters are always *capital* once we press the CAPS (or CAPS LOCK) key and the caps light is lit.

Type the following Line, *exactly* as shown:

```
10 PRINT "YOU ARE A COMPUTER PROGRAMMER."
```

Do **not** hit the ENTER key yet!

If you made a typing error, don't worry. Just use the BACKSPACE key. (On the 3000s, this key is labeled [←] and is located in the top row above [ENTER ↵].) Each time you press this key, the rightmost character will be erased. If the error was at the beginning of the Line, erase way back to that point, then retype the rest of the Line. If you hold the backspace key down longer than a second, it will erase many letters very quickly.

Study **carefully** what you typed:

1. Is everything after the word PRINT enclosed in quotation marks?

2. Are there any extra quotation marks?

If everything's okay, press **ENTER**. The flashing cursor moves to the left edge telling us, "I got the message."

If It's Too Late

If you found an error **after** pressing **ENTER**, the backspace key cannot correct it. The best way to fix it is by correctly retyping the **entire** Line. When the **ENTER** key is pressed, this new Line will replace the old one since they both share the same Line number (in this case, 10). In a few Chapters we'll learn how to "EDIT" out errors instead of retyping entire Lines.

"Allow Me to Introduce You"

Let's tell the Computer to execute, or RUN, this program. The BASIC command is simply: RUN. So type:

```
RUN
```

and press **ENTER**.

If you made no mistakes, the bottom Line will read:

```
YOU ARE A COMPUTER PROGRAMMER.
OK
_
```

If it didn't work, try typing RUN **ENTER** again. If RUN still doesn't produce the statement, there's something wrong in your program. Type NEW **ENTER** to clear it out, then type it back in, and RUN again.

If it did work -- let out a yell!

"I are now a computer programmer!"

This is important because now that you have tasted success with computer programming, it may be the last you are heard from in some time.

OKAY, OKAY! SO YOU LEARNED RUN-YOU GONNA SIT THERE ALL AFTERNOON?

In Summary

Note that the word PRINT is not displayed, nor are the Line number nor the quotation marks. They are part of the BASIC language program's *instructions*. Everything inside the quote marks is printed including blank spaces and the period.

Whether typing in a program or giving direct commands like RUN, we have to follow up each action by hitting **ENTER**. This makes the Computer accept what we typed and act accordingly.

Type the word RUN again and hit **ENTER**.

Type RUN **ENTER** to your heart's content, and watch the magic machine do as it's told. When you feel you've got the hang of this, get up and stretch, walk around the room, look out the window -- the whole act. You'll soon be absorbed in programming and won't have time for such things.

Learned in Chapter 2

Commands	Statements	Miscellaneous
NEW	PRINT	**BACKSPACE**
RUN		Cursor
		" " quotation marks
		ENTER
		CTRL **BREAK**
		CTRL **ALT** **DELETE** (reset)

Commands (like NEW) are executed as soon as we type them and press **ENTER**.

Statements (like PRINT) are executed only **after** we type RUN and press **ENTER**.

Special message for people who can't resist the urge to play around with the Computer and skip around in this book. (There always are a few!)

It is possible to "lose control" of the Computer so it won't give an OK message. To regain control, just press the CTRL and BREAK keys at the same time. If that doesn't work, push the reset button, or press the CTRL, ALT and DELETE (or Del) keys at the same time. If that doesn't work, turn the Computer OFF for 10 seconds, then turn it back ON again.

Return to DOS, and be sure to remove all diskettes **before** turning the Computer OFF!

Chapter 3

Expanded Program

We now have a program in the Computer. It's only a one-Liner, so let's expand it by adding a second Line. In BASIC, every Line in the program *must* be numbered, and the instructions are executed in order from the lowest Line number to the highest. Type:

```
20 PRINT "YOU HAVE A COMMAND, MASTER?"    ENTER
```

Check it carefully -- especially the quote marks, then:

```
RUN        ENTER
```

Have you noticed that we use Ø for the number zero so we can distinguish between the letter O and number Ø? The Video Display does it this way -- and it's standard throughout Computerdom.

If all was correct, the screen will read:

```
YOU ARE A COMPUTER PROGRAMMER.
YOU HAVE A COMMAND, MASTER?
OK
_
```

BIG DEAL! YOU MASTER, ME SLAVE.

If it ran Ok, answer the question by typing:

```
YES          ENTER
```

Oh -- sorry about that! It "bombed," didn't it? The screen says:

```
Syntax error
```

We deliberately "set you up" to demonstrate the Computer's *error* trouble-shooter. The Computer is smart enough to know when **we've** made a mistake in telling it what to do, and it PRINTs a clue as to the nature of the error.

Syntax is an obscure word that refers to the pattern of words in a language. *Error* means we have made one. The Computer is expecting a new program Line or a BASIC command. The word "YES" is neither. Later on we'll learn how to make the Computer accept a "YES" or "NO" and respond accordingly.

There are many possible errors we can make, and in time we will learn to understand the built in "Error Codes."

A complete listing of Error Codes is provided in Appendix C.

Meanwhile, there is one other important error situation we must be able to recognize to be able to pry ourselves out of accidental trouble. Type this temporary Line 30 and deliberately make the spelling error:

```
30 PRIMT "TESTING."          ENTER
```

and

```
RUN          ENTER
```

Again we get an error message:

```
Syntax error in 30
```

but after OK, we see:

```
30 PRIMT "TESTING"
```

The cursor in Line 3Ø tells us BASIC found the word PRIMT there and has no idea what to do with it.

Pressing the ENTER key a few times will move the cursor down and provide us some breathing room. (Shhh! If you know what the flashing cursor in Line 3Ø will let us do, don't say anything. We don't want to confuse anyone with too much too soon.)

To erase the bad Line, type:

```
3Ø        ENTER
```

and it's gone.

And the Program Grows

It is customary to space the Lines in a program 10 numbers apart. Note that our two-Line program uses the numbers 1Ø and 2Ø. The reason ... it's much easier to modify a program if we leave room to insert new Lines between the old ones. There is no benefit to numbering the Lines more closely (like 1,2,3,4). DON'T DO IT.

RUN again and look at the video display. Suppose we don't want the two Lines PRINTed so close together, but would rather have a space between them? Type in the new Line:

```
15 PRINT        ENTER
```

Then:

```
RUN        ENTER
```

It now reads

```
YOU ARE A COMPUTER PROGRAMMER.
```

```
YOU HAVE A COMMAND, MASTER?
```

Note: To make this book easier to read, we put in a little more space than you actually see on the screen between all our program Lines.

Looks neater, doesn't it? But what about Line 15? It says PRINT. PRINT what? Well -- PRINT "nothing." That's what followed PRINT, and that's just what it PRINTed. But in the process of PRINTing nothing, it automatically inserted a space between the PRINTing ordered in Lines 10 and 20. (Hmmm ...so **that's** how we space between lines.)

Didn't that room between Lines 10 and 20 come in handy?

Another important program statement is REM which stands for REMark. It is often convenient to insert REMarks into a program.

Why? So you or someone else can refer to them later to help remember complicated programming details or even identify what the program's for and how it should be used. It's like having a scratch pad or notebook built into the program. When we tell the Computer to execute the program by typing RUN **ENTER**, it skips right over any numbered Line which begins with a REM. **A REM statement has no effect whatsoever on the program**. Insert the following:

```
5 REM *THIS IS MY FIRST COMPUTER PROGRAM* ENTER
```

You might wonder why the asterisks(*) in Line number 5? The answer is ... they're just for decoration. Remember, **everything** on a line that follows REM is ignored by the Computer.

Then:

```
RUN          ENTER
```

The *video printout* reads just like the last one, totally unaffected by the presence of Line 5. Did it work that way for you?

Well, this programming business is getting complicated, and I've already forgotten what is in our program. How can we get a LISTing of what the program now contains? Easy. A new BASIC command. Type:

```
LIST        ENTER
```

The screen reads:

```
5 REM *THIS IS MY FIRST COMPUTER PROGRAM*
10 PRINT "YOU ARE A COMPUTER PROGRAMMER."
15 PRINT
20 PRINT "YOU HAVE A COMMAND, MASTER?"
```

Where Is the END of the Program?

The end of a program is the last statement we want the Computer to execute. Many computers require placing an END statement at this point so the Computer will know when to stop. But with our Computers, an END statement is optional.

By tradition, END is given the number 99 or 999 or 9999 (or larger) depending on the largest number the specific computer will accept. Our Computers accept Line numbers up to 65529.

Let's add an END statement:

Type:

```
99 END        ENTER
```

Then:

```
RUN        ENTER
```

The sample RUN should read:

```
YOU ARE A COMPUTER PROGRAMMER.
```

```
YOU HAVE A COMMAND, MASTER?
```

Question: Why didn't the word END PRINT? **Answer:** Because nothing is PRINTed unless it is the "object" of a PRINT statement. So, how could we make the Computer PRINT THE END at the end of the program's execution? Think for a minute before typing the next Line.

```
98 PRINT "THE END"        ENTER
```

...and RUN.

We now have an END statement (Line 99) and a PRINT "THE END" statement (Line 98). 98 says it; 99 does it.

Erasing Without Replacing

Just for fun, move the END statement from Line 99 to the largest usable Line number, 65529. Two separate steps are required.

First, erase Line 99. Note that we're not just making a change or correcting an error in Line 99 -- we want to completely eliminate it from the program. Easier done than said.

Type:

```
99        ENTER
```

The Line is erased. How can we be sure? Think about it. Sure -- "pull" a LISTing of the entire program by typing:

```
LIST        ENTER
```

The screen should show the program with Lines 5, 10, 15, 20, and 98. Line 99 should be gone. Any Line can be erased this way.

The second step is just as easy. Type:

```
65529 END        ENTER
```

...and the new Line is entered. Pull a LISTing of the program to see if it was. RUN the program to see if moving the END statement changed anything. Did it? It shouldn't have.

Other Uses for END

Move END from number 65529 to Line number 17, LIST, then RUN.

What happened? It ENDed the RUN after PRINTing Line 10 and a space.

Now move END to Line 13, LIST, and RUN. Then to Line 8, LIST, and RUN.

Do you see the effect END has, depending where it is placed (even temporarily) in a program? Feel like you are starting to gain control over the machine?

Learned in Chapter 3

Commands	Statements	Miscellaneous
LIST	PRINT (Space)	Error Messages
	REM	Line numbering
	END	Erasing program Lines

Chapter 4

Using the EDITor

A valuable part of our BASIC is a feature called the EDITor. Its purpose is as simple as its name. It lets us "EDIT," or make changes to program lines.

The Tandy EDITor gives us the best of 2 worlds. We get the ease of use of a *Line editor* plus the power of a *screen editor*. Since it edits letters and numbers in only one Line at a time, we have nearly the power of a "word processor" on that one Line. It is easy to use but so powerful you'll never again want to use a computer without one.

Clear out the current program by typing NEW **ENTER**. Then type in this Line (errors and all):

```
10 PRINT "THIS HEAR ARE SHORE A FLOXY CONFUSER."
```

ENTER and RUN.

NOTE: From this point on we will not specify **ENTER** except in special circumstances. We all know that a RUN or LIST requires an **ENTER** to make it work.

The program should RUN just fine, and if that's the way you usually talk, you probably don't see any need for EDITing. If, on the other hand, you wish to change the sentence to something like:

```
THIS IS SURE A FOXY COMPUTER.
```

then some EDITing is needed in Line 10.

In the earlier Chapters we made changes by retyping the entire Line, hoping to not make more mistakes than we eliminated. This particular example has so much to change it might be easier to retype it, but our purpose here is to "exercise" the EDITor, so type:

`EDIT 10` **ENTER** (Don't omit the space before the 10!)

and see what happens.

We get:

```
10 PRINT "THIS HEAR ARE SHORE A FLOXY CONFUSER."
```

Don't panic if your Line 10 looks slightly different. Your cursor might look different, but will appear in the same position and work the same.

The flashing cursor on the `1` is a good (but not perfect) sign the Computer is in the EDITor mode. To *exit the EDITor* we can simply hit **ENTER** like we did several Chapters ago when we blundered into it by mistake.

But being in the EDITor is not like being in BASIC. We only use **ENTER** when we are **done** EDITing and want to **return** to BASIC. The EDITor is a special feature included within BASIC which we can call up by using the word EDIT. Don't hit **ENTER** until the EDITing is finished.

Since we want Line 10 to read `THIS IS SURE A FOXY COMPUTER`, let's first get rid of the words `HEAR ARE`. Tap (or hold down) the right arrow ➧ key and watch the cursor move. When it is at the `H` in `HEAR`, stop.

The arrow, or cursor, keys are clustered on the right side of the keyboard. On the 3000 Series Computers, they are on the numeric keypad. To use them as arrow keys, be sure the **NUM LOCK** light is off.

```
10 PRINT "THIS HEAR ARE SHORE A FLOXY CONFUSER."
```

Press the key that says **DELETE** (or **Del**) 9 times. It will delete the H and the 8 characters to its right. Line 10 now reads:

```
10 PRINT "THIS SHORE A FLOXY CONFUSER."
```

We now must insert the word IS between THIS and SHORE. The blinking cursor should be on the second S. Press **INSERT** (or **Ins**). Notice that the cursor has changed its appearance. (On the 2000, the cursor does not change.) This means the EDITor is in *Insert* mode. Type the letters:

```
IS
```

and press the space bar once. The screen now reads:

```
10 PRINT "THIS IS SHORE A FLOXY CONFUSER."
```

We inserted the IS and a space following it, but must now **leave** the *Insert* mode. We can leave the EDITor at any time by hitting **ENTER**, but since there's a lot more work to do on this Line, press the right arrow to move the cursor to the H in SHORE. Hitting any of the EDITor arrow keys bails us out of *Insert*, as does hitting the **INSERT** key again.

Press **DELETE** to get rid of the H and type the letter U. By typing U we **changed** the O to a U. **Changing** a letter or number is done simply by *over-striking*. It now reads:

```
10 PRINT "THIS IS SURE A FLOXY CONFUSER."
```

If it seems we're going slowly, you're right! The EDITor is so simple but so important we may as well learn to use it right the first time. You know the old story, "There's never time to do it right the first time, but always time to do it over."

Hit the right arrow 6 times to put the cursor under the L in FLOXY.

```
10 PRINT "THIS IS SURE A FLOXY CONFUSER."
```

Think for a moment. How can we change FLOXY to FOXY?

TO CHANGE "FLOXY" TO "FOXY"? SIMPLE GET THE L OUTTA HERE! HEH, HEH, NO OFFENSE, MASTER.

The easiest way is to just press **DELETE** to erase the L. Next, move the cursor to the N.

```
10 PRINT "THIS IS SURE A FOXY CONFUSER."
```

Only one final change is needed, changing CONFUSER to COMPUTER. Should we go into the word CONFUSER and delete the N and F and insert M and P, or would it be easier to just **change** those letters instead?

What about the S? Think it through.

Of course! It usually takes fewer keystrokes to **change** than to **delete** then **insert**, so we always change, or overstrike, when possible. Move the cursor under the N and type MPUT.

Whew! Finally done. But wait -- we're still in the EDITor. Press **ENTER**, see the cursor drop down, and know that we're back in BASIC. RUN to be sure all is well.

It is **very important** to hit **ENTER** when done EDITing a Line. This tells the Computer:

"Ok, I'm done EDITing this Line. Lock the changed Line in as the NEW program Line."

It is a **very** common mistake to EDIT a Line, then use the down arrow to move to EDIT another Line. If you do that, the Computer has no way of remembering the changes you made on the first Line. You **must** hit **ENTER** to save the changes!

Despite our taking each editing task one step at a time, it is possible to make all these EDITing changes in only one pass through the Line. The purpose of an EDITor is to save time.

Since you now know what the EDITor does, type:

NEW **ENTER**

type in old Line 10 again, then EDIT it in one pass.

```
10 PRINT "THIS HEAR ARE SHORE A FLOXY CONFUSER."
```

If you mess it up, start all over by retyping Line 10. With some practice, the complete edit will take you less than 10 seconds.

From here on, always use the EDITor for changes, especially in long Lines. Compare the time it takes to change only one letter or number in a very long and complex Line by retyping it, with the speed of doing it with the EDITor.

The EDITor -- Second Semester

Several other keys help EDIT. Type:

```
LIST
```

and tap the ENTER key until Line 10 is at the top of the screen.

The cursor is now at the bottom of the screen. But suppose you want to EDIT Line 10. Instead of typing EDIT 10, hit the HOME key. This moves the cursor immediately to the top left-hand corner of the screen, or sends it HOME, to Line 10. Try it!

If you use the CTRL key with either the right or left arrows, the cursor will jump to the **beginning** of each word in those directions. Try it. (The CTRL key doesn't work with the up or down arrows.)

After the Computer has been turned on or reset, special functions or characters sharing the numeric keypad keys are active. To use these keys as a standard numeric keypad, the NUM LOCK must be pressed. Notice that the NUM LOCK light goes on to indicate that the keypad is LOCKed in the NUMbers mode. Go ahead and press NUM LOCK a couple of times, then leave it in the *alternate key mode* with the light out.

Find the END key on the right side of the keyboard. The END key moves the cursor to the END of the Line, and CTRL END **erases** to the END of the Line. Position the cursor in the middle of the Line and try it.

We often clear the screen because the clutter gets confusing while we're EDIT-ing. Hitting CTRL HOME moves the cursor up to the top left **and** clears the entire screen. It doesn't erase the program, just the screen. Try it.

EXERCISE 4-1: Type NEW **ENTER**, then use the EDITor to change:

```
10 PAINT "WE CAN TAKE CREDIT FOR CONSUMER PROGRESS."
```

to:

```
10 PRINT "WE CAN EDIT COMPUTER PROGRAMS."
```

Work out this one on your own. The answers to it and later Exercises are found in Section B, along with some notes and ideas.

We could probably live happily ever after with what we've learned about the EDITor, but it has a couple of other powerful features. One which will force itself upon us is shown by the following. Erase the memory with NEW and type:

```
10 PRIMT "THAT ISN'T HOW TO SPELL PRINT!"
```

...and RUN.

```
Syntax error in 10
OK
10 PRIMT "THAT ISN'T HOW TO SPELL PRINT!"
```

means there is a syntax error in Line 10. The Computer is telling us:

What? -- I don't understand what you are saying,

and **automatically** puts BASIC in the EDITor mode at the Line containing the error. This always happens when there is a syntax error. (More on Syntax and other errors in later Chapters.) Proceed normally to change the "M" to an "N" and press:

ENTER

to return to BASIC.

There is a third and often convenient way to enter the EDIT mode. It is particularly valuable when experimenting ... switching back and forth between BASIC and EDIT to test programming changes.

For example, we just EDITed Line 10. To enter EDIT 10 again, type:

`EDIT .` **ENTER** (Note the space and the period.)

Try it.

EDIT followed by a period is an abbreviation for EDIT followed by the Line number of the Line **last** EDITed.

Learned in Chapter 4

Commands	Miscellaneous
EDIT	Editing features
EDIT .	

Chapter 5

AUTOmatic Line Numbering and RENUM

They Laughed When I Sat Down at the Computer to Play

Clean out the old program by typing:

```
NEW          ENTER
```

then:

CTRL HOME

to clear the screen.

As the artist approaches a blank canvas with only a gleam in his eye, so we approach our empty Computer and type:

```
AUTO         ENTER
```

It responds with:

```
10 _
```

We are in the AUTOmatic Line numbering mode. Type:

```
PRINT "WHAT IS GOING ON HERE?"        ENTER
```

and

```
20 _
```

pops up on the screen.

Type:

```
PRINT "THIS IS RIDICULOUS."        ENTER
```

and

```
30 _
```

appears.

It's obvious that we're being fed new Line numbers as fast as we can use them. Hit the ENTER key a few more times and watch the numbers jump up.

Okay -- how do we get **out** of AUTO? Hit:

CTRL BREAK or CTRL C

Type LIST and see that only those Line numbers we actually used (1Ø and 2Ø) contain anything.

Type NEW, then:

```
AUTO 1ØØØ        ENTER
```

and ENTER a few times. Line numbering *defaults* to 1Ø. Hit CTRL BREAK, then:

```
AUTO 1ØØØ,2ØØ
```

Hit the ENTER key a half dozen times or so, and the pattern becomes clear. The "1ØØØ" established the **beginning** Line number, and the "2ØØ" determined the **spacing** between Lines.

CTRL **BREAK** out of AUTO and start again with:

```
AUTO 3000,5
```

and a few **ENTER** s. Very handy for very big programs requiring lots of Line numbers.

CTRL **BREAK** again, and:

```
AUTO 17,4
```

plus a few **ENTER** s, then **CTRL** **BREAK**.

You get the idea. Unless you specify otherwise, AUTO will always begin numbering with Line 10 and always increment the Line numbers by 10.

One important caution: Whenever fooling with something that's automatic, a degree of personal control is lost. Enter this quickie, using AUTO and the Line numbers shown:

```
10 PRINT "NOW WHAT ARE WE UP TO?"
20 PRINT "BEATS ME!"
40 REM
80 REM
90 END
```

CTRL **BREAK**

Then type:

```
AUTO
```

Oh, oh! What does the `10*` mean?

The asterisk means there is **already** a Line number 10. If you type anything, the existing line will be changed. If you hit **ENTER** without typing anything, the cursor will advance to Line 20 without altering the existing Line 10. Do it.

NOW WHAT ARE WE UP TO?
"BEATS ME"
THAT'S MY LINE!

The AUTO command is not just for the lazy. It can be a real time saver (and can save mental energy as well). For the touch typist who doesn't have to look at the screen, it's a real delight.

Insert Line 60 by pressing **ENTER** four times, then type:

```
REM          ENTER
```

Press **CTRL** **BREAK** and type:

```
AUTO .    ENTER
```

(Put a space between AUTO and the period.)

AUTO . starts automatic Line numbering with the **highest** or **last** Line number in the program.

CTRL **BREAK** out of it.

RENUMbering

In addition to the AUTOmatic Line numbering feature, we also have a feature for RENUMbering program Lines. It can be exceedingly helpful. Simply type:

```
RENUM        ENTER
```

and our entire program is RENUMbered by tens, starting with Line 10. Try it, then LIST to see the result.

To RENUMber by fives, try:

```
RENUM ,,5        ENTER
```

Try it, and LIST.

If you only need to RENUMber part of a program, use:

```
RENUM 5000,25        ENTER
```

This command will RENUMber from Line 25 to the end of the program, starting with a new Line 5000. The RENUMbering will be by tens. Line 25 needn't actually be in the program. If it isn't, renumbering will start with the next highest existing Line number. Try it and LIST.

RENUM also changes all of the GOSUBs and GOTOs (yet to be studied) along with the new Line numbers.

If you thrive on cryptics, the entire RENUM syntax is:

```
RENUM newLine,startLine,increment
```

Learned in Chapter 5

Commands	Miscellaneous
AUTO	AUTOmatic Line numbering
AUTO . (include space)	Line RENUMbering
RENUM	

Chapter 6

The Keyboard

Special Function Keys

Locate the keys labeled F1 to F12 (or F1 to F10). These are the *Special Function Keys*, sometimes called *Soft Keys*. Each can call up an entire command or series of commands with just a touch, and you can easily reprogram them. The current function of each is displayed at the bottom of the screen.

F11 and F12 are not programmed with a specific function. To see them listed on the screen, hold down the CTRL key and press T. Press CTRL T again to clear the screen; then CTRL T a third time to return the F1 through F10 listing to the bottom of the screen.

So far, the only two that look familiar are LIST and RUN, but we will discover the uses for the rest of the keys as needed.

Type in the following NEW program:

```
10 PRINT "I WONDER WHAT THESE KEYS ARE FOR?"
20 PRINT "MAYBE THEY'RE GOOD FOR SOMETHING."
```

Now hit the key labeled F1.

```
LIST _
```

appears on the screen. Since we want to LIST the entire program, just hit ENTER.

It worked.

Now hit F2 .

What happened? Why didn't we have to hit ENTER ? The F2 key types RUN on the screen **plus** hits ENTER . Keys F5 , F7 , and F8 also include an ENTER. More on them in due course.

The Whole Enchilada

Hit F9 then F1. The screen displays:

```
KEY LIST
```

Hit ENTER . The instructions associated with each key are PRINTed out in complete detail. Notice that F10 says `SCREEN 0,0,0`. However, on the bottom right hand side of the screen, only part of that is visible.

Each soft key is allowed to store up to 15 characters, but only the first few of each can be displayed in the limited screen space.

The soft keys are meant to aid the programmer in writing and executing programs. If we want to assign **our** own set of characters to these keys, the Computer is willing. That's why the keys are called "soft." Unlike the rest of the keys, they can be easily reprogrammed in BASIC to do special things. (Keys 11 and 12 were left undefined so we could program them any way we like).

Suppose for example, you want Key 10 to say MY TANDY 1000!. All you have to do is type:

```
KEY 10, "MY TANDY 1000!"          ENTER
```

Do it, then look at the bottom of the screen after the number 10.

Type KEY LIST again (or F9 F1) and hit ENTER .

This time Key 10 displays MY TANDY 1000!

NO, THAT'S NOT A SOFT KEY! YOU'VE GOT SOME GUM ON YOUR FINGER.

To prove that this really works, type:

```
30 PRINT "F10"          ENTER
```

F10 means, **"Press key F1Ø here."** Don't type in F1Ø! **Do** include the quotes.

and RUN. (F2 does RUN ENTER , remember?)

To return F10 to its original use, type:

```
KEY 1Ø, "SCREEN Ø,Ø,Ø"     ENTER
```

Alternate Keys

In addition to the special function keys, almost every letter key has a BASIC keyword associated with it. A keyword is a BASIC *command, function* or *statement*. We will make the distinctions in future Chapters.

In the last Chapter we learned about AUTOmatic Line numbering. Here's an easier way to do it. Type NEW.

Hold down the ALT key and hit the letter A. AUTO appears on the screen. Hit ENTER a few times to convince yourself that we're really in AUTO Line numbering mode, then CTRL BREAK out of it.

This chart shows the ALT keywords corresponding to letter keys A-Z.

A - AUTO	B - BSAVE	C - COLOR
D - DELETE	E - ELSE	F - FOR
G - GOTO	H - HEX$	I - INPUT
J - (not used)	K - KEY	L - LOCATE
M - MOTOR*	N - NEXT	O - OPEN
P - PRINT	Q - (not used)	R - RUN
S - SCREEN	T - THEN	U - USING
V - VAL	W - WIDTH	X - XOR
Y - (not used)	Z - (not used)	

*MOTOR is not used in this BASIC but is still a reserved word.

If you can remember the keywords, the Alternate keys can be great time savers.

Special Effects Dept.

One additional ALT key feature that exists only on the Tandy 2000 is the ability to "toggle" a smooth scrolling screen. Press the ALT and right arrow keys at the same time. Now type KEY LIST a few times to get the screen to scroll.

To switch back to the normal scroll, press ALT ➧ again.

The CTRL Key

The CTRL key on the left side of the keyboard is used for special purposes. For example, hold down the CTRL key and hit G. This is pronounced Control Gee. The speaker speaks!

Now try CTRL I . The cursor moves over 8 spaces at a time (the same as pressing the TAB key). And CTRL H moves the cursor back one space (the same as the BACKSPACE key). For the finale, hit CTRL L , and the screen is cleared (the same as CTRL HOME). The program, however, is unchanged.

Take a quick look back at Appendix A, the ASCII chart. Notice the relationship between codes 7-13. CTRL G made a beep. G is the seventh letter of the alphabet, and code 7 is a beep. H is the eighth letter, and CTRL H performed a backspace. Appendix A says code 8 is a backspace. We will study this chart intensively, later.

There are several more important keys. On the right side is a key that says NUM LOCK . Hit NUM LOCK and as with CAPS (or CAPS LOCK), and a light comes on. In this mode we get numbers by pressing the numbered keys. To get the special characters and functions above the numbers, we use SHIFT . When NUM LOCK is hit again, the light goes off, and we're in the opposite mode. Now we need SHIFT to get the numbers but not for the special characters or functions.

As we saw earlier, the HOLD key (when available) can suspend the DIRectory listing. When we create longer programs, we will use it to HOLD long program LISTings and to suspend the action of programs while they are RUNning. (Use Ctrl Num Lock if there's no HOLD.)

ESC is the ESCape key. It erases everything on the Line containing the cursor. Set the cursor on a Line then hit **ESC**. The Line disappears from the screen **only**; the program is not affected.

We'll discuss the **PRINT** (or **Prt Sc**) key in a later chapter when we talk about printers.

There are several other keyboard keys, but we don't need them for BASIC. They are used primarily with word processor and electronic spreadsheet programs.

Learned in Chapter 6

Miscellaneous

Special Function keys
Alternate keys (**ALT**)
CTRL
ESC
NUM LOCK

PART 2

BASIC FUNDAMENTALS

Chapter 7

Math Operators

But Can It Do Math?

Yes, it can. Basic arithmetic is a snap for Tandy Computers. So are highly complex math calculations -- when we write special programs to perform them -- and we will.

The BASIC Computer language uses the 4 fundamental arithmetic operations, plus 4 more complex ones which are just modifications of the others:

1. ADDITION, using the symbol +

2. SUBTRACTION, using the symbol −

3. MULTIPLICATION, using the special symbol *

4. DIVISION, using the symbol /

and

5. EXPONENTIATION, using ^ (unveiled in the next chapter)

6. NEGATION, (meaning "multiply times minus one") using the − symbol

7. MODulo. Of interest primarily to pure math-computer types. (We'll discuss it in Chapter 30.)

I DON'T CARE WHAT YOUR DADDY USES IN HIS COMPUTER-- THE TEACHER WANTS YOU TO USE × and ÷ !

8. INTEGER DIVISION, using the backslash \ (taught in Chapter 18.)

Of course, we also need that old favorite, the equals sign (=). But the BASIC language is very particular about how we use this sign! Math expressions (like 1 + 2 * 5) can only go on the **right-hand** side of the equals sign; the left-hand side is reserved for the **result** of the math equation. We say 4 = 2 + 2. (This may seem a little strange, but it's really quite simple, as we'll discover in the next few pages.)

We **cannot** use an "X" for multiplication. Unfortunately, a long time ago a mathematician decided to use "X," which is a letter, to mean multiply. We use letters for other things, so it's much less confusing to use a "*." Confusion is one thing a computer can't tolerate. To computers, "*" is the **only** symbol which means multiply. After using it a while, you, too, may feel we should do away with X as a multiplication symbol.

Putting all this together in a program is not difficult, so let's do it. First, we have to erase the *resident program* from the Computer's memory.

Resident program is computer talk for "what's already in there."

Type the command:

```
NEW        ENTER
```

Then type:

```
LIST       ENTER
```

to check that it's really gone. The Computer responds with:

```
OK
_
```

Putting the Beast to Work

Using the Computer for some very simple problem solving means using equations. (Oh -- panic.) But then, an equation is just a little statement that says,

"What's on one side of an equals sign amounts to the same as what's on the other side." That can't get too bad.

We'll start with that old standby equation,

"*Distance* traveled equals *Rate* of travel times *Time* spent traveling."

If it's been a few years, you might want to contemplate that.

To shorten the equation, let's choose letters (called variables) to stand for the 3 quantities. Then we can rewrite the equation as a BASIC statement acceptable to the Computer. Type in:

```
40  D = R * T          ENTER
```

Remember, you have to use a * to specify multiplication.

What's that 40 doing in our equation? That's the program Line number. Remember, every step in a program has to have one. We chose 40, but another number would have done as well.

The extra spaces in the Line are there just to make the equation easier for us to read; BASIC ignores them. Later, when writing very long programs, you may want to eliminate extra spaces because they take up memory space. For learning, they are helpful, so leave them in.

Here's what Line 40 means to the Computer: "Take the values of R and T, multiply them together, and assign the resulting value to the variable D." So until further notice, D is equal to the result of R times T.

We could **not** reverse the equation and write R*T=D. It has no meaning to the Computer. Remember, the left-hand side of the equation is reserved for the Line Number and the value we are **looking for.** The right-hand side is the place to put the values we **know.**

Any of the 26 letters from A through Z can be used to identify the values we know, as well as those we want to figure out. Whenever possible, it's a good idea to choose letters that are abbreviations of the things they stand for -- like the D, R, and T in the Distance, Rate, Time equation.

To complicate this very simple example, there's an optional way of writing the equation using the BASIC statement LET:

```
40  LET D = R * T
```

This use of LET reminds us that making D equal R times T was **our** choice rather than an eternal truth like 2 = 1 + 1. Some computers are fussy and require the use of LET. Tandy Computers do not.

Okay -- let's complete the program.

Assume:

> Distance (in miles) = Rate (in miles per hour) multiplied by Time (in hours). How far is it from San Diego to London if a jet plane traveling at an average speed of 500 miles per hour makes the trip in 12 hours?

Yes, I know you can do that one in your head but that's not the point!

Use AUTO, and type in the following:

```
10 REM  * DISTANCE, RATE, TIME PROBLEM *  ENTER
20 R = 500    ENTER
30 T = 12    ENTER
40*    CTRL BREAK
```

LIST and check the program carefully, then:

```
RUN        ENTER
```

Hum de dum...ho-hum...(this sure is a slow computer).

```
OK

_
```

All it says is Ok. **The Computer Doesn't Work!**

Yes, it does. **It worked just fine.** The Computer multiplied 500 times 12 just like we told it and came up with the answer of 6000 miles. But **we** forgot to tell it to give **us** the answer. Sorry about that.

> **EXERCISE 7-1:** Can you finish this program without help? It only needs one more Line. Give it a good try before reading on for the answer. That way, the answer will mean more to you.
>
> (Hint: We've already used PRINT to PRINT messages in quotes. What would happen if we said `50 PRINT "D"`? ... No, we want the *value* of D, not "D" itself. Hmmmm, what happens when we get rid of the quotes?)

Do not Read Beyond This Point Until You've Completed Exercise 7-1!

Well, the answer 6000 is correct, but its "presentation" is no more inspiring than the readout on a hand calculator. This inevitably leads us back to where we first started this foray into the unknown -- the PRINT statement.

> Did you find out the hard way that a space must be placed between the PRINT and the variable D? It **cannot** be eliminated.

Note that we said `50 PRINT D`. There were no quotes around the letter D like we had used before. The reason is simple but fairly profound. If we want the Computer to PRINT **the exact words** we specify, we enclose them in quotes. If we want it to PRINT the **value** of a variable, in this case D, we leave the quotes off. That simple fact is worth serious thought before continuing on.

> Did you think seriously about it? Then on we go!

Now suppose we want to include both the **value** of something and some **words** on the same Line. Pay attention, as you will be doing more and more program designing yourself, and PRINT statements give beginners more trouble than any other single part of computer programming. Type in the following:

```
50 PRINT "THE DISTANCE (IN MILES) IS",D    ENTER
```

Then:

```
RUN    ENTER
```

REMEMBER: Typing in a statement with a Line number that already exists erases the original Line completely -- and that's what we want to do here. Could we have used the EDITor instead of retyping? Yes.

The display says:

```
THE DISTANCE (IN MILES) IS   6000
```

How about that! The message enclosed in quotes is PRINTed exactly as we specified, and the letter gave us the value of D. The comma told the Computer to PRINT two separate items on the **same** Line. (We can PRINT up to **5** items on the **same** Line, simply by inserting commas between them.)

With this in mind, see if you can change Line 50 so the Computer finishes the program with the following message:

```
THE DISTANCE IS               6000          MILES.
```

Answer: Break up the message words into two parts, and put the number variable in between them on the same PRINT Line. (Use the EDITor.)

```
50 PRINT "THE DISTANCE IS",D,"MILES."
```

Why is there all that extra space on both sides of the 6000 in the PRINTout? The reason is that the Computer divides up the screen width into 5 zones of 14 characters each. When a PRINT statement contains two or more items separated by commas, the Computer automatically PRINTs them in adjacent PRINT zones. *Automatic zoning* is a convenient method of outputting TABular information, and we'll explore the subject in detail later on.

It's possible to eliminate the extra spaces in the display. EDIT the last version of Line 5Ø, substituting semicolons (;) for the 2 commas.

Careful -- don't replace the period with a semicolon.

```
RUN          ENTER
```

Perfection, at last:

```
THE DISTANCE IS 6ØØØ MILES.
```

Look carefully at the new Line 5Ø. There is no blank space between the S in IS, the D, and the M in MILES. But in the display printout, there **is** a space between IS and 6ØØØ, and another space between 6ØØØ and MILES. Why?

Reason: When a **number** is PRINTed, leading and trailing blank spaces are automatically inserted. As we do more programming, this feature will become very important.

WHEW!

Well, we have already covered more than enough commands, statements and math operators to solve a myriad of problems.

Math operators? -- they're the = + - * ^ / and \ symbols we mentioned earlier.

Now let's spend some time actually writing programs to solve problems. There is no better way to learn than by doing, and **everything** covered so far is fundamental to our success in later Chapters. Don't jump over these exercises! They will plunge you right into the thick of programming where you belong. Remember, sample answers are in Section B along with further comments.

EXERCISE 7-2: Write a program which will find the TIME required to travel by jet plane from London to San Diego, if the distance is 6000 miles and the plane travels at 500 MPH.

EXERCISE 7-3: If the circumference of a circle is found by multiplying its diameter times π (3.14), write a program which will find the circumference of a circle with a diameter of 35 feet.

EXERCISE 7-4: If the area of a circle is found by multiplying π times the square of its radius, write a program to find the area of a circle with a radius of 5 inches.

EXERCISE 7-5: Your checkbook balance was $225. You've written three checks (for $17, $35 and $225) and made two deposits ($40 and $200). Write a program to adjust your old balance based on checks written and deposits made, and PRINT out the new balance.

Learned in Chapter 7

Statements	Math Operators	Miscellaneous
LET (optional)	=	, (comma)
	+	; (semicolon)
	−	Variable Names
	*	
	/	
	\	
	^	

Remember, we can use any of the 26 letters as variables, not just D, R, and T (they were just convenient for our problem).

Chapter 8

Scientific Notation

Are There More Stars or Grains of Sand?

In this mathematical world we are blessed with very large and very small numbers. Millions of these and billionths of those. To cope with all this, our Computers use "exponential notation," or "standard scientific notation," when the number sizes start to get out of hand. The number 5 million (5,000,000), for example, can be written "5E+06" (E for Exponential). This means, "the number 5 followed by six zeros."

Technically, $5*10^6$, which is 5 times ten to the sixth power: 5*10*10*10*10*10*10

If an answer comes out "5E-06," that means we must shift the decimal point, which is after the 5, six places to the **left** inserting zeros as necessary. Technically, it means 5 X 10^{-6}, or 5 millionths, (.000,005).

In our BASIC, that's 5/10/10/10/10/10/10.

This is really pretty simple once you get the hang of it, and makes it very easy to keep track of the decimal point. Since the Computer **insists** on using it with very large and very small numbers, we can just as well get used to it right now.

Type NEW, then type and RUN the following:

```
10 PRINT 5*10^7
```
(The caret ^ is located above the 6 key.)

T-T-THAT'S 5 MILLION?
5E+06
YEP, NOW LET'S TRY SOMETHIN' DIFFICULT!
(CLOSE YOUR MOUTH, BOY, YOU'LL DRAW FLIES!)

The answer is:

```
5E+07
```

Type NEW before solving the following exercise:

EXERCISE 8-1: If 1 million cars each drove 10 thousand miles in a certain year, how many miles did they drive altogether that year? Write and run a simple program using zeros (not exponential notation) which will give the answer.

Didn't forget the ENTER did you? We've been reminding you to ENTER after each Line or command -- but from now on, we'll assume that you'll remember.

LIST your program. Then check it against the "official" answer in Section B. Look at Line 20. What's that exclamation point doing at the end of the Line? It turns out that the Computer automatically stores numbers in variables as *single precision* values (between −32768 and +32767). The exclamation point is a *Type Declaration Character* that means the number has exceeded the *single precision* limitations. Don't worry about it! We'll explain it in Part 4.

Learned in Chapter 8

Miscellaneous

E - notation
^ (caret)

Chapter 9

Using ( ) and the Order of Operations

Parentheses play an important role in computer programming, just as in ordinary math. They are used here in the same general way, but there are important exceptions.

1. In BASIC, parentheses can enclose operations to be performed. Those operations which are within parentheses are performed before those **not** in parentheses.

2. Operations buried deepest within parentheses (that is, parentheses inside parentheses) are performed first.

To be sure equations are calculated correctly, use ( ) around the operations which must be performed first.

---

3. When there is a "tie" as to which operation the Computer should perform **after** it has solved all problems enclosed in parentheses, it works its way along the program Line from **left to right** performing the *multiplication* and *division*. It then starts at the left again and performs the *addition* and *subtraction*.

Recall the old memory aid, "**M**y **D**ear **A**unt **S**ally"? In math we do **M**ultiplication and **D**ivision first (from left to right), then come back for **A**ddition and **S**ubtraction (left to right). Our BASIC does it the same way.

INT, RND and ABS functions are performed before multiplication and division. (We haven't used them yet, but we're just mentioning them to be completely accurate...)

4. An operation written as (X)(Y) will **not** tell the Computer to multiply. X * Y is the only recognized scheme for multiplication.

EXAMPLE: To convert temperature expressed in degrees Fahrenheit to Celsius (Centigrade), the following relationship is used:

The Fahrenheit temperature equals 32 degrees plus nine-fifths of the Celsius temperature. Or, maybe you're more used to the simple formula:

$$F = \frac{9}{5} * C + 32$$

Assume we have a Celsius temperature of 25. Type in this NEW program and RUN it:

```
10 REM * CELSIUS TO FAHRENHEIT CONVERSION *
20 C = 25
30 F = (9/5)*C + 32
40 PRINT C;"DEGREES (C) =";F;"DEGREES (F)."
```

SAMPLE RUN:

```
25 DEGREES (C) = 77 DEGREES (F).
```

Remember what the semicolons are for?

Notice first that Line 40 consists of a PRINT statement followed by 4 separate expressions -- 2 variables and 2 groups of words in quotes called "literals," or "strings." Notice also that everything within the quotes (including spaces) is PRINTed.

SHOOT! AN' I WAS JUST GETTIN' TO THE GOOD PART!
YOUR DINNER'S GETTING COLD!

Next, note how the parentheses are placed in Line 30. With the 9/5 securely inside, we can multiply its quotient times C, then add 32.

Now, remove the parentheses in Line 30 and RUN again. The answer comes out the same. Why?

1. On the first pass, the Computer started by solving all problems within parentheses, in this case (9/5). It came up with (but did not PRINT) 1.8. It then multiplied the 1.8 times the value of C and added 32.

2. On the next pass, without the parentheses, the Computer simply moved from left to right performing first the division problem (9 divided by 5), then the multiplication problem (1.8 times C), then the addition problem (adding 32). The parentheses really made no difference in this example.

Next, change the `+32` to `32+` and move it to the front of the equation in Line 30 to read:

```
30 F = 32 + (9/5)*C
```

RUN it again, without parentheses.

Did it make a difference in the answer? Why not?

Answer: Execution proceeds from left to right, multiplication and division first, then returns and performs addition and subtraction. This is why the 32 was *not* added to the 9 before being divided by 5. **Very Important!** If they had been added, we would, of course, have gotten the wrong answer.

EXERCISE 9-1: Write and RUN a program which converts 65 degrees Fahrenheit to Celsius. The rule tells us that "Celsius temperature is equal to five-ninths times what's left after 32 is subtracted from the Fahrenheit temperature."

$$C = (F - 32) * \frac{5}{9}$$

____

____

EXERCISE 9-2: Remove the first set of parentheses in the Ex. 9-1 answer and RUN again.

EXERCISE 9-3: Replace the first set of parentheses in program Line 3Ø and remove the second pair of parentheses, then RUN. Note how the answer comes out -- correctly!

EXERCISE 9-4: Insert parentheses in the following equation to make it correct. Write a program and check it out on your Computer.

30 - 9 - 8 - 7 - 6 = 28

Learned in Chapter 9

Miscellaneous

( )
Order of Operations

Chapter 10

Relational Operators

If you liked the preceding Chapters, **then** you're going to love the rest of this book!

...because we're just getting into the good stuff like IF-THEN and GOTO statements that let the Computer make decisions and take "executive action." But first, a few more operators.

Relational Operators allow the Computer to compare one value with another. There are only 3:

1. Equals, using the symbol =

2. Is greater than, using the symbol >

3. Is less than, using the symbol <

Combining these 3, we come up with 3 more operators:

4. Is not equal to, using the symbol <>

5. Is less than or equal to, using the symbol <=

6. Is greater than or equal to, using the symbol >=

Example: A<B means A is less than B. To help distinguish between < and >, remember that the **smaller** (pointed) end of the < symbol points to the **smaller** of the two quantities being compared.

By adding these 6 *relational* operators to the *math* operators we already know, plus new *statements* called IF-THEN & GOTO, we create a powerful system of comparing and calculating that becomes the central core of everything that follows.

The IF-THEN statement, combined with the 6 relational operators above, gives us the **action** part of a system of logic. Enter and RUN this NEW program:

```
10 A = 5
20 IF A = 5 THEN 50
30 PRINT "A DOES NOT EQUAL 5."
40 END
50 PRINT "A EQUALS 5."
```

The screen displays:

```
A EQUALS 5.
```

This program is an example of using an IF-THEN statement with only the most fundamental relational operator, the equals sign.

The Autopsy

Let's examine the program Line by Line.

Line 10 — establishes the fact that A has a value of 5.

Line 20 — is an IF-THEN statement which directs the Computer to GOTO Line 50 **if the value of A is exactly 5**, skipping over whatever might be in between Lines 20 and 50. Since A **does** equal 5, the Computer jumps to Line 50 and does as it says, PRINTing `A EQUALS 5`. Lines 30 and 40 were not used at all.

Now, change Line 10 to read:

```
10 A = 6
```

...and RUN.

The screen says:

```
A DOES NOT EQUAL 5.
```

Taking it a Line at a time:

Line 10	establishes the value of A to be 6.
Line 20	tests the value of A. If A equals 5, THEN the Computer is directed to GOTO Line 50. But the test fails, that is, A does **not** equal 5, so the Computer proceeds as usual to the next Line, Line 30.
Line 30	directs the Computer to PRINT the fact that A DOES NOT EQUAL 5. It does not tell us what the **value** of A is, only that it does **not** equal 5. The Computer proceeds to the next Line.
Line 40	ENDs the program's execution. Without this statement separating Lines 30 and 50, the Computer would charge right on to
Line 50	and PRINT its contents, which obviously are in conflict with the contents of Line 30.

IF-THEN vs. GOTO

IF-THEN is what is known as a *conditional* branching statement. The program will "branch" to another part of the program **on the condition that** it passes the IF-THEN test. If it fails the test, program execution simply passes to the next Line.

GOTO is an *unconditional* branching statement. If we were to replace Line 40 with:

```
40 GOTO 99
```

LISSEN! IF YOU FAIL ONE MORE "IF-THEN" TEST, I'M GOIN' TO TELL YOU WHERE TO GOTO!

and add Line 99:

```
99 END
```

...whenever the Computer hit Line 40 it would *unconditionally* follow orders and GOTO 99, ENDing the RUN. Change Line 40 as discussed above and run.

Did the program work Ok as changed? Did you try it with several values of A? Be sure you do! We will find many uses for the GOTO statement in the future.

Optional THEN with GOTO

When the IF-THEN statement is used with a GOTO statement, either `THEN` or `GOTO` or both can be used. This can be useful in long program lines. For example, either of these Lines will work in place of Line 20 in our program:

```
20 IF A = 5 THEN GOTO 50
```

or

```
20 IF A = 5 GOTO 50
```

EXERCISE 10-1: Change the value of A in Line 10 back to 5 then rewrite the resident program using a "does-not-equal" sign in Line 20 instead of the equals sign. Change other Lines as necessary, so the same results are achieved with your program as with the one in the example.

____

____

____

____

____

EXERCISE 10-2: Change Line 1Ø to give A the value of 6. Leave the other four Lines from Exercise 10-1 as shown. Add more program Lines as necessary so the program will tell us whether A is larger or smaller than 5 and RUN.

EXERCISE 10-3: Change the value of A in Line 1Ø at least three more times, RUNning after each change to ensure that your new program works correctly.

No sample answers are given since you are choosing your own values of A. It will be obvious whether or not you get the right answer.

Learned in Chapter 10

Statements	Relational Operators	Miscellaneous
IF-THEN	=	Conditional branching
GOTO	>	Unconditional branching
	<	Optional THEN
	<>	
	<=	
	>=	

Chapter 11

It Also Talks and Listens

By now you have probably become tired of retyping Line 1Ø each time you wish to change the value of A. The INPUT statement is a simple, fast and more convenient way to accomplish the same thing. It's a biggie, so don't miss any points.

Enter this NEW program:

```
10 PRINT "THE VALUE I WISH TO GIVE A IS"
20 INPUT A
30 PRINT "A =";A
```

...and RUN

The Computer will PRINT:

```
THE VALUE I WISH TO GIVE A IS
? _
```

See the question mark on the screen? It means, "It's your turn -- and I'm waiting..."

Type in a number, press **ENTER** and see what happens. The program responds exactly the same way as when we changed values within a program Line. RUN several more times to get the feel of the INPUT statement.

Powerful, isn't it?

Let's add a touch of class to the INPUT process by changing Line 1Ø as follows:

```
1Ø PRINT "THE VALUE I WISH TO GIVE A IS";
```

Look at that Line very carefully. Do you see how it differs from the earlier Line 1Ø? It is different -- a *semicolon* was added at the end.

Did you use the EDITor to add the semicolon?

Think back a bit. We used semicolons before in PRINT statements, but only in the **middle,** to hook several together to PRINT them on the same Line. In this case, we put a semicolon at the **end,** so the *question mark* from the Line 1Ø will PRINT on the **same** display Line rather than on a second line. After changing Line 1Ø as above, RUN. It should read:

```
THE VALUE I WISH TO GIVE A IS? _
```

We cannot use a semicolon indiscriminately at the end of a PRINT statement. It is only meant to hook two Lines together, **both** of which will PRINT something. The INPUT Line PRINTs a question mark. We will later connect two long PRINT Lines starting with "trailing semicolon" so as to PRINT everything on the same Line.

The Tandy BASIC *interpreter* speaks "The King's BASIC" as well as a variety of dialects.

INTERPRETER -- is the program we loaded in from disk which allows us to communicate with the Computer in an English-like language. The program is called BASIC, which stands for **B**eginners **A**ll-purpose **S**ymbolic **I**nstruction **C**ode.

Sometimes the word "dialect" is used when talking about the different variations of a computer language. Just as with dialects in "human" languages, there are differences in the way different computers use BASIC words. That's why I wrote **The BASIC Handbook, An Encyclopedia of the BASIC Computer Language** available at better Computer and Bookstores everywhere in English, and translated into French, German, Swedish, Norwegian, Dutch, Italian, and Spanish.

I SAY, OL' BOY, I SPEAK NOTHING BUT THE KING'S BASIC!
WELL, LA DEE DA AN' PIN A MONOCLE ON ME!

The first of the many "short-cuts" we will learn combines PRINT and INPUT into one statement.

Change Line 10 to read:

```
10 INPUT "TYPE IN A VALUE FOR A";A
```

delete Line 20 by typing:

```
20        ENTER
```

...and RUN.

The results are exactly the same, aren't they? Here is what we did:

1. Changed PRINT to INPUT
2. Placed both statements on the same Line
3. Eliminated an unnecessary Line

In the long programs which we will be writing, running and converting, this shortcut will be valuable.

Endless Love

Up to now, all our programs have been strictly one-shot affairs. You type RUN, the Computer executes the program, PRINTs the results (if any) and comes back with an OK. To repeat the program, you have to type RUN again. Can you think of another way to make the Computer execute a program two or more times?

No -- don't enlarge the program by repeating the same Lines over and over again. That's not very creative!

We'll answer that question by upgrading our Celsius-to-Fahrenheit conversion program (Chapter 9). If you think GOTO is a powerful statement in everyday life, wait 'til you see what it does for a computer program!

Type NEW and the following:

```
10 REM * IMPROVED (C) TO (F) CONV. PROGRAM *
20 INPUT "WHAT IS THE TEMP IN DEGREES (C)";C
30 F = (9/5)*C + 32
40 PRINT C;"DEGREES (C) =";F;"DEGREES (F)."
50 GOTO 20
```

...and RUN.

Hit CTRL BREAK to exit the program loop.

The Computer will keep asking for more until we get tired or the power goes off. This is the sort of thing a computer is best at -- doing the same thing over and over. Modify some of the other programs to make them self-repeating. They're often much more useful this way.

These have been 4 long and "meaty" lessons, so go back and review them, repeating those assignments where you feel weak. We are moving out into progressively deeper water, and complete mastery of these fundamentals is your only life preserver.

Learned in Chapter 11

Statements

INPUT
INPUT with built-in PRINT

Miscellaneous

Trailing semicolon

Chapter 12

Calculator or Immediate Mode

Two Easy Features

Before continuing exploration of the nooks and crannies of the Computer acting as a **computer**, we should be aware that it also works well as a **calculator**. If we **omit** the Line number before certain statements and commands, the Computer will execute them and display the answer on the screen. What's more, it will work as a calculator even when another computer program is loaded, **without disturbing that program**. All we need, to be in the calculator mode, is the cursor.

EXAMPLE: How much is 3 times 4? Type in:

```
PRINT 3 * 4        ENTER
```

...the answer comes back:

```
12
```

EXAMPLE: How much is 345 divided by 123?

Type:

```
PRINT 345/123        ENTER
```

...the answer is:

```
2.8Ø4878
```

Spend a few minutes making up routine arithmetic problems of your own, and use the calculator mode to solve them. Any arithmetic expression which can be used in a program can also be evaluated in the calculator mode. This includes parentheses and chain calculations like A*B*C.

Try the following:

```
PRINT (2/3)*(3/2)        ENTER
```

The answer is:

```
1
```

Immediate Mode for Troubleshooting

Suppose a program isn't giving the answers we expect. How can we troubleshoot it? One way is to ask the Computer to tell us what it knows about the variables used in the resident program.

EXAMPLE: If our program uses the variable X, we can ask the Computer to:

```
PRINT X        ENTER
```

The Computer will PRINT the present value of X.

Keep this handy tip in mind as you get into more complex programs.

Another thought: **Something** is stored in every memory cell (even if **you** have not put anything there). Type this instruction in the immediate mode:

```
PRINT A,B,C,D,E,F,G,H,I,J,K,L,M,N,O,P,Q,R,S,T,
U,V,W,X,Y,Z      ENTER
```

The answers depend on the values last given those variables -- even from much earlier programs. When we turn the Computer off, then on again, all variables are reset to 0. Typing RUN also "initializes" all variables to 0.

The FRE(0) Function

Since programs **do** occupy space in the Computer's memory, and program size is limited by how much memory is installed, it may be important to know how much memory is left. That's what the FRE(0) function is for.

In a "256K" computer there are about 256,000 different memory locations available to store and process programs. "256K" is just a shortcut phrase for the exact amount of memory which is 262144.

This book is for the computer operator and programmer, so we are studiously avoiding computer electronics theory -- when possible.

The Computer uses some of the memory to store the BASIC interpreter and for program control. To see the actual amount of memory available for programming, type:

```
NEW              ENTER

PRINT FRE(0)     ENTER
```

...and the answer is:

```
61109
```

With no program loaded, it means there are 61109 memory locations available for use. Note that the amount of usable memory will change with different versions of BASIC. The difference in memory space between 61109 and 262144 is used by the BASIC language interpreter and by the Computer for overall management and "monitoring".

Type in this simple program:

```
10 A = 25
```

then measure the memory remaining by typing:

```
PRINT FRE(Ø)        ENTER
```

Ø is a "dummy" value used with FRE. Any number or letter can be used.

...the answer is:

```
61Ø98
```

The program we entered took 611Ø9 - 61Ø98 = 11 bytes of space. Here is how we account for it:

1. Each Line number and the space following it (regardless of how small or large that Line number is) occupies 4 memory cells. The "carriage return" at the end of the Line takes 1 more byte even though it does not PRINT on the screen. Thus, memory "overhead" for each Line, short or long, is 5 bytes.

2. Each letter, number and space takes 1 byte. In the above program 5 bytes for overhead + 6 bytes for the characters = 11 bytes.

Now, type RUN, then check the memory again with PRINT FRE(Ø). It changed to 61Ø9Ø, 8 more bytes! When RUN, a simple variable like the A takes up 4 bytes and the numerical value takes another 4, totaling 8.

BYTE -- is the basic unit of storage for most microcomputers. In the Tandy MS-DOS Computers, it is a string of eight **bi**nary digi**ts** (bits). Thus a byte = 8 bits.

We will be studying memory requirements in more detail later.

Obviously, the short learning programs we have written so far are not taking up much memory space. This will change quickly as we move to more sophisticated programming. Make a habit of typing `PRINT FRE(Ø)` when completing a program to develop a sense of its size and memory requirements.

"BYTES and BITS"— IT SOUNDS LIKE A DOG FOOD COMMERCIAL!
WOOF

Learned in Chapter 12

Functions

FRE(Ø)

Miscellaneous

Immediate Mode
Memory
Byte

Chapter 13

SAVEing and LOADing Using Disk

A big advantage of having disk drives is that programs can be SAVEd on or LOADed from disk very quickly and reliably.

On a one-drive system, programs are automatically SAVEd on the diskette in Drive A unless it has a write-protect tab on it. In multi-drive systems, we must specify use of any other drive.

Remember: Diskettes must be "formatted" before they can be used. The MS-DOS disk is, of course, already formatted. See Chapter 1 for use of the FORMAT command.

Type in this short BASIC program:

```
10 REM * DISK BASIC PROGRAM *
20 PRINT "HELLO THERE, DISK DRIVE!"
99 END
```

then type:

```
SAVE "PROGRAM1"
```

Users with 2 drives type:

```
SAVE "B:PROGRAM1"
```

to save on the second drive.

If you placed a write-protect tab on your working master, the Computer will let you know there's a problem. (The message displayed will vary depending on the Computer.)

Remember, this prevents you from accidentally adding to, or deleting from, files on this disk. Remove the write-protect tab, and again type:

`SAVE "PROGRAM1"` (Use the **F4** key for `SAVE"`.) **ENTER**

Aha. It worked.

How do we know it worked? Easy. Type:

`FILES "*.BAS"` **ENTER**

`FILES "B:*.BAS"` for 2-drive computers.

and see the name:

```
PROGRAM1.BAS
```

listed. But where did the `.BAS` come from? The Computer automatically adds `.BAS` to any program saved from the BASIC interpreter. We don't have to use it when either SAVEing or LOADing a program to or from disk. When the disk has many programs on it, it's nice to be able to look at a FILES listing and know which ones are written in BASIC.

The `*.BAS` is a "wild card." It lists **all** BASIC programs of whatever name **before** the period.

WHERE DID THE .BAS COME FROM? ...and IF YOU SAY "THE LAKE", I'LL PULL YOUR PLUG!
MY LIPS ARE SEALED...

With the program SAVEd and the FILES checked, let's see if we can LOAD the program back from disk into memory. Type NEW to remove it from memory first. LIST to be sure it's gone, then:

`LOAD "PROGRAM1"` (Use the **F3** key for `LOAD"`.) **ENTER**

2-drive users:

`LOAD "B:PROGRAM1"`

---

and the Computer says Ok. Type LIST to see if it's back in memory. How about that?

Just for fun, let's see what's on the disk drive. Type:

`FILES` **ENTER**

2-drive users:

`FILES "B:"`

---

and there they are. Do you remember how we listed files from the MS-DOS command level? Right. Using DIR. From BASIC we use the FILES command. Don't study the list very hard. Most files are the subject of a whole different book.

As a final test, load our PROGRAM1 again.

`LOAD "PROGRAM1"` **ENTER**

2-drive users:

`LOAD "B:PROGRAM1"`

---

and

`LIST` **ENTER**

How sweet it is!

Learned in Chapter 13

Commands

SAVE
LOAD
FILES

Miscellaneous

"Pulling a DIRectory" from BASIC
Wild Card

Chapter 14

FOR-NEXT Looping

A major difference between a Computer and a calculator is the Computer's ability to do the same thing over and over an outrageous number of times! This single capability (plus a larger display) more than any other feature distinguishes between the two.

The FOR-NEXT loop is of such overwhelming importance in putting our Computer to work that few of the programming areas we explore from here on will exclude it. Its simplicity and variations are the heart of its effectiveness, and its power is truly staggering.

Type NEW, then this program:

```
20 PRINT "HELP! MY COMPUTER IS BERSERK!"
40 GOTO 20
```

...and RUN.

The Computer is PRINTing:

```
HELP! MY COMPUTER IS BERSERK!
```

and will do so indefinitely until we tell it to STOP. When you have seen enough, hit **CTRL** **BREAK**. This "breaks" the program RUN.

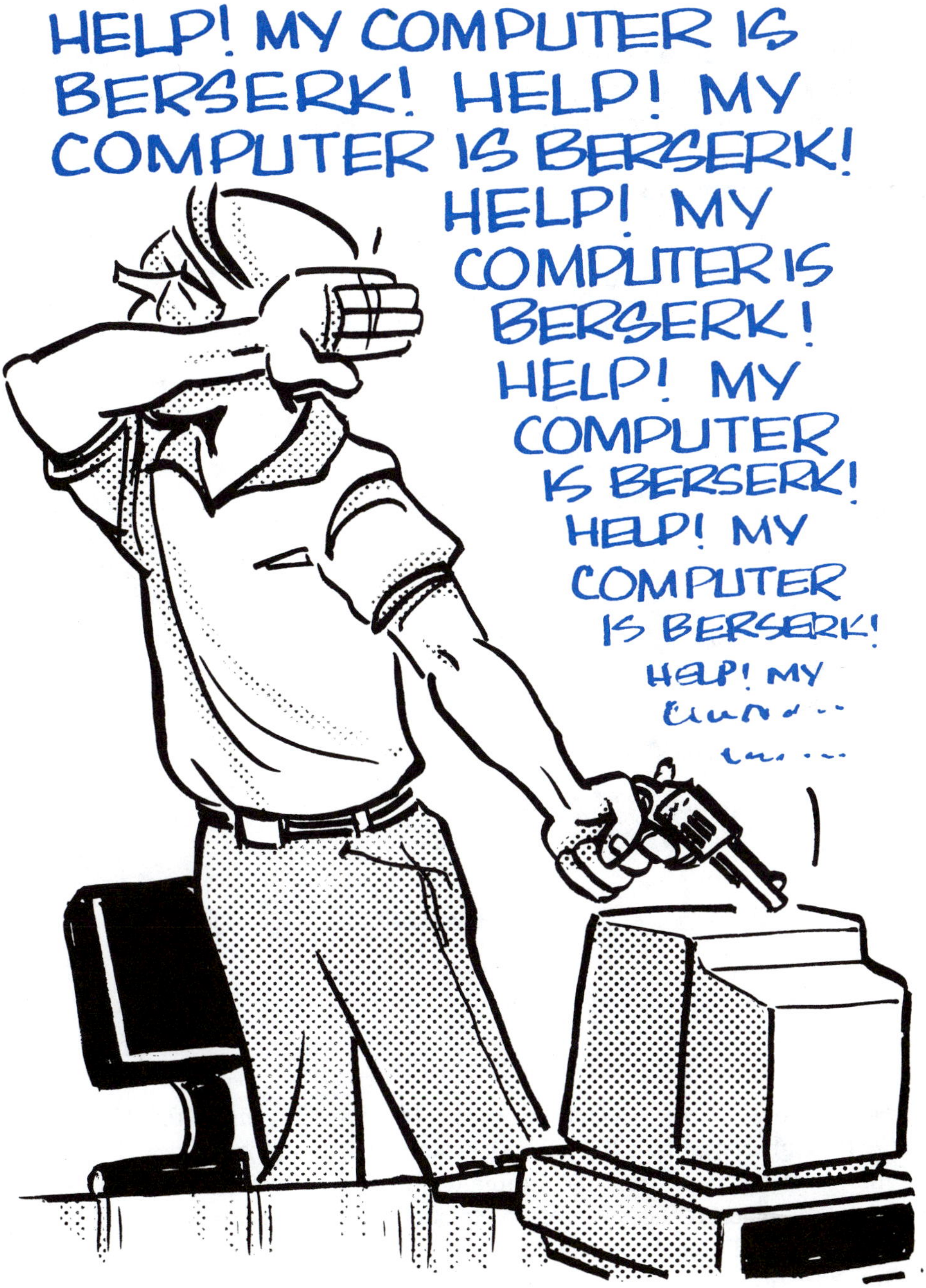
HELP! MY COMPUTER IS BERSERK! HELP! MY COMPUTER IS BERSERK!
HELP! MY COMPUTER IS BERSERK!
HELP! MY COMPUTER IS BERSERK!
HELP! MY COMPUTER IS BERSERK!
HELP! MY

Endless Loop

We created what is called an "endless loop". Remember our earlier programs which kept coming back for more INPUT? They had a very similar "loop."

Line 40 is an unconditional GOTO statement which causes the Computer to cycle back and forth ("loop") between Lines 20 and 40 forever, if not halted. This idea has great potential if we can harness it.

Modify the program to read:

```
10 FOR N = 1 TO 5
20  PRINT "HELP! MY COMPUTER IS BERSERK!"
40 NEXT N
60 PRINT "NO --- IT'S UNDER CONTROL."
```

...and RUN it.

The line:

```
HELP! MY COMPUTER IS BERSERK!
```

was PRINTed 5 times, then:

```
NO --- IT'S UNDER CONTROL.
```

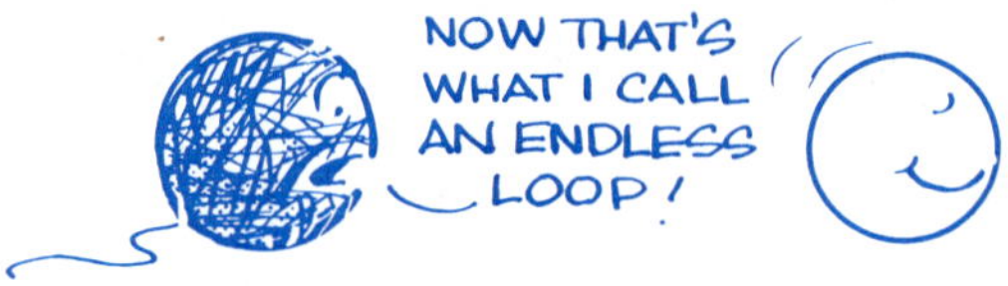

The FOR-NEXT loop created in Lines 10 and 40 caused the Computer to cycle through Lines 10, 20, and 40 exactly 5 times, then proceed to the rest of the program. Each time the Computer hit Line 40, it saw "NEXT N." The word NEXT caused the value of N to increase (or STEP) by exactly 1. The Computer "conditionally" went back to the `FOR N =` statement that **began** the loop.

Execution of the NEXT statement is "conditional" on N being less than or equal to 5 because Line 10 says FOR N = 1 TO 5. After the 5th pass through the loop, N = 6. The built-in test fails, the loop is broken, and program execution moves on. The FOR-NEXT statement harnessed the endless loop!

The STEP Function

There are times when it is desirable to increment the FOR-NEXT loop by some value other than 1. The STEP function allows it. Change Line 10 to read:

```
10 FOR N = 1 TO 5 STEP 2
```

...and RUN.

Line 20 was PRINTed only 3 times (when N=1, N=3, and N=5). On the first pass through the program, when NEXT N was hit, it was incremented (or STEPped) by the value of 2 instead of the default value of 1. On the second pass through the loop, N equaled 3. On the third pass, N equaled 5.

FOR-NEXT loops can be STEPped by any decimal number, even negative numbers. Why we would want to STEP down with negative numbers might seem vague at this time, but that too will be understood when needed. Meanwhile, change the following Line:

```
10 FOR N = 5 TO 1 STEP -1
```

...and RUN.

Five passes through the loop stepping **down** from 5 to 1 is exactly the same as stepping **up** from 1 to 5. Line 20 was still PRINTed 5 times. Change the STEP from -1 to -2.5 and RUN again.

Amazing! It PRINTed exactly twice. Smart Computer. Change the STEP back to -1.

You **are** using the EDITor, aren't you?

Modifying the FOR-NEXT Loop

Suppose we want to PRINT both Lines 20 and 60 five times, alternating between them. How will you change the program to accomplish it? Go ahead and make the change.

HINT: If you can't figure it out, try moving the NEXT N Line to another position.

Right -- we moved Line 40 to Line 70 and the screen reads:

```
HELP! MY COMPUTER IS BERSERK!
NO --- IT'S UNDER CONTROL.
HELP! MY COMPUTER IS BERSERK!
NO --- IT'S UNDER CONTROL.
```

... etc., 3 more times.

How would you modify the program so Line 20 is PRINTed 5 times, then Line 60 is PRINTed 3 times? Make the changes and RUN.

The new program might read:

```
10 FOR N = 1 TO 5
20  PRINT "HELP! MY COMPUTER IS BERSERK!"
40 NEXT N
50 FOR M = 1 TO 3
60  PRINT "NO --- IT'S UNDER CONTROL."
70 NEXT M
```

We now have a program with **two** controlled loops, sometimes called *DO-loops*. The first do-loop *DOes* something 5 times; the second one *DOes* something 3 times. We used the letter N for the first loop and M for the second, but any letters can be used. In fact, since the two loops are totally separate, we could have used the letter N for both of them -- not an uncommon practice in large programs where many of the letters are needed as variables.

RUN the program. Be sure you understand the fundamental principles and the variations. Then SAVE on disk as DOLOOP.

Incremental Looping

There is nothing magic about the FOR-NEXT loop; in fact, you may have already thought of another (longer) way to accomplish the same thing by using techniques we learned earlier. Stop now, and see if you can figure out a way to construct a workable do-loop by substituting something else in place of the FOR-NEXT statement.

Answer:

```
10 N = 1
20 PRINT "HELP! MY COMPUTER IS BERSERK!"
30 N = N + 1
40 IF N < 6 THEN 20
60 PRINT "NO --- IT'S UNDER CONTROL."
```

Line 10 *initializes* the value of N giving it an *initial*, or beginning, value of 1. Without initializing, N could have been any number from a previous program or program Line. Note that typing RUN automatically resets all variables back to 0 before the program executes.

Initialize: initially, or at the beginning, establish the value of a variable.

Line 30 *increments* it by 1, making N one more than whatever it was before. Line 40 uses one relational operator, <, to check that the new value of N is within the bounds we have established. If not, the test fails and the program continues.

Increments: STEPs (increases or decreases) values by specific amounts: by 1's, 3's, 5's, or whatever.

Note that in this system of *incrementing* and testing we do not send the program back to Line 10 as was the case with FOR-NEXT. What would happen if we did?

Answer: We would keep re-initializing the value of N to equal 1 and would, again, form an endless loop.

The opposite of *incrementing* is *decrementing*. Change the program so Line 30 reads:

```
30 N = N - 1
```

To *decrement* is to make smaller.

... then make other changes as needed to make the program work.

The changed Lines read:

```
10 N = 6
30 N = N - 1
40 IF N>1 THEN 20
```

Putting FOR-NEXT to Work

It isn't very exciting just seeing or doing the same thing over and over. The FOR-NEXT loop has to have a more noble purpose. It has many, and we will be learning new ones for a long time.

Suppose we want to PRINT out a chart showing how the time it takes to fly from London to San Diego varies with the speed at which we fly. (Remember, the formula is D = R*T). Let's PRINT out the flight time required for each speed between 100 mph and 1500 mph in increments of 100 mph. The program might look like this:

```
10 REM * TIME VS RATE FLIGHT CHART *
```

```
20 CLS
30 D = 6000
40 PRINT "      LONDON TO SAN DIEGO"
50 PRINT "    DISTANCE =";D;"(MILES)"
60 PRINT "RATE (MPH)","TIME (HOURS)"
70 PRINT
80 FOR R=100 TO 1500 STEP 100
90   T = D/R
100  PRINT R,T
110 NEXT R
```

Type in the program and RUN.

How about that? Try doing that one on the old slide rule or hand calculator!

It solved the D = R*T problem 15 times in a row for different values and PRINTed out the result. The screen should look like this:

```
      LONDON TO SAN DIEGO
    DISTANCE = 6000 (MILES)
RATE (MPH)      TIME (HOURS)

 100             60
 200             30
 300             20
 400             15
 500             12
 600             10
 700             8.571428
 800             7.5
```

```
900          6.666667
1000         6
1100         5.454546
1200         5
1300         4.615385
1400         4.285714
1500         4
```

Analyzing the Program

Look through the program and observe these many features before we do some exercises to change it:

Line 10	contains the REM statement identifying the program.
Line 20	uses the CLS (CLear Screen) statement to erase the screen so we have a nice place to write. It allows us to write in a *top-down* manner. (RUN the program again leaving out this Line to contrast *top-down* with *scroll* mode, then, put it back in.) CLS is a very unfussy statement which you will want to use often to make your PRINTouts neat and impressive.
Line 30	*initializes* the value of D. D will remain at its initialized value.
Lines 40 - 70	PRINT the chart heading.
Line 60	uses *automatic zone spacing* to position those column headings.

Remember *zone spacing?* The comma (,) in a PRINT statement automatically moves PRINTing over to the next 14-space PRINT zone.

Line 80 established the FOR-NEXT loop complete with a STEP. It says, "Initialize the rate (R) at 100 mph and make passes through the 'do-loop' with values of R incremented by values of 100 mph until a final value of 1500 mph is reached." Line 110 is the other half of the loop.

Line 90 contains the actual formula which calculates the answer.

Line 100 PRINTs the two values. They are positioned under their headings by automatic zone spacing (the commas).

Lines 90 and 100 are indented from the rest of the program text. This is a simple programming technique which highlights the do-loop and makes reading the program and troubleshooting it easier. **Try to adopt good programming practices like this** as you do the exercises. Indenting does take up a little memory space and on long programs is sometimes omitted.

Take a deep breath and go back over any points you might have missed in this lesson. SAVE the program onto disk as LONDON1 because we will use it in the next Chapter continuing our study of FOR-NEXT loops.

Learned in Chapter 14

Statements	Miscellaneous
FOR-NEXT	Increment
CLS	Decrement
STEP	Initialize
	"Top down"Display
	"Scroll" Display
	"Do-Loop"

Chapter 15

Son of FOR-NEXT

This is heady stuff. If you turned the Computer off between Chapters, LOAD in the LONDON1 program which we SAVEd in the last Chapter.

Modify the program so the rate and time are calculated and PRINTed for every 25 mph increment instead of the 100 mph increment presently in the program.

...and RUN.

Answer: `80 FOR R = 100 TO 1500 STEP 25`

Trouble in the Old Corral

What a revolting development! The PRINTout goes by so fast we can't read it, and by the time it stops, the top part is cut off.

Solutions for Sale

Several solutions are available:

1. Pressing the **HOLD** key (or **Ctrl** **Num Lock** keys) will halt program execution or LISTing. Pressing the key(s) again will start it. RUN the program several times, and practice stopping and starting using this method.

There's another solution we must try. While the program is RUNning, press CTRL BREAK for an execution BREAK. While Ctrl Num Lock or HOLD can be thought of as just pressing in the clutch, a BREAK is more like turning off the engine.

To restart execution after a BREAK, either type RUN to start over again from the beginning, or type CONT to CONTinue execution from the "break-point." CONTinue does **not** reset all variables back to zero, which can be an important consideration. F5 does the same as CONT ENTER.

2. For a classy display, we can build a "pause" **into the program**. The screen will fill, pause a moment, then automatically continue if we don't interrupt execution.

The Timing Loop

It takes time to do everything. Even this foxy box takes time to do its thing, though we may be awed by its speed.

We are going to write and experiment with a timing program using Lines 1-9 without erasing the one already resident. The new one must END without plowing ahead into the LONDON1 program, thus, Line 9. Type:

```
4 PRINT "DON'T GO AWAY"
5 FOR X = 1 TO 6800
6 NEXT X
7 PRINT "TIMER PROGRAM ENDED."
9 END
```

...and RUN.

On the 1000 SX, use:

```
5 FOR X = 1 TO 8200
```

On the 2000, use:

```
5 FOR X = 1 TO 2000
```

And on the 3000s, use:

```
5 FOR X = 1 TO 28000
```

Remember back when we learned **not** to do this (number Lines in tight sequence)? If we **hadn't** followed that rule with our LONDON1 program, we wouldn't have this nice space to demonstrate the point.

How long did it take? Well, it did take time, didn't it? About 10 seconds? The 1000 and 1000 EX can execute approximately 680 FOR-NEXT loops per second (the 1000 SX, 820 loops; the 2000, 2000 loops; and the 3000s, 2800 loops). That means, by specifying the number of loops, we can build in as long a time-delay as we wish.

Change the program to create a 30-second delay. Time it against your watch or clock to see how accurate it is.

Answer: `5 FOR X = 1 TO 20400` (`TO 60000` on the 2000)

`TO 24600` on the 1000 SX.

`TO 84000` on the 3000s.

EXERCISE 15-1: Using the space in Lines 1 through 8, design a program which:

1) Asks us how many seconds delay we wish, allows us to enter a number, then executes the delay and reports back at the end that the delay is over, and how many seconds it took. A sample answer is in Section B.

How to Handle Long Program LISTings

We now have **two** programs in the Computer. Let's pull a LIST to look at them. Oh, oh -- they almost fill the screen. Wonder what would we do if the programs were a few Lines longer so they couldn't both fit on the screen at the same time?

Rather than wring our hands about the problem, let's add some dummy Lines and learn how. Add:

Remember how to use AUTO?

```
1000 REM
2000 REM
3000 REM
4000 REM
5000 REM
6000 REM
7000 REM
8000 REM
9000 REM
10000 REM
```

and LIST. Sure enough, the first Lines of the first program are chopped off.

For Every Problem, a Solution

Try each of the following variations of the LIST command, and study the screen very carefully as each one does its thing:

LIST 50 (Lists only Line 50)

LIST -50 (Lists all Lines up through 50)

LIST 50- (Lists all Lines from 50 to end)

LIST 30-70 (Lists all Lines from 30 thru 70)

LIST 15-85 (Note that these numbers are not even in the program)

LIST . (Lists 80, the last Line number ENTERed or LISTed)

LIST .- (Lists the current or last Line number ENTERed or LISTed to end)

Question: How would you look at the resident program only up through Line 9?

Answer: Type LIST -9 (Talk about a give-away!)

Is There No End to This Magic?

To RUN the first program resident in the Computer -- we just type RUN. To RUN the second one we have an interesting variation of RUN called:

```
RUN ###
```

The ###'s represent the number of the Line we want the RUN to start with.

...and as you might suspect, it is similar to LIST ###. To RUN the program starting with Line 1Ø, type:

```
RUN 1Ø
```

...and that's just what happened.

Don't forget the space between RUN and 1Ø. Note that we can't use key F2 since it always starts RUNs with the first program Line. By pressing the ALT and R keys together, then typing in the Line number and pressing ENTER, you can start RUN at any line.

If there are 20 or 30 programs in the Computer at the same time, we can RUN just the one we want, provided we know its starting Line number. What's more, we can start any program in the middle (or elsewhere) for purposes of troubleshooting.

Meanwhile, Back at the Ranch

We got into this whole messy business trying to find a way to slow down our RUN on the flight times from London to San Diego. In the process we found out a lot more about the Computer and learned to build a timer loop. Now let's see if we can build a pause right into the Distance program. First erase the test program by typing:

```
DELETE 1-9          ENTER
```

and

```
DELETE 1000-10000          ENTER
```

Don't forget the space after DELETE.

Now:

```
LIST
```

How's that for power? It DELETEd those Lines without having to type each individual Line number.

Wrong Way Computer

One way to STOP the fast parade of information is to put in a STOP. Type in:

```
85 IF R = 500 THEN STOP
```

...and RUN.

We know R is going to increment from 100 to 1500. 500 is about a third of the way to the end. See how the chart PRINTed out to 475 mph, then hit the STOP as 500 came racing down to Line 85? The screen displays the first third of the chart and:

```
Break in 85
```

This means the program is STOPped, or broken in Line 85. To restart the program merely type:

CONT   ENTER   (or press F5.)

WOW! YOU PRINTED OUT TO 475 mph!
S'NUTHIN'. I CAN HIT MACH 2 ON A GOOD DAY!

...and execution picks up where it left off and PRINTs the rest of the chart, or executes until it hits another STOP. Where would you place the next STOP?

Yep.

```
87 IF R = 1000 THEN STOP
```

...and RUN.

At Last

The ultimate plan is to build timers into the program so as not to completely STOP execution, but merely delay the display long enough for study.

For the first timer, add:

```
83 IF R<> 500 THEN 90
84  FOR X = 1 TO 2100
85  NEXT X
```

On the 1000 SX, type:
```
84  FOR X = 1 TO 2500
```

On the 2000, type:
```
84 FOR X = 1 TO 6000
```

On the 3000s, type:
```
84 FOR X = 1 TO 8400
```

...and RUN.

It really works! As long as R does **not** equal 500 the program skips over the delay loop in Lines 84 and 85. When R **does** equal 500, the test "falls through" and Lines 84 and 85 "play catch" 2100 times, delaying the program's execution for about 3 seconds.

You have learned enough to design the 2nd delay when the Rate (R) reaches 1000. Have fun.

HINT: You'll need to make a small change in the first delay loop.

Time for a Cool One

It's been a long and tortuous route with numerous scenic side trips, but we made it. You picked up so many smarts in these 2 lessons on FOR-NEXT that it's your turn to put them to work.

EXERCISE 15-2: Modify the resident program so (MPH) appears **below** the heading. RATE, and (HOURS) appears **below** TIME. (It should be a breeze.)

EXERCISE 15-3: Design, write and RUN a program which will calculate and PRINT income at yearly, monthly, weekly and daily rates, based on a 40-hour week, a 1/12th-year month, and a 52-week year. Do this for yearly incomes between $5,000 and $25,000 in $1,000 increments. Document your program with REM statements to explain the equations you create.

Some of the exercise programs are becoming too long to leave work space for your ideas. From now on, use a pad of paper for working up the answers.

EXERCISE 15-4: Here's an old chestnut the Computer really eats up: Design, write, and RUN a program which tells how many days you have to work, starting at a penny a day, so if your salary doubles each day, you'll know which day you earn at least a million dollars. Include columns which show each day number, its daily rate, and the total income to-date. Make the program stop after PRINTing the first day your daily rate is a million dollars or more. (After that ... who cares?)

Answers to these exercises are found in Section B.

The "Brute Force" Method (Subtitled: Get A Bigger Hammer)

Much to the consternation of some teachers, a great value of the Computer is its ability to do the tedious work involved in the "cut and try," "hunt and peck" or other less respectable methods of finding an answer (or attempting to prove the correctness of a theory, theorem or principle). This method involves trying many possible solutions to see if one fits or to find the closest one or to establish a trend. Beyond that, it can be a powerful learning tool by providing reams of data in chart or graph form which would simply take too long to generate by hand. For example:

EXERCISE 15-5: You have a 1000 foot roll of fencing wire and want to make a **rectangular** pasture.

Using all of the wire, determine what length and width dimensions will allow you to enclose the maximum number of square feet. Use the brute force method; let the Computer try different values for L and W and PRINT out the Area fenced by each pair of L and W.

The formula for area is Area = Length times Width, or A=L*W.

EXERCISE 15-6: Extra credit problem for "electronics types"

Don't necessarily shy away from this problem if electricity isn't your bag. The principle, the optimizing of a value, is applicable to many fields of endeavor and is little short of profound. Enough information is given so that anyone can write the program.

This exercise involves a problem confronted by every electricity student who studies SOURCES (batteries, generators) and LOADS (lights, resistors).

The *Maximum D.C. Power Transfer Theorem* states,

"Maximum DC power is delivered to an electrical load when the resistance of that load is equal in value to the internal resistance of the source."

And then the arguments begin...

> "Use a HIGH resistance load because it will drop more voltage and accept more power." ($P=V^2/R$)
>
> "No, use a LOW resistance load so it will draw more current and accept more power." ($P=I^2*R$)
>
> "Use a load value somewhere in between." ($P=I*V$)

(continued)

With the values given in the schematic, design, write and RUN a program which will try out values of load resistance ranging from 1 to 20 ohms, in 1 ohm increments, and PRINT the answers to the following:

1. Value of Load Resistance (from 1 to 20 ohms)

2. Total circuit power (circuit current squared, times total circuit resistance) = $I^2 * (10 + R)$

3. Power lost in source (circuit current squared, times source resistance) = $I^2 * 10$

4. Power delivered to load (circuit current squared, times load resistance) = $I^2 * R$

Note: Circuit current is found by dividing source voltage (120 volts) by total circuit resistance (load resistance + 10 ohms source resistance). Everything follows Ohms Law (V=I*R) and Watts Law (P=I*V).

GOOD LUCK! Don't look at the answer until you've got it whipped.

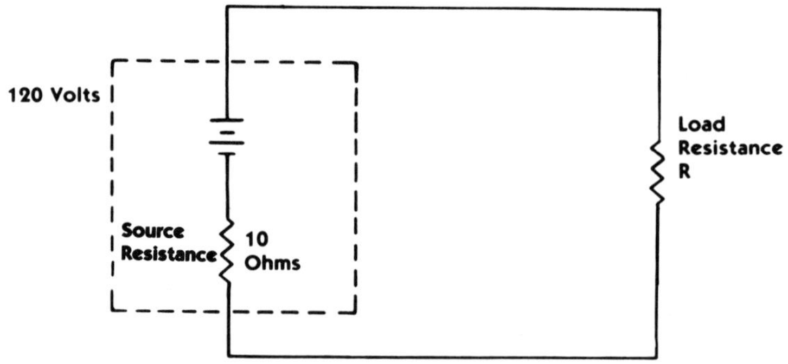

Learned in Chapter 15

Commands	Statements	Miscellaneous
LIST ###	STOP	Timing Loop
RUN ###		"Brute Force" method
DELETE ###		Ctrl Num Lock (HOLD)
CONT		

Chapter 16

Formatting with TAB

After those last few Chapters it's time for an easy one.

We already know 3 ways to set up the output PRINT format.

We can:

1. Enclose what we want to say in quotes, inserting blank spaces as necessary.

2. Separate the objects of the PRINT statement with semicolons so as to PRINT them tightly together on the same line.

3. Separate the objects of the PRINT statement with commas to PRINT them on the same line in the 5 different PRINT "zones."

A 4th way is by using the TAB function, which is similar to the TAB on a typewriter. TAB is especially useful when the output consists of columns of numbers with headings. Type in the following NEW program and RUN:

```
10 PRINT TAB(5);"THE";TAB(20);"TOTAL";
        TAB(35);"SPENT"
20 PRINT TAB(5);"BUDGET";TAB(20);"YEAR'S";
        TAB(35);"THIS"
```

```
30 PRINT TAB(5);"CATEGORY";TAB(20);"BUDGET";
         TAB(35);"MONTH"
```

The RUN should appear:

```
THE             TOTAL           SPENT
BUDGET          YEAR'S          THIS
CATEGORY        BUDGET          MONTH
```

EXERCISE 16-1: EDIT the above program to use the following 3 ways to format PRINTing. Here is a start:

```
10 PRINT"THE                 TOTAL                SPENT"
20 PRINT"BUDGET","YEAR'S","THIS"
30 PRINT TAB( );"CATEGORY";TAB( );
"BUDGET";TAB( );"MONTH"
```

Use ordinary spacing for the first Line of the heading, zone spacing for the second Line and TABbing for the third Line.

HINT: This isn't as easy as it looks, so it may require extensive editing. Since automatic zone formatting is not adjustable, the other formats will have to be keyed to it.

A semicolon is traditionally used following TAB, as shown above. Most newer BASIC interpreters permit quote marks, a blank, or even no space, instead.

```
10 PRINT TAB(10) "OOPS, NO SEMICOLON!"
```

RUNs just fine, but **leave out semicolons at your own peril.**

The number inside the parentheses of the TAB function tells the Computer how many spaces to the right of the left margin to start PRINTing. It is important to remember when using TABs that whenever numbers or numeric variables are PRINTed, the Computer inserts one additional space to the left of the number to allow for the − or + sign.

Type this NEW program:

```
10 A = 3
20 B = 5
30 C = A + B
40 PRINT TAB(10);"A";TAB(20);"B";TAB(30);"C"
50 PRINT TAB(10);A;TAB(20);B;TAB(30);C
```

...and RUN.

```
A          B          C
 3          5          8
```

The numbers are indented one space beyond the TAB value. Keep this in mind when lining up (or indenting) headings and answers.

Change Line 20 to read:

```
20 B = -5
```

...and RUN.

See why numbers indent one space?

Whole numbers are most commonly used as TAB values, but on those rare occasions when a fraction is used, the Computer rounds the fraction to the nearest whole number before TABbing.

All of the rules we have seen so far for TABbing apply whether the TAB value is an actual number or a numeric variable.

The Long Lines Division

Have you ever wondered what would happen if we had to PRINT a great number of headings or answers on the same line -- but didn't have enough room on the program Line to neatly hold all the TAB statements? You have? Really? It's easy. Type and RUN the following NEW program. It stretches the "leaving out of semicolons" to the limits of prudence.

```
10 A = 0
20 B = 1
30 C = 2
40 D = 3
50 E = 4
60 F = 5
70 G = 6
80 H = 7
90 I = 8
100 PRINT "A"TAB(10)"B"TAB(20)"C"TAB(30);
110 PRINT "D"TAB(40)"E"TAB(50)"F";
120 PRINT TAB(60)"G"TAB(70)"H"TAB(80)"I"
130 PRINT A;TAB(10)B;TAB(20)C;TAB(30)D;
140 PRINT TAB(40)E;TAB(50)F;TAB(60)G;
150 PRINT TAB(70)H;TAB(80)I
```

The trailing semicolons (;) in Lines 100, 110, 130 and 140 do the trick. They make the end of one PRINT Line continue right on to the next PRINT Line without activating a carriage return. The combination of TAB and trailing semicolon allows us almost infinite flexibility in formatting the output.

But do you see a problem in the display?

LISTEN, MR. PROGRAMMER! THE NEXT TIME YOUR SCREEN OVERFLOWS — YOU CLEAN IT UP!
ACTUALLY, HE STEPPED IN THE DOG'S WATER DISH.

The number 8 is printed one Line too low and indented one space. When we specified TAB(8Ø) in Line 15Ø, we pushed the number 8, with its leading and trailing space, beyond the right hand side of the screen causing it to be printed on the next Line. To print it on the same Line as the other numbers, change Line 150 to:

```
150 PRINT ... TAB(78)I
```

...and RUN.

2000 users change Lines 12Ø and 15Ø to:

```
120 PRINT ... TAB(78)"I"
150 PRINT ... TAB(78)I
```

...and RUN.

These extra lessons from the program are timely and raise the flag of caution whenever the limits of either a screen or printer width are pushed. Plan ahead...

Finally, to see the program crash when one too many liberties are taken with semicolons, remove the only one in Line 15Ø and RUN.

That's enough fooling around with Mother Nature.

EXERCISE 16-2: Rework the answer to Exercise 15-3 to include the *hourly* rate of pay in the PRINTout. Use the TAB Function to have the chart display all 5 columns side by side.

EXERCISE 16-3: (Optional) Rework the special program 15-6 answer using the TAB Function so the PRINTout includes the internal resistance in a fifth column.

Learned in Chapter 16

Print Modifiers	Miscellaneous
TAB	Trailing semicolon

Chapter 17

Grandson of FOR-NEXT

The FOR-NEXT loop didn't go away for long. It returns here more powerful than ever. Type this NEW program:

```
10 FOR A = 1 TO 3
20  PRINT "A LOOP"
30   FOR B = 1 TO 2
40    PRINT ,"B LOOP"
50   NEXT B
60 NEXT A
```

...and RUN.

For good program readability, add 2 blank spaces in Line 20 before PRINT; 3 in Line 30 before FOR; 4 in 40 before PRINT; and 3 in 50 before NEXT.

The result is:

```
A LOOP
              B LOOP
              B LOOP
```

```
A LOOP
                    B LOOP
                    B LOOP
A LOOP
                    B LOOP
                    B LOOP
```

This display vividly demonstrates operation of the nested FOR-NEXT loop. "Nesting" is used in the same sense that drinking glasses are "nested" when stored to save space. Certain types of portable chairs, empty cardboard boxes, etc. can be nested. They fit one inside the other for easy stacking.

Let's analyze the program a Line at a time:

Line 10 — establishes the first FOR-NEXT loop, called A, and directs that it be executed 3 times.

Line 20 — PRINTs `A LOOP` so we will know where it came from in the program. See how this program Line is indented to make it stand out as being nested in the A loop?

Line 30 — establishes the second loop, called B, and directs that it be executed twice. It is indented even more so we can instantly see that it is buried even deeper in the A loop.

Line 40 — PRINTs two items: "nothing" in the 1st PRINT zone, then the comma kicks us into the 2nd PRINT zone where `B LOOP` is PRINTed. Makes for a clear distinction on the screen between A loop and B loop, eh?

Line 50 — completes the B loop and returns control to Line 30 for as many executions of the B loop as Line 30 directs. (So far we have PRINTed one "A" and one "B".)

Line 60 — ends the first pass through the A loop and sends control back to Line 10, the beginning of the A loop. The A loop has to be executed 3 times before the program RUN is complete, PRINTing "A" 3 times and "B" six times (3 times 2).

Study the program and the explanation until you completely comprehend. It's simple but powerful magic.

To get a better feel for this nested loop (or loop within a loop) business, let's play with the program. Change Line 10 to read:

```
10 FOR A = 1 TO 5
```

...and RUN.

Right! A was PRINTed 5 times, meaning the A loop was executed 5 times, and B was PRINTed 10 times -- twice for each pass of the A loop. Now change Line 30 to read:

```
30 FOR B = 1 TO 4
```

...and RUN

Nothing to it! A was PRINTed 5 times and B PRINTed 20 times. Do you remember what to do if the A's and B's whiz by too fast? Press the **HOLD** key to temporarily freeze the display.

How to Goof-Up Nested FOR-NEXT Loops

The most common error beginning programmers make with nested loops is improper nesting. Change these Lines:

```
50  NEXT A
60 NEXT B
```

...and RUN.

The Computer says:

```
NEXT without FOR in 60
```

Looking at the program we quickly see that the B loop is *not* nested within the A loop. The FOR part of the B loop is inside the A loop, but the NEXT part is outside it. That doesn't work! A later chapter deals with something called "flow charting," a means of planning programs to avoid this type of problem. Meanwhile we just have to be careful.

Breaking Out of Loops

Improper nesting is illegal, but breaking out of a loop when a desired condition has been met is OK. Add and change these Lines:

```
50    NEXT B
55   IF A = 2 GOTO 100
60 NEXT A
99 END
100 PRINT "A EQUALLED 2. RUN ENDED."
```

...and RUN.

As the screen shows, we "bailed out" of the A loop when A equaled 2 and hit the test Line at 55. The END in Line 99 is a precautionary block set up to STOP the Computer from executing Line 100 unless specifically directed to go there. That would never happen in this simple program, but we will use *protective ENDs* from time to time to remind us that Lines which should be reached only by specific GOTO or IF-THEN statements must be protected against accidental "hits."

We'll be seeing a lot of the *nested* FOR-NEXT loop now that we know what it is and can put it to use.

EXERCISE 17-1: Re-enter the original program found at the beginning of this Chapter. It contains a B loop nested within the A loop. Make the necessary additions to this program so a new loop called "C" will be nested within the B loop, and will PRINT "C LOOP" 4 times for each pass of the B loop.

EXERCISE 17-2: Use the program which is the answer to Exercise 17-1. Make the necessary additions to this program so a new loop called "D" will be nested within the C loop, and will PRINT "D LOOP" 5 times for each pass of the C loop.

WHILE - WEND

A variation on the FOR-NEXT idea is the WHILE-WEND statement. WHILE is the beginning statement in a series which is executed repeatedly until a certain WHILE condition becomes **false**.

LET ME GUESS ...
YOU'RE BAILING OUT
OF A NESTED LOOP!
BINGO!

The loop which begins with WHILE must be closed by a WEND. Type in this NEW program:

> When writing programs, be sure to indent Lines to highlight nesting or program flow. It helps when reading them -- and is a great aid when debugging (troubleshooting) programs. End of message.

```
10 X = 1
20 WHILE X<>Ø
30   INPUT X
40   S = S + X
50 WEND
60 PRINT "SUM =";S
```

...and RUN.

INPUT several non-zero numbers, then INPUT a Ø. As long as X does not = Ø, WEND keeps returning execution to WHILE. When X is INPUT as Ø, the WHILE statement in Line 2Ø interprets the Ø as its "bail-out" cue and exits the loop via WEND. Line 6Ø PRINTs the sum of the numbers INPUT.

And with that, let's WEND our way towards the next Chapter.

Learned in Chapter 17

Statements	Miscellaneous
WHILE-WEND	Nested FOR-NEXT loops
	Protective END blocks

Chapter 18

The INTeger Function

Integer? "I can't even pronounce it, let alone understand it." Oh, come, come. Don't let old nightmares of being trapped in Algebra class stop you **now**. It's pronounced (IN-teh-jur) and simply means a *whole number* like -5, 0, or 3, etc. How difficult can that be? Come to think of it, some folks make a whole career out of complicating simple ideas. We try to do just the opposite.

The INTeger function, INT(X), allows us to "round off" any number, large or small, positive or negative, into an INTeger, or *whole* number.

Careful -- we're not talking about ordinary rounding. Ordinary rounding gives us the **closest** whole number, whether it's larger or smaller than X. INT(X) gives us the **largest** whole number which is **less than** or **equal to** X. This is a very versatile form of rounding -- in fact, we can use it to produce the other "ordinary" kind of rounding.

Type NEW to clear out any old programs, then type:

```
10 X = 3.14159
20 Y = INT(X)
50 PRINT "Y =";Y
```

...and RUN.

The display reads:

```
Y =  3
```

Oh -- success is so sweet! It rounded 3.14159 off to the whole number 3. Change Line 1Ø to read:

```
1Ø X = -3.14159
```

...and RUN.

Good Grief! It rounded the answer **down** to read:

```
Y = -4
```

What kind of rounding is this? Easy. The INT function **always** rounds **down** to the next **lowest whole number**. Pretty hard to get that confused! It makes a positive number less positive, and makes a negative number more negative (same thing as less positive). At least it's consistent.

Taking it a Line at a time:

Line 1Ø	set the value of X equal to the value we specified, in this case π.
Line 2Ø	found the INTeger value of X and assigned it to variable Y.
Line 5Ø	PRINTed an identification label (Y =) followed by the value of Y.

Not Content to Leave Well Enough Alone

We can do some foxy things by combining a FOR-NEXT loop with the INTeger function.

Change the program to read:

```
1Ø X = 3.14159
```

```
20 Y = INT(X)

30 Z = X - Y

40 PRINT "X =";X

50 PRINT "Y =";Y

60 PRINT "Z =";Z
```

SAVE this as INTEGER1...and RUN.

AHA! I don't know what we've discovered, but it must be good for something. It reads:

```
X = 3.14159

Y = 3

Z = .1415901
```

We've split the value of X into its INTeger (whole number) value (called it Y) and its decimal part (called it Z).

Lines 40, 50, and 60 merely PRINTed the results.

Hold the Phone

Oh - oh! Why doesn't Z equal the exact difference between X and Y? Where did that "01" in the decimal value come from?

The slight difference has nothing to do with the INT function. You have discovered the Computer's limit of accuracy. Just like a calculator (or a person), a computer can never be perfectly accurate all the time. For short arithmetic expressions, our Computer is accurate to six digits. In longer, more complex expressions, such a minute error in the sixth digit can be magnified to where it becomes significant. All programmers have to cope with this kind of built-in error.

There **is** a way to control the accuracy of our results. It involves artificially rounding the fraction to the desired number of decimal places, and then forcing the Computer to PRINT out only those digits which are "properly rounded."

DOING? WELL, I WAS WORKING WITH 3.14159 A LOT and SMAK ONE THING LED TO ANOTHER...
ULP

For example, suppose we need π accurate to only 3 decimal places. (Of course, we can specify it as 3.142, but that's not the point.) Type NEW, then enter and RUN the following program:

```
10 X = 3.14159
20 X =  X + .0005
30 X = INT(X * 1000)/1000
40 PRINT X
```

Adding .0005 in Line 20 gives our fraction a "push in the right direction." If this fraction has a digit greater than 4 in its 10-thousandths-place, then adding .0005 will effectively increase the thousandths-place digit by 1. Otherwise, the added .0005 will have no effect on the final result. This results in what's called "4/5 rounding."

Try using other values than π for X (just make sure X*1000 isn't too large for the INT function to handle).

It's easy to change the program to round accurately to a number of decimal places. For example, to round X off at the hundredths-place (2 digits to the right of the decimal point), change Lines 20 and 30 to read:

```
20 X = X + .005
30 X = INT(X * 100)/100
```

...and RUN using several values for X.

This trick is very useful when PRINTing dollars-and-cents. It prevents $39.995 type prices.

Hmmmm!!!

Do you suppose there is a way to separate each of the digits in 3.14159, or in any other number? Do you think I would have brought it up if there wasn't? After all...(mumble, mumble).

It's really your turn to do some creative thinking, but we'll get it started and see if you can finish this idea. First wipe out the resident program and reLOAD and RUN INTEGER1.

```
20 Y = INT(X)
30 Z = X - Y
40 PRINT "X =";X
50 PRINT "Y =";Y
60 PRINT "Z =";Z
```

It split X into INTeger and decimal parts.

Now, if we multiply Z by 10, then Z will become a whole number plus a decimal part, 1.4159. We can then take *its* INTeger value and strip off the decimal part leaving the left hand digit standing alone. Let's label the Left-hand digit L, and see what happens. Enter:

```
70 Z = Z * 10
80 L = INT(Z)
90 PRINT "L =";L
```

...and RUN.

Hmmm! It reads:

```
X = 3.14159
Y = 3
Z = .1415901
L = 1
```

We peeled off the leftmost digit from the decimal. Can you think of a way we might use a FOR-NEXT loop in order to strip off the rest?

Time Out For Creative Thinking!

(...brief interlude of recorded music...)

After all, these digits might not be just an accurate value of pi, but a coded message from a cereal box. If you don't have the decoder ring, you need a computer!

(...more recorded music...)

Enough thinking there on company time! Add these Lines:

```
75 FOR A = 1 TO 5
100 Z = Z - L
110 Z = Z * 10
120 NEXT A
```

SAVE as INTEGER2 and RUN.

VOILA! The "PRINTout" reads:

```
X = 3.14159
Y = 3
Z = .1415901
L = 1
L = 4
L = 1
L = 5
L = 9
```

OK. Now let's analyze the program.

Line 75	began a FOR-NEXT loop, one pass for each of the 5 digits right of the decimal.
Line 100	creates a new decimal value of Z by stripping off the INTeger part. (Plugging in the values, Z = 1.415901 − 1 = .415901)
Line 110	does the same as Line 70 did, multiply the new decimal value times 10 so as to make the left-hand digit an INTeger and vulnerable to being snatched away by the INT function. (Z = .415901 * 10 = 4.15901)
Line 120	sends control back to Line 75 for another pass through the clipping program, and the rest is history.

We already talked about the accuracy of the Computer. To understand it better, change Line 75 to read:

```
75 FOR A = 1 TO 10
```

...and RUN.

Where did all those extra numbers come from? Again, the last digit or two at the end of a number is not to be trusted.

But there is a solution. Change Line 75 back as it was, then change Line 10 to read:

```
10 X = 3.1415900
```

...and RUN.

Whew! Was a little nervous there for a minute. By declaring the accuracy of X to be a few decimal places greater than actually needed, digits we **do** need will be reliable. There are better ways to do this, and we will learn to use them later.

Now "pull" a LIST of the program. Line 10 says:

```
10 X = 3.14159#
```

The # sign at the end is a "Type Declaration" character. Since we typed in more than 6 digits, the Computer is indicating that the number has exceeded the limits of "Single Precision" and has become "Double Precision." We'll talk **much** more about this concept in a later Chapter, but let's not be diverted from the main theme of **this** Chapter.

Is This Too Hard to Follow?

No -- it isn't hard to follow. We could go through and calculate every intermediate value just like before, and it would be perfectly clear. Let's learn a way to let the Computer help us understand what it is doing, instead.

We can insert temporary PRINT Lines anywhere in any program to follow every step in its execution. The Computer can actually overwhelm us with data. By carefully indicating exactly what we want to know, it will display the inner details of any process. Start by adding this Line:

```
72 PRINT "#72 Z =";Z
```

...and RUN.

The essentials of this "test," or "debugging" or "flag," Line are:

1. It PRINTs something.
2. It gives the *Line number*, for analysis and easy location for later erasure.
3. It tells the *name* of the variable we are watching at that point in the program.
4. It gives the *value* of that variable at **that point**.

"Flagging" is such a wonderful tool for troubleshooting stubborn programs that you will make a habit of using it whenever the going gets tough.

It can be very helpful when inserted in FOR-NEXT loops -- so:

```
77 PRINT "#77 A =";A
```

...and RUN.

Wow! The information comes thick and fast! It tells what is happening during each pass of the loop. Hard to keep track of so much, and we've barely begun. Is there some way to make it more readable?

Yes, there are lots of ways. Indenting is a simple way to separate the answers from the troubleshooting data. Edit Lines 72 and 77 as follows:

```
72 PRINT ,"#72 Z =";Z
77 PRINT ,,"#77 A =";A
```

...and RUN.

Ahh. That is so easy to read. Let's monitor some more points in the program. Type in:

```
105 PRINT ,,,"#105 Z =";Z
115 PRINT ,,,,"#115 Z =";Z
```

SAVE as INTEGER3

...and RUN.

Egad, Igor! We've created a monster!

Well, there it is. All the data we can handle (and then some). By using the **HOLD** (or **Ctrl** **Num Lock**) keys to temporarily halt execution, we can study the data at every step to understand how the program works (or doesn't). Do it. Understand this program and all its little lessons completely. When you are satisfied, go back and erase the "flags."

INTeger Division

If that isn't quite enough to keep the mind reeling, there **is** another way to get the INTeger value of the result of an equation without using the INT function! It is called "INTeger division," and instead of using the normal slash /, we use a backslash \ (located on the keypad or in the upper right above the ENTER key).

Type NEW. Then enter this example:

```
10 X = 23.987
20 Y = 2.567
30 PRINT "X/Y =";X/Y
40 PRINT "INT(X/Y) =";INT(X/Y)
50 PRINT "X\Y =";X\Y
```

...and RUN. It should produce:

```
X/Y = 9.344371
INT(X/Y) = 9
X\Y = 8
```

8? Is that right? Yep. INTeger division actually modifies the value of each variable in the equation **before the calculation is made**. In this case, both X and Y are rounded to the nearest whole numbers, 24 and 3, then division is performed producing the INTeger value of 8. Hmmm.

Take a breather and do the exercises. You have learned enough for one Chapter.

EXERCISE 18-1: Enter this straightforward NEW program for finding the area of a circle.

```
10 P = 3.14159
20 PRINT "RADIUS", "AREA"
30 PRINT
40 FOR R=1 TO 10
50  A = P * R * R
60  PRINT R,A
70 NEXT R
```

...and RUN.

Area equals π times the radius squared (that is, the radius times itself).

Modify the program to suppress all the numbers to the right of the decimal point.

EXERCISE 18-2: Knowing just enough to be dangerous, and in need of some humility, change Line 55 so each value of *area* is rounded (down) to be accurate to one decimal place. For example:

```
RADIUS                  AREA
 1                       3.1
```

> **EXERCISE 18-3:** Carrying the above Exercise one step further, modify the program Line 55 to round down the value of area to be accurate to 2 decimal places.

Learned in Chapter 18

Functions	Math Operators	Miscellaneous
INT(X)	\	Flags INTeger Division

Chapter 19

More Branching Statements

It Went That-A-Way

Enter this NEW program:

```
10 INPUT "TYPE A NUMBER BETWEEN 1 AND 5";N
20 IF N = 1 GOTO 100
30 IF N = 2 GOTO 120
40 IF N = 3 GOTO 140
50 IF N = 4 GOTO 160
60 IF N = 5 GOTO 180
70 PRINT "THE NUMBER YOU TYPED WAS"
80 PRINT "NOT BETWEEN 1 AND 5!"
90 END
100 PRINT "N = 1"
110 END
120 PRINT "N = 2"
130 END
140 PRINT "N = 3"
150 END
```

```
160 PRINT "N = 4"

170 END

180 PRINT "N = 5"
```

SAVE as ONGOTO1 and RUN it a few times to feel comfortable and be sure it is "debugged." Be sure to try numbers outside the range of 1-5 including 0 and a negative number.

Debugged means "getting all the errors out of a computer program."

This program works fine for examining the value of a variable, N and sending the Computer off to a certain Line number to do what it says there. If there are lots of possible directions in which to branch, however, we will want to use a greatly improved test called ON-GOTO, which cuts out lots of Lines of programming.

DELETE Lines 20, 30, 40, 50 and 60. Remember how? (Type DELETE 20-60).

Enter this new Line:

```
20 ON N GOTO 100,120,140,160,180
```

SAVE as ONGOTO2 and RUN a few times, as before.

Works fine until a negative number or a number greater than 255 is entered. Then the Computer responds with an Illegal function call error.

Using the ON-GOTO statement is really pretty simple, though it looks hard. Line 20 says:

IF the "rounded" value of N is 1, THEN GOTO Line 100.

IF the "rounded" value of N is 2, THEN GOTO Line 120.

IF the "rounded" value of N is 3, THEN GOTO Line 140.

IF the "rounded" value of N is 4, THEN GOTO Line 160.

IF the "rounded" value of N is 5, THEN GOTO Line 180.

IF the "rounded" value of N is not one of the numbers LISTed above, THEN move on to the next Line ... Line 70.

The ON-GOTO statement has a built-in standard rounding system. If the number INPUT is less than halfway between 2 INTegers, rounding is downward to the **lower** INTeger. If it is halfway or larger, rounding is to the next **higher** INTeger.

RUN again and type in the following values of N to prove the point:

```
2.4

1.5

3.7

4.499

4.5

0.5
```

Get the picture?

Variations on a Theme

Lots of tricks can be played to get the most from ON-GOTO. For example, if you wanted to branch out to 15 different locations but didn't want to type that many different numbers on a single ON-GOTO Line, you could use several Lines like this (don't bother to do it):

```
20 ON N GOTO 100,120,140,160,180

30 ON N-5 GOTO 200,220,240,260,280

40 ON N-10 GOTO 300,320,340,360,380
```

and, of course, fill in the proper responses at those Line numbers.

In Line 3Ø, it was necessary to subtract 5 from the number being INPUT as N, because each new ON-GOTO Line starts counting again from the number 1.

In Line 4Ø, since we had already provided for INPUTs between 1 and 10, we subtract 10 from N to cover the range from 11 through 15.

We could have used any letter after "ON," not just N. N can be the value of a letter variable or a complete expression, either calculated in place or calculated in a previous Line.

Give Me a SGN(X)

Using ON-GOTO along with a new function called SGN (it's pronounced "sign") plus a modest amount of imagination produces a useful little routine. But first, let's learn about SGN.

The SGN function examines number to see whether it is negative, zero, or positive. It tells us the number is negative by giving us a −1. (In computer language, "It returns a −1.") If the number is zero, it returns a Ø. If positive, it returns a +1. SGN is a very simple function.

In order to ease into the next concept, we will simulate the built-in SGN function with a SUBROUTINE.

So What Is a Subroutine?

A subroutine is a short but very specialized program (or routine) which is built into a large program to meet a specialized need. The BASIC interpreter incorporates many of them which we never see.

As an example of how to create functions that are **not** included in our BASIC, we will use a 5-Line subroutine instead of the SGN function to accomplish the same thing. (Even though our BASIC has its own SGN function, you should complete this Chapter to be sure you understand subroutines.)

"Scratch" the program now in memory by typing NEW, then type in this SGN subroutine:

```
30000 END

30010 REM SGN(X), INPUT X, OUTPUT T=-1,0, OR +1
```

```
30020 IF X < 0 THEN T = -1
30030 IF X = 0 THEN T = 0
30040 IF X > 0 THEN T = +1
30050 RETURN
```

"Calling" a Subroutine

GOSUB directs the Computer to go to a Line number, execute what it says there and in the following Lines, and when done, RETURN to the Line containing that GOSUB statement. We'll use Line 20:

```
20 GOSUB 30020
```

RETURN is to GOSUB what NEXT is to FOR.

A RETURN statement always ends a subroutine, and ours is in Line 30050. We have reserved Line number 30000 to hold a protective END block for our subroutine, so the Computer doesn't come crashing into it when done with the main program. (Try taking it out when we're done to see what happens.)

Getting Down to Business

Okay, now let's combine GOSUB with the SGN subroutine to see what this is all about. Add:

```
10 INPUT "TYPE ANY NUMBER";X
20 GOSUB 30020
30 ON T+2 GOTO 50,70,90
40 END
50 PRINT "THE NUMBER IS NEGATIVE."
60 END
70 PRINT "THE NUMBER IS ZERO."
```

```
80 END
90 PRINT "THE NUMBER IS POSITIVE."
```

...and RUN.

Try entering zero and positive and negative numbers to be sure it works. Most of the program workings are obvious, but here is an analysis:

Line 10 INPUTs any number.

Line 20 sends the Computer to Line 30020 by a GOSUB statement. This is different from an ordinary GOTO, since a GOSUB will return control to the originating Line like a boomerang when the Computer hits a RETURN. The call to GOSUB is not complete and will not move on to the next program Line until a RETURN is found. Lines 30020 through 30040 contain this simple logic routine.

Line 30050 holds RETURN, which sends control back to Line 20, which silently acknowledges the return and allows execution to move to the next Line.

Line 30 is an ordinary ON-GOTO statement, but adds 2 to the value of its variable, in this case "T". Line 30 really says:

"If T is -1, THEN GOTO Line 50. If it is zero, THEN GOTO Line 70, and if it is +1, GOTO Line 90."

By adding 2 to each of the values from SGN, we "matched" them up with the 1, 2, and 3 series which is built into the ON-GOTO statement.

Lines 40, 60, and 80 are routine protective END blocks.

By the way, many subroutines are not this simple -- as a matter of fact, they often contain very complex mathematical derivations. We won't bother trying to explain any of them -- if you're heavily into math, you go right ahead and play with the numbers.

ON-GOSUB

ON-GOSUB is a variation on the ON-GOTO and GOSUB schemes. It allows branching to a variety of *subroutines* from a single GOSUB statement. If we had 3 subroutines and had to decide which one to use based on the value of X, here is how the program might be structured. (Don't bother to type it in.)

```
10 INPUT X
20 ON X GOSUB 1000,2000,3000
30  REM - CALCULATIONS HERE
60  REM - PRINT RESULTS HERE
99 END
1000 REM - 1ST ROUTINE GOES HERE.
1099  RETURN
2000 REM - 2ND ROUTINE GOES HERE.
2099  RETURN
3000 REM - 3RD ROUTINE GOES HERE.
3099  RETURN
```

Preview of Coming Attractions?

Like so much of what we are learning, this is just the tip of the iceberg. The ON-GOTO and ON-GOSUB statements have many more clever applications, and they will evolve as we need them. As a hint, note that the *value* of X (which we INPUT) was not used, but it didn't go away. All we did was find its SGN. Hmmm...

Routines vs. Subroutines

In this Chapter we studied a special-purpose routine used as a SUBroutine. Routines can be built directly into any program instead of being set aside and "called" as subroutines. The main value of subroutines is that they can be called repeatedly from different parts of a program, which is often desirable. Ordinary routines are usually only used once, so use of GOSUB and RETURN with them often doesn't make good programming sense.

ON-GOSUB?
ON-GOTO?
NEXT, IT'LL BE
DONNER and BLITZEN!
DON'T BE
INSUBORDINATE!

One value of using routines as subroutines is that some are exceedingly complex to type without error, and if each is typed once and SAVEd on disk, it can be quickly and accurately LOADed back into the Computer as the first step in creating a new program or added to an existing one.

Now it's your turn.

> **EXERCISE 19-1:** Remove all traces of the subroutine from the resident program. Use the SGN function to accomplish the same thing as the subroutine. Hint: T = SGN(X)

Learned in Chapter 19

Functions	Statements	Miscellaneous
SGN(X)	ON-GOTO	Debugging
	GOSUB	Calling a subroutine
	ON-GOSUB	Routines
	RETURN	

Chapter 20

Random Numbers

At Random

A *random* number is one with an unpredictable value. A "Random Number Generator" is a device which pulls *random numbers* "out of a hat." Our Computer has an RND generator, and it works this way:

```
N = RND(X)
```

where N is the *random number*.

RND is the symbol for *RaNDom* function, and

X is a dummy value, either negative, zero, or positive, which can either be placed between the parentheses or brought in as a variable from elsewhere in the program.

Type this NEW program:

```
20 FOR N = 1 TO 10
30  PRINT RND(1)
40 NEXT N
```

...and RUN. Did you observe:

1. A different number appeared each time?

2. All numbers were between 0 and 1?
3. **Very** small numbers were expressed in Exponential notation?

RND behaves exactly the same as RND(X) when X is a positive number. Since this is almost always how it is used, we almost always omit (X). Put a semicolon at the end of the PRINT statement and increase the FOR-NEXT loop to 100 passes to put more numbers on the screen at one time.

```
20 FOR N = 1 TO 100
30  PRINT RND;
40 NEXT N
```

...and RUN.

The Computer uses an internal "seed number" to produce a "random number" series. The seed for RND is always the same.

You get the idea.

Now type:

```
PRINT RND(0)        ENTER
```

and the **last** RaNDom number PRINTed is repeated. Hmmm...

This Is Fairly Exciting!

Well, maybe so, but you ain't seen nothin' yet! Virtually all computer games are based on RND(X), and we'll soon design and play our own.

RND with Racing Stripes

In most real-life cases, we need a Random INTeger not a Random Number between 0-1. To create numbers larger than 1, we have to resort to mathematical chicanery.

Change Line 30 to read:

```
30  PRINT INT(RND * 15 + 1);
```

...and RUN.

That's more like it -- real random INTegers. They all have values between 1 and 15. Figured out the scheme? Pretty simple, isn't it?

This equation specifies the *range* of INTegers RND will output:

```
R = INT(RND * (B-A+1) + A)
```

where R = the RaNDom number,
B = the **largest** INTeger, and
A = the **smallest** INTeger.

Pseudo-Random

Random numbers are unpredictable; properly functioning computers are not. So how do we get truly random numbers from the Computer? We usually don't; we get *pseudo-random* numbers.

RUN the program several times and study the screen. The numbers from each RUN are the same as from the previous RUN! They may be random but not unpredictable!

Change Line 30 and RUN the program several times using negative seed numbers like:

```
30  PRINT RND(-20);
```

We get different sets of numbers -- but all with the same value. RUN again; the numbers are unchanged. Using a different negative seed with RND produces the same result, but the value will change slightly.

When RUNning game programs using RND, it's a good idea to set the *seed* to an unpredictable value. To ensure that a different pseudo-random number sequence is used each time the Computer uses RND(X), we need to find a source of unpredictable numbers somewhere in the Computer.

Type the following:

```
PRINT TIME$        ENTER
```

Hmmm, that's interesting. If we could somehow separate the seconds from the rest of the time, we would have essentially unpredictable numbers between 0 and 59. That would give us 60 different seed numbers. Here's how to do it:

```
PRINT VAL(RIGHT$(TIME$,2))
```

The mechanics of that statement will be covered in detail in a later Chapter, but for those too curious to wait, here is a short analysis: RIGHT$(TIME$,2) means, "Peel off the 2 right-most characters from TIME$." VAL means, "Make sure those 2 characters are numbers so we can use them in a numeric variable."

We now have the tools to write a subroutine for "randomizing" the INPUT to RND. Type the following and RUN:

```
10 GOSUB 10000          (to our own Randomizer)
20 FOR N = 1 TO 10
30  PRINT RND;
40 NEXT N
99 END
10000 S = VAL(RIGHT$(TIME$,2))
10010 FOR N = 1 TO S
10020  D = RND
10030 NEXT N
10040 RETURN
```

Here's how it works:

Line 10000	picks off a number between 0-59.
Lines 10010-10030	"burn off" the first "S" numbers in the RND series.
Line 10040	RETURNs execution to the main program where
Line 30	continues RND, and PRINTs the next 10 numbers.

If you don't believe any of this, insert a temporary Line:

```
10005 S = 25
```

which sets the number of burn-offs to a specific value. Then RUN several times. The same 10 numbers appear each time, so it must be working.

Remove Line 10005 and RUN a few more times. Ahhh! Now we've got it. Instead of only one, we now have 60 versions. We have developed a viable RANDOMIZER routine.

Randomizer

With a RANDOMIZE statement at the beginning of the program, the Computer will "shuffle," or "reseed," the series of random numbers. Type this NEW program:

```
10 RANDOMIZE
20 FOR N = 1 TO 10
30  PRINT RND;
40 NEXT N
```

...and RUN.

Oh, Oh! More decisions needed. RANDOMIZE allows the selection of 65536 different seed values. Even so, whoever picks the seed controls the numbers series.

Variable Randomizer

To increase the possibility that a different seed number will be selected each time RANDOMIZE is encountered, we can let the Computer make that selection for us. The RANDOMIZE statement can be followed by a variable. A numeric value between −32768 and +32767 can be read into that variable. In the routine below, we set up a simple FOR-NEXT loop between those extremes and start it RUNning. When the ENTER key is pressed, execution breaks out of the loop and the value of R **at that time** is picked up by RANDOMIZE.

Since it takes a few minutes for the loop to execute from one extreme to the other, there's plenty of time to press **ENTER**.

```
10 GOSUB 20000
19999 END
20000 CLS : PRINT "PLEASE PRESS ENTER"
20010 FOR R = -32768 TO 32767
20020  R$ = INKEY$
20030  IF R$ = "" THEN  20050
20040  GOTO 20060
20050 NEXT R
20060 RANDOMIZE R
20070 RETURN
```

We will study INKEY$ in detail in a future Chapter, but for now just understand that if we press the **ENTER** key, execution will break out from Line 20030 to 20050. The value of R at breakout will seed RANDOMIZE, and upon RETURN to the main program, a string of random numbers from a variety of over 65,000 choices will be executed.

The "randomness" of this scheme is based on the unpredictability of the time from the start of RUN to the pressing of the **ENTER** key. Over 500 values of R whiz by each second. That's random enough to satisfy an eagle-eyed Las Vegas pit boss!

The Old Coin Toss Gambit

We could toss a thousand heads in a row, and the odds on the next toss are **exactly 50/50** that a head will come up. The outcome of every toss is totally independent of what happened before. **It is too!**

In the long run however, the number of heads and tails should be exactly the same. (Casinos live off people who go broke waiting for their particular scheme to pay off ... "in the long run.") The Computer can provide an education in "odds" and various games of chance and allow us to prove or disprove many ideas involving probability. This is known as computer "modeling," or "simulation."

Type NEW, then type in this coin toss simulation:

```
10 RANDOMIZE
20 INPUT "NUMBER OF COIN FLIPS";F
30 PRINT "STAND BY WHILE I'M FLIPPING"
40 FOR N=1 TO F
50  X = INT(RND * 2 + 1)
60  ON X GOTO 90,110
70  PRINT "WAS NEITHER A HEADS NOR TAILS."
80  END
90  H = H + 1
100  GOTO 120
110  T = T + 1
120 NEXT N
130 PRINT "HEADS","TAILS","TOTAL FLIPS"
140 PRINT H,T,F
150 PRINT 100*H/F;"%",100*T/F;"%"
```

...and RUN.

Seed the generator with the number 1, and "flip the coin" 100 times. RUN a number of times changing the seed. When it's time for lunch, try 25,000 flips or more.

Line 10	allows INPUT of a seed value.
Line 20	INPUTs the number of flips desired.
Line 30	PRINTs a "standby" statement.
Line 40	begins a FOR-NEXT loop that RUNs "F" times.
Line 50	is the RND generator. It's set to generate INTegers between 1 and 2. Heads is "1" and Tails is "2."

Line 60	has an ON-GOTO test that sends X=1 to Line 90 where the "Heads" are counted and X=2 to Line 110 where the "Tails" are counted.
Line 70	is the default Line. If X = other than 1 or 2, the error message will be PRINTed and execution will END. It will never happen, but here is the proof.
Line 90	sets up H as a counter. Each time the ON-GOTO tests sends control to this Line because X=1, H is incremented by one and keeps count of the "Heads."
Line 100	sends control to Line 120 where NEXT N is executed. When the N Loop has gone through "F" number of passes, control drops to Line 130.

Until then, Line 50 generates another RaNDom number (1 or 2). If the next X = 2,...

Line 60	sends control to Line 110.
Line 110	keeps track of the "Tails."
Line 130	PRINTs the Headings.
Line 140	PRINTs the values of H, T and F.
Line 150	calculates and PRINTs the percentage of heads and percentage of tails.

SAVE this program as COINTOSS.

More Than One Generator at a Time

It is possible to generate more than one random number in a program by using more than one generator. This has special value when the ranges of the generators are different but is helpful even if their ranges are the same.

It could also be done with a single generator, but that wouldn't make the point.

To make the point, we will simulate the game of "Craps" -- where 2 dice are "rolled." Each "die" has six sides, and each side has 1,2,3,4,5 or 6 dots.

WE'RE PLAYIN' RANDOM NUMBERS...
?
YEH, I GOT 'IM—25,000 FLIPS TO 10 SO FAR.

When the 2 dice are rolled, the number of dots showing on their top sides are added. That sum is important to the game. Obviously, the lowest number that can be rolled is 2, and the highest number is 12. We will set up a separate Random Number Generator for each die, give each a range from 1 to 6, and call them die "A" and die "B."

Type NEW, then the following:

```
10 A = INT(RND*6+1)
20 B = INT(RND*6+1)
30 N = A + B
40 PRINT N,
50 GOTO 10
```

...RUN.

Each number PRINTed falls between 2 and 12. We only need to PRINT N since the dice are both thrown at the same time, and only the **sum** of the 2 is what counts.

Remember to press CTRL BREAK to stop the Computer.

Why would the following be wrong?

```
10 PRINT INT(RND*11+2)
```

It creates numbers between 2 and 12.

Answer: Adding random numbers created by two generators, each picking numbers between 1 and 6, will create many more sums which equal 3,4,5,6,7,8,9,10 and 11 than a single generator which picks an equal amount of numbers 0 through 10 to which we add 2 to make the range 2 through 12. To simulate 2 dies, the generator range must be 1-6, twice.

Rules of the Game

In its simplest form, the game goes like this:

1. The player rolls the two dice. On the first roll, if the sum is 2 (called "snake eyes"), a 3 ("cock-eyes"), or a 12 ("boxcars"), he loses, and the game is over. That's "craps."

2. If the player rolls 7 or 11 (called "a natural") on the first throw, he wins, and the game is over.

3. If any other number is rolled, it becomes the player's "point." He must keep rolling until he either "makes his point" by getting the same number again to win or rolls a 7 and loses.

> **EXERCISE 20-1:** You already know far more than enough to complete this program. Do it. Put in all the tests, PRINT Lines, etc. to meet the rules of the game and tell the player what is going on. It will take you awhile to finish, but give it your best before you turn to Section C (User's Programs) for a sample solution. Good luck!

> **EXERCISE 20-2:** Add a RANDOMIZE subroutine to the CRAPS game. Test the game to be sure it's different each time it's RUN.

Learned in Chapter 20

Functions	Miscellaneous
RND(X)	Seed numbers
RANDOMIZE	Pseudo-random

Chapter 21

READing DATA

We have learned how to insert numeric values into programs by two different methods. The first is by building them into the program:

```
10 A = 5
```

The second is by using an INPUT statement to enter them through the keyboard:

```
10 INPUT A
```

The third principal method uses the DATA statement.

Type in this NEW program:

```
10 DATA 1,2,3,4,5
20 READ A,B,C,D,E
30 PRINT A;B;C;D;E
```

...and RUN.

The DATA statement is, in some ways, similar to the first method in that a Line holding the values is part of the program. It's different, however, since each DATA Line can contain many numbers, or pieces of data, each separated by a comma. Each piece of data must be read by a READ statement. Each READ Line can hold a number of READ statements, each separated by a comma.

The display shows that all 5 pieces of DATA in Line 10, the values 1,2,3,4 and 5, were READ by Line 20, assigned to variables A through E, and PRINTed by Line 30.

Keep in mind these important distinctions: DATA Lines can be read *only* by READ statements. If more than one piece of DATA is placed on a DATA Line, they must be separated by commas. INPUT statements are used to enter data directly from the keyboard.

DATA Lines are always read from left to right by READ statements, the first DATA Line first (when there is more than one), *no matter where they are in the program*. This may seem startling, but do the following and see:

1. Move the DATA Line from Line 10 to Line 25 and RUN. No change in the PRINTout, right?

2. Move the DATA Line from Line 25 to Line 10000. Same thing -- no change in the PRINTout.

DATA Line(s) can be placed anywhere in the program.

This fact leads different programmers to use different styles. Some place all DATA Lines at the beginning of a program so they can be read first in a LISTing and found quickly to change the DATA.

Others place all DATA Lines at a program's end where they are out of the way and where there are additional Line numbers available to add more DATA Lines as the need arises. Still others scatter the DATA Lines throughout the program next to the READ Lines. The style you select is of little consequence -- **but consistency is comfortable**.

The Plot Thickens

Since we now know all about FOR-NEXT loops, let us see what happens when a DATA Line is placed in the middle of a loop. Erase the old program with NEW and type in this program:

```
10 DATA 1,2,3,4,5
20  FOR N = 1 TO 5
30   READ A
40   PRINT A;
50  NEXT N
```

...and RUN.

That DATA Line is outside the loop. Now move it to Line 25 and RUN. What happened?

Nothing different! It is important to absorb this fact or we wouldn't have gone to the trouble to prove it. We went through the N loop 5 times, READ a value for the variable A 5 times, and the PRINT statement PRINTed A 5 times, but A's value was **different** each time. Its value was what it last READ from the DATA Line. The reason -- each piece of DATA in a DATA Line can only be read **once** each time the program is RUN. The next time a READ statement requests a piece of DATA, it will read the NEXT piece of DATA in the DATA Line or, if that Line is all "used up," move on to the next DATA Line and begin READing it.

Change Line 2Ø in the program to:

```
20 FOR N = 1 TO 6
```

...and RUN.

The READ statement was instructed to read 6 pieces of DATA, but there were only 5. An error statement caught it, as the screen shows.

```
1 2 3 4 5
Out of DATA in 30
```

Change Line 2Ø so the number of READs is **less** than the DATA available.

```
20 FOR N = 1 TO 4
```

...and RUN.

No problem. It works just fine even if we don't use all the available DATA. The point is, each piece of data in a DATA statement can only be READ once during each run.

Exceptions, Exceptions!

Because it is sometimes necessary to read the same DATA more than once without RUNning the entire program over, a statement called RESTORE is available. Whenever the program comes across a RESTORE, **all** DATA Lines are RESTOREd to their original "unread" condition, both those that have been READ and those that have not, and all are available for reading again. Change Line 20 back to:

```
20 FOR N = 1 TO 5
```

and insert:

```
35 RESTORE
```

...and RUN.

Oh-oh! The screen PRINTs five 1's instead of 1 2 3 4 5. Can you figure out why?

Answer: Line 30 READ A as 1, but Line 35 immediately RESTOREd the DATA Line to its **original unREAD condition**. When the FOR-NEXT loop brought the READ Line around for the next pass, it again read the first piece of data which was that same 1. Same thing happened with the remaining passes.

RESTOREing One Line

By placing a number after RESTORE, we can RESTORE one Line of DATA while leaving the others alone. Change the program to:

```
20 FOR N = 1 TO 10
```

```
30  READ A
40  PRINT A;
50 NEXT N : PRINT
60 RESTORE 120
70 FOR N = 1 TO 5
80  READ A
90  PRINT A;
100 NEXT N
110 DATA 1,2,3,4,5
120 DATA 6,7,8,9,10
```

...and RUN.

Line 60 RESTOREd the Computer's pointer in Line 120 so the next READ statement in Line 80 read the DATA in Line 120. Try RUNning the program again after changing the RESTORE Line number from 120 to 110.

READ and DATA statements are extremely common. RESTORE is used less often.

Do you begin to see some distant glimmer involving the storing of business or technical DATA in DATA Lines where they're easily changed or updated without affecting the rest of the program or its formulas?

String Variables

We have been using the letters A through Z to hold number values. They are called *numeric variables*. We can use the same 26 letters to hold *string variables* by just adding a "$."

A$, for example is called "A String." String variables can be assigned to indicate **letters**, **words** and/or **combinations** of letters, numbers, spaces and other characters. Type NEW then type in:

```
10 INPUT "WHAT IS YOUR NAME";A$
```

```
20 PRINT "HELLO THERE, ";A$
```

...and RUN.

How's that for a grabber? If that, along with what we have learned in earlier Chapters, doesn't make the creative juices flow, nothing will.

That's Two....

We now know two ways to PRINT words. The first, learned long ago, is to imbed words in PRINT statements (and is called "PRINTing a string"). The second is to bring word(s) in through an INPUT statement (called "INPUTting a string"). If you can't think of the third way, go back and check the title at the beginning of this Chapter.

Change the program to read:

```
10 READ A$
20 DATA TANDY PERSONAL COMPUTER
30 PRINT "SEE MY FOXY ";A$
```

...and RUN.

```
SEE MY FOXY TANDY PERSONAL COMPUTER
```

Let's use 2 string variables to accomplish the same thing to see how they work with each other. Reword the program to read:

```
10 READ A$
15 READ B$
20 DATA TANDY, PERSONAL COMPUTER
30 PRINT "SEE MY FOXY ";A$;" ";B$
```

...and RUN.

I KNOW IT'S YOUR PERSONAL COMPUTER, BUT THIS IS JUST TOO MUCH!

Analyzing the program:

Line 20 contains two pieces of string DATA separated by a comma.

Line 10 READs the first one.

Line 15 READs the second one.

Line 30 contains 4 PRINT expressions.

The first one PRINTs "SEE MY FOXY" leaving a space behind the "Y" since, unlike numeric variables, string variables do *not* insert leading and trailing spaces. This gives excellent control over PRINT spacing.

The second PRINT expression is A$, and it prints "TANDY."

The third PRINT inserts the space which is enclosed in quotes.

The fourth PRINT expression is B$ which PRINTs "PERSONAL COMPUTER."

Together, they PRINT the entire message on the same line.

A semicolon between STRING variables does **not** cause a space to be PRINTed between them. We have to insert a space using " " marks.

Learned in Chapter 21

Statements

READ
DATA
RESTORE

Miscellaneous

String Variables A$, B$,...
Numeric Variables

PART 3
STRINGS

Intermediate BASIC

Intermediate Features of BASIC

Now that we've learned the rudiments of "Elementary" BASIC, we can get serious about "Intermediate" BASIC. The next Chapter is a kind of "catch-up" and "catch-all," explaining a lot of little unrelated features that didn't conveniently fit in the previous Chapters. Study each of them, do the sample programs, and think about them. Each Chapter is brief but important.

Chapter 22

Smörgåsbord

Multiple Statement Lines : (Now he tells us!)

BASIC allows us to put more than one consecutive statement on each numbered Line by separating them with a colon (:). For example, a timer loop such as:

```
100 FOR N = 1 TO 500
110 NEXT N
```

can become...

```
100 FOR N = 1 TO 500 : NEXT N
```

Caveat Emptor *(Don't buy a used computer from a stranger.)*

It's easy to get carried away with this exciting feature. While we will use multiple statement Lines often from here on, you will quickly find that it's possible to pack the information so tightly it becomes hard to read and also very hard to modify.

More Caveat *(or is it more Emptor?)*

Multiple statement Lines require careful understanding. Especially critical are statements of the IF-THEN variety.

Enter the following NEW but **incorrect** program:

```
10 INPUT "TYPE IN A NUMBER";X
20 IF X = 3 THEN 50 : GOTO 70
30 PRINT "HOW DID YOU GET HERE?"
40 END
50 PRINT "X=3"
60 END
70 PRINT "CAN'T GET FROM THERE TO HERE."
```

...and RUN it several times with different INPUT values including 3.

Line 20 has an error in logic. If the IF-THEN test passes, control moves to Line 50. That's OK.

If the test fails, however, control drops to the next Line in the program, Line 30, not to the 2nd statement in Line 20. **There is no way the 2nd statement in Line 20 (GOTO 70) can ever be executed**.

The Message -- if you put an IF-THEN (or ON-GOTO) test in a multiple statement Line, it must be the **last** statement in that Line.

Next Message -- we cannot send control to any point in a multiple statement Line except to its FIRST statement. Look at Line 20. There is no way to address the GOTO 70 portion. It shares the same Line number as the first statement in the same Line. Only the first statement is addressable by a GOTO or IF-THEN. Other statements in the Line are accessed in sequence, IF each prior test is passed.

New Numeric Variables

We know we can use the 26 letters of the alphabet as names for variables. We can also use the numbers 0 through 9 in conjunction with these letters:

```
A3 = 65
F9 = 37
```

etc.

Although the 26 letter variables are usually enough, adding the numbers gives us an additional 26*10 = 260. They can be very handy, particularly if we want to label a number of "sub" variables (D1,D2,D3,etc.) which combine to make a grand total which we can just call D.

```
PI = 3.14159
```

```
C = PI*D
```
(Circumference = 3.14159 * Diameter)

In addition, we can use any combination of upper case letters, numbers and periods for a name up to 40 characters long. For example:

```
BUSHEL.OF.100.BANANAS = 23.95
```

Now that really looks valuable.

If that doesn't provide enough variables to solve your problems, nothing will.

New String Variables

So far we've used only A$ and B$ as string variables. We actually have **all** the letters of the alphabet available for strings. And the numbers 0 through 9, too, plus any letter-number combination. These are valid string names:

```
X$

D8$

PI$

WHAT.A.GREAT.BOOK$
```

etc.

As with numeric variables, string variables can have any combination of up to 40 upper case letters, numbers, and periods followed by the $ sign.

Shorthand

There are several little "shorthand" tricks available.

The first is the use of ? in place of the very common word PRINT. Type NEW, then this Line:

```
10 ? "QUESTION MARK"
```

...and LIST it.

The pumpkin turned into a coach! The Computer rewrote it to read:

```
10 PRINT "QUESTION MARK"
```

It also works at the command level. Try:

```
? 3*4
```

and we get:

```
12
```

Try `? FRE(0)`.

The ' is shorthand for REM and is especially nice when documenting the purpose of a Line. It makes program Lines into multiple statement Lines. ' = :REM.

```
50 X = Z*C/4 + 33          'THE SECRET EQUATION
```

The only place ' can't be used unaided is in a DATA Line, and that problem can be overcome by actually adding a : (colon).

```
1000 DATA 102,3,9,105,10,1 : 'DATA IS IN
1010 DATA 108,7,3,111,6,1 : 'SEQUENCE
```

50x=Z*C/4+33 ?
WATCH THAT QUESTION MARK, FRIEND, OR I'LL PRINT IT!

The Enter Key

If you're the very observant type, you noticed that program execution begins when the ENTER key is **pressed**, not when it's released.

Use of Quotes

Technically, it is not necessary to use quotes to close off many PRINT statements or LOADs and SAVEs.

```
10 PRINT "WHERE IS THE END QUOTE?
```

Note lack of second ".

RUNs just fine, but leave it off at your own peril.

A BASIC interpreter that is "too forgiving" is like an airplane that is "too forgiving." It allows us to become sloppy, and when we need all the skill we can muster, it is gone from the lack of practice. You are strongly encouraged **not** to take these and other "cheap" short-cuts.

INPUT

It's possible to INPUT several variables with a single INPUT statement. Type this program, and respond with a cluster of 3 numbers separated by commas. It will "swallow" them all in one gulp.

```
10 INPUT A,B,C
```

...and RUN.

If we fail to INPUT them all, separated by commas, the error:

```
?Redo from start
? _
```

points out that more DATA must be INPUT. To see the error message, RUN again, but INPUT only one number. Then ENTER, then CTRL BREAK.

RUN again and try to INPUT letters instead of numbers. Same error message.

There is extensive information in Appendix C dealing with error messages. Most often, *Redo* reminds us that we can't INPUT a string variable into a request for a numeric variable.

Optional NEXT

FOR-NEXT loops don't always have to specify which FOR we are NEXTing. This can be useful when dealing with nested loops.

Type this NEW program:

```
10 FOR A = 1 TO 2 : PRINT A
20   FOR B = 1 TO 3 : PRINT ,B
30      FOR C = 1 TO 4 : PRINT ,,C
40 NEXT : NEXT : NEXT
```

RUN it several times to get the flavor. Note how commas were used to place PRINTing in different zones.

This method of NEXTing should not be used if the program contains tests which might allow a loop to be broken out of. Better then to be specific or to use this little short-cut.

```
40 NEXT C,B,A
```

IF-THEN-ELSE

ELSE is an interesting addition to conditional branching statements. It allows an option other than dropping to the next Line if a test fails. Try this NEW one:

```
10 INPUT "ENTER A NUMBER";N
20 IF N=0 THEN PRINT "0" ELSE PRINT "NOT 0"
30 PRINT : LIST
```

...and RUN.

See how we can use LIST in a program so after the RUN, it LISTs itself? Great for learning and troubleshooting.

---

255 Characters per Line

On Tandy Computers, BASIC permits up to 255 characters in a program Line.

Learned in Chapter 22

Statements

IF-THEN-ELSE

Miscellaneous

Multiple statement Lines
Variable Names
Some Shorthand
Quotes
Multiple INPUTting
Optional NEXT
String Variables

Chapter 23

The ASCII Set

The purpose of this Chapter is to learn how to use ASC and CHR$. Before doing so, however, we must learn about something called "the ASCII set."

ASCII is pronounced (ASK'-EE) and stands for **A**merican **S**tandard **C**ode for **I**nformation **I**nterchange. Since a computer stores and processes only numbers, not letters or punctuation, it's important that there be some sort of uniform system to specify which numbers represent which letters and symbols. The ASCII Chart in Appendix A shows the relationship between the number system and symbols as used in the Tandy Computers. Take a minute to review the chart.

Type in this short program:

```
10 CLS
20 FOR N = 1 TO 255
30  PRINT "ASCII NUMBER";N;
40  PRINT "STANDS FOR",CHR$(N)
50  FOR T = 1 TO 500 : NEXT T
60 NEXT N
```

SAVE as ASCII

...and RUN.

THE ASCII SET? ACTUALLY, IT'S A CUT ABOVE THE JET SET, MARK!

Observe that the characters between ASCII code numbers 97 to 122 are lowercase duplicates of ASCII numbers 65 to 90.

Numbers 128 to 168 are foreign language characters.

Code numbers 176 to 223 are special graphics characters.

Codes 224-254 are special technical characters.

ASCII Codes 1-6 and 14-27 are special characters.

ASCII Chart

Some of the ASCII numbers between 0 and 31 are used by the Computer for special control purposes:

Code	Function
7	Beep
9	Tab
10	Move cursor to beginning of next Line
11	Move cursor to upper left corner
12	Clear Screen
13	Carriage Return
28	Advance cursor without erasing
29	Backspace without erasing
30	Move cursor up
31	Move cursor down

There is very little uniformity internationally (or even within the U.S.) in the assignment of ASCII code numbers except those used for the roman letters and arabic numbers. Fortunately, they handle most of our everyday needs. If we contemplate the problems faced by the Japanese, Arabs, and others who need special letters and characters, it's easy to see how good use can be found for the ASCII values between 128 and 255.

Line Graphic Characters

While we are nosing around this region of the ASCII set, let's see what we can do with those Line Graphic characters the Tandy Computers have bestowed on us.

Enter this NEW program:

```
10 REM  * LINE GRAPHIC CHARACTER PROGRAM *
20 CLS
30 FOR I=1 TO 4 : FOR J=1 TO 8
40  READ N : PRINT CHR$(N);
50  NEXT J : PRINT : NEXT I
70 DATA 218,196,196,191,218,196,196,191
80 DATA 179,218,191,179,179,218,191,179
90 DATA 179,192,193,193,180,195,217,179
100 DATA 192,196,194,194,180,195,196,217
```

...and RUN.

Line 30	starts two loops: one for the 4 rows and the other for the 8 characters per row.
Line 40	reads the code numbers from the DATA Lines and PRINTs the ASCII characters.
Line 50	closes both loops and adds a PRINT at the end of each row.

Now that our fingers are rested, change Line 30 to:

```
30 FOR I=1 TO 8 : FOR J=1 TO 8
```

and add the rest of the DATA:

```
110 DATA 218,196,180,195,193,193,196,191
120 DATA 179,218,180,195,194,194,191,179
130 DATA 179,192,217,179,179,192,217,179
140 DATA 192,196,196,217,192,196,196,217
```

Besides the Line Graphic characters, there are lots of other weird characters between 128-255. The Computer allows us to type some characters (33-127) from the keyboard using the ALT key. Referring to Appendix A, we see the ASCII chart and the codes of all the special characters.

Suppose we want to PRINT the tilde (˜), code 126. Hold down the ALT key and type 126 with the numbers on the *numeric keypad*. Then release the ALT key and presto, the tilde appears on the screen. This technique can be used with characters 33-127 although these can just as easily be entered directly from the regular keyboard.

So What Is CHR$(N)?

We have used CHR$ (pronounced CHaRacter String) without describing it, but you've undoubtedly figured it out anyway. CHR$(N) produces the ASCII character (or control action) specified by the code number N. It is a one-way converter from the ASCII *code number* to the ASCII *character* and allows us to throw characters around with the ease of throwing around numbers. The word "string" refers to any character or mixture of characters (letters, numbers or punctuation).

Enter this simple program:

```
10 INPUT "TYPE ANY NUMBER (33-126)";N
20 PRINT CHR$(N)
30 PRINT : RUN
```

...and RUN.

See how RUN can be used **inside** a BASIC program? Remember to use CTRL BREAK to stop the program.

Almost all of our activity with ASCII numbers will be confined to this range.

EXERCISE 23-1: Using the ASCII chart (Appendix A) and the CHR$ function, create a program which will PRINT the name: TANDY.

ASCII Applications

If we end up in the Big House serving time for computer fraud, the following little program will make up our license plate combinations, putting CHR$ to good use.

Enter this NEW program:

```
10 REM * LICENSE PLATE NUMBER GENERATOR *
20 FOR N=1 TO 3 : PRINT INT(RND(1)*10);
30 NEXT N : PRINT "   ";
40 FOR N=1 TO 3
50  PRINT CHR$(INT(RND(1)*26+65));"   ";
60 NEXT N : PRINT : GOTO 20
```

SAVE as LICPLATE

...and RUN.

The RND generator in Line 20 PRINTs numbers between 0 and 9. Line 50 spits out numbers between 0 and 25, and we add 65 to each of them to make the sum fall between 65 and 90. What do we see on the ASCII conversion chart between 65 and 90? Hmmmm???

What Then Is ASC($)?

ASC is the exact opposite of CHR$(N). ASC is a one-way converter from the ASCII *character* to its corresponding ASCII *number*.

Type:

```
10 INPUT "TYPE NEARLY ANY CHARACTER";A$
20 PRINT "ITS ASCII NUMBER IS";ASC(A$)
30 PRINT : GOTO 10
```

...and RUN.

It will PRINT the ASCII number of almost any character. It doesn't work with the comma (,), the quotation mark ("), the space bar and a few others, but then strings can be a real mystery at times, as we will see.

To get around this and other problems, we use an advanced form of INPUT called LINE INPUT. LINE INPUT allows us to INPUT **any** character (that is assigned an ASCII code) as a string. Notice that the Computer will not insert a question mark when it asks for the text.

Change Line 10 to:

```
10 LINE INPUT "TYPE IN ANYTHING ";A$
```

...and RUN. Try comma, quote, space bar, etc.

An obscure way to use ASC is to imbed the character within quotes, thus:

```
10 PRINT ASC("A")
```

but this latter method is rarely convenient.

Home Base

So far we have talked exclusively about *decimal* numbers. But our BASIC has two intrinsic functions which convert decimal numbers to numbers with Hexadecimal and Octal Bases. Whereas the Decimal system is built on the base 10 (10 digits, 0-9), Octal is base 8 (8 digits, 0-7) and Hexadecimal is base 16 (16 digits, 0-9 and A-F).

Type in the following:

```
10 LINE INPUT "TYPE ANY LETTER, NUMBER OR
   CHARACTER ";A$
20 PRINT "ITS ASCII VALUE IS";ASC(A$)
30 A = ASC(A$) : PRINT
40 PRINT,A,"DECIMAL"
```

```
50 PRINT, HEX$(A),"HEXADECIMAL"
60 PRINT, OCT$(A),"OCTAL"
70 PRINT : GOTO 10
```

SAVE as BASECONV

...and RUN.

Before we can really understand the importance of CHR$ and ASC, we must learn a lot more about strings. Before we could learn about strings we had to learn something about ASCII. It's like "catch Tandy."

EXERCISE 23-2: Input a single character from the keyboard and test its ASCII value to determine IF it is a number. If not, return program control to the INPUT statement. Hint: use two IF statements and ASC.

Learned in Chapter 23

Statements	Functions	Miscellaneous
LINE INPUT	CHR$	ASCII Codes
	ASC	
	HEX$	
	OCT$	

Chapter 24

Strings in General

It was not our intention to "string you along" in the previous Chapter, but we really can't understand how strings work without first understanding the ASCII concept of numbers standing for letters, numbers, and other characters and controls.

Comparing Strings

One of the most powerful string handling capabilities is the ability to **compare** them. We compare the values of *numeric* variables all the time. How can we compare *strings* of letters or words? Well, why do you suppose we put the ASCII Chapter just before this one? **Right!** The Computer can compare the ASCII *code numbers* of letters and other characters. The net result is a comparison of what's in the corresponding strings.

Type in this NEW program:

```
1 CLS
10 INPUT "WHAT IS YOUR NAME";A$
20 IF A$ = "ISHKIBIBBLE" THEN 50
30 PRINT "SORRY, WRONG NAME!"
40 END
50 PRINT "FINALLY GOT IT!"
```

...and RUN.

If the Computer can compare A$ against **that** name, it should be able to compare anything!

During the process of comparing what you enter as A$ in Line 10 to what's already in quotes in Line 20, the ASCII code numbers of each letter found in one string are compared, letter for letter, from left to right, with those in the other. Every one must match, or the test fails.

Strings and quotes are inseparable. You know this from earlier Chapters where every PRINT "XXX" has its string enclosed in quotes.

PRINT "XXX" is called a string *constant*. A$ is a string *variable*.

RUN the above program again, this time answering the question with "ISHKIBIBBLE" (enclosed in quotes).

Sure -- it ran OK.

READing Strings

A string can be INPUT with or without quotes. BASIC has become increasingly lenient about this matter, but every once in a while the rules come up from behind and bite us if we play fast and loose with them.

If we READ a string from a DATA Line, and it has no commas, semi-colons, leading or trailing spaces in it, we don't **have** to enclose it in quotes. We will never go wrong by **always** enclosing strings in quotes, but that can be a nuisance.

EXERCISE 24-1: Write a program that will compare two strings entered from the keyboard and PRINT them in alphabetical order.

Erase the resident program, and type in this next one, which READs string data from a DATA Line.

```
10 CLS
20 READ A$,B$,C$
30 PRINT A$
```

```
40 PRINT B$
50 PRINT C$
100 DATA COMPUSOFT, SAN DIEGO, CA, 92128
900 PRINT : LIST
```

...and RUN.

Look carefully at the results. The screen shows:

```
COMPUSOFT
SAN DIEGO
CA
```

That's nice, but where is the ZIP Code? And why weren't SAN DIEGO and CA PRINTed on the same line? The answer is in the commas.

Because of the commas in the DATA Line, the READ statement sees 4 pieces of DATA, but only READs 3 of them. What do we have to do in order to PRINT a comma as part of a string? Right -- enclose it, or the string containing it, in quotes.

```
EDIT 100
```

and change Line 100 to read:

```
100 DATA COMPUSOFT, "SAN DIEGO, CA", 92128
```

...and RUN.

That's more like it. Notice that we didn't have to enclose **all** pieces of string DATA in separate quotes but could have.

What would happen if we also enclosed the **entire** DATA Line in quotes, leaving the existing quotes in there? (Think about it, then try it. Every question raised has a specific purpose.)

Our EDITor is so easy to use. Make Line 100 read:

```
100 DATA "COMPUSOFT, "SAN DIEGO, CA", 92128"
```

...and RUN.

Oh, oh! A Syntax error in Line 100. There is no straightforward way to READ quotes as part of a string, even by enclosing them inside another pair of quotes. The Computer just isn't smart enough to figure out which quote mark is which. The usual way to overcome this BASIC language deficiency is to substitute ' for each " imbedded inside other quotes. Let's try it:

```
100 DATA "COMPUSOFT, 'SAN DIEGO, CA', 92128"
```

...and RUN.

Ooops. Out of DATA in 20? Of course. With quotes surrounding the whole works there is now just one piece of DATA, and we are trying to read 3 pieces. Change Line 20 to just read one piece:

```
20 READ A$
```

...and RUN.

B$ and C$ are PRINTed as "blanks" since they are empty.

There we go. Might look a little strange, but it demonstrates the point and warns us a little about the "touchiness" of strings.

As we modify this program "over the cliff," that classic ballad from the hills is heard echoing:

> *"Ah-cigareets, and whusky, and wild computers, they'll drive you crazy, they'll drive you insane!"*

But undaunted by this high class philosophy, we steer our vessel towards the next Chapter.

Ah-cigareets, whusky and wild computers, they'll drive you crazy, they'll drive you insane!
YOU'RE STRAINING OUR USER-FRIENDLY RELATIONSHIP!

Learned in Chapter 24

Miscellaneous

String comparison
INPUTting strings
READing strings

Chapter 25

Measuring Strings

One of the most frequently needed facts about a string is its length. Fortunately, the LEN function makes it easy to find. Type:

```
10 INPUT "ENTER A STRING OF CHARACTERS";A$
20 L = LEN(A$)
30 PRINT A$;" HAS";L;"CHARACTERS"
90 PRINT : LIST
```

RUN several times, entering your name and other combinations of letters and numbers. Try entering your name, last name first, with a comma after your last name.

AHA! Can't INPUT a comma. How about if we put it all in quotes? Try again.

Yep. Just like we learned in the last Chapter.

LEN has only one significant variation, and it's not all that useful -- unless it's really needed. Change Lines 10-30 to read:

```
10 INPUT "ENTER A NUMBER";A
20 L = LEN(A)
```

```
30 PRINT A;" HAS";L;"CHARACTERS"
```

...and RUN.

Crash time again! "Type mismatch" means we tried to INPUT a *number* into LEN -- but it requires a *string*.

Letters cause a "?Redo from start" since they need to be INPUT by an A$ or equivalent. RUN again, and INPUT a letter. Is there no justice here? OK, let's change LEN to make it a string:

```
20 L = LEN("A")
```

...and RUN entering a Number. Then try bigger numbers.

Hmmm. Doesn't seem to matter what number we INPUT, it always comes back saying that we have only 1 character.

The answer is, LEN evaluates the LENgth of what is actually between its parentheses (or quotes). At first we brought in a string from outside the program and measured its length. That worked fine. We are now measuring the length of what's actually between the quotes, and that *length* doesn't change with the *value* of A. We are using A as a "literal string constant," not a variable string.

Like we said, this second way to use LEN has its limitations, but don't lose any sleep over it. (Change the resident program back to the way it appears at the beginning of the Chapter.)

DEFSTR -- For Thrill Seekers

Those among us who attract trouble will love this next one. As if handling strings isn't complex enough, this very powerful statement looks nice and clean but in long, complex programs can be the source of endless problems and frustrations.

DEFSTR (pronounced "DEFine STRing") allows us to define **which** variables are to be *string* variables, so we don't have to use the $ any more. Add this Line:

```
5 DEFSTR A
```

and use the EDITor to change Line 20 to:

```
20 L = LEN(A)
```

Then RUN.

Works fine, doesn't it. A was declared by Line 5 to be a string variable. So what's all the fuss about?

Well, this is a very simple program, but let's change 5 to read:

```
5 DEFSTR A-Z
```

which makes *all* letters string variables.

...and RUN.

Crasho again! **Too much** of a good thing. Because of Line 5, the L in Line 20 is now **also** a string. Since LEN gives us the length of a string as a number, it doesn't set at all well with L (really L string). Imagine the fun this can create in a long program.

Good thing we can learn by our errors!

DEFSTR is best used to define individual variables. For example:

```
DEFSTR A,N,Z
```

defines only A, N and Z as string variables. EDIT Line 5 to read:

```
5 DEFSTR A
```

...and RUN.

That's a short course in what DEFSTR is all about.

Concatenation

Concatenation? Concatenation??? Now what is that supposed to mean?

Concatenation (pronounced con-cat-uh-na'shun) is a national debt-sized word which means ADD, as in "add strings together." It's easier to do than to pronounce.

Type this NEW program:

```
10 CLS : FOR N = 1 TO 15
20  READ A$ : B$ = B$ + A$
30 PRINT B$ : NEXT N
100 DATA ALPHA,BRAVO,CHARLIE,DELTA
110 DATA ECHO,FOXTROT,GOLF,HOTEL
120 DATA INDIA,JULIETT,KILO,LIMA
130 DATA MIKE,NOVEMBER,OSCAR
```

Check it carefully, but don't RUN it yet. The key Line is 20, which simply says B$ (a new variable) equals the old B$ (which starts out as nothing) plus whatever is in A$. The program cycles around and keeps adding what is in B$ to what is READ from DATA as A$. Now RUN.

The point of all this is *concatenation*. Line 20 just did it, and that's about all there is to it. We added strings together.

EXERCISE 25-1: Use the LEN function to check the length of a string INPUT from the keyboard. PRINT a message telling us if the string exceeded 10 characters.

EXERCISE 25-2: INPUT a word from the keyboard, and compare it to a secret password. If there is a match, PRINT "CORRECT PASSWORD, YOU MAY ENTER". If not, PRINT "WRONG PASSWORD. TRY AGAIN!" Store the ASCII number for each letter of the password in a DATA Line. READ each value and use CHR$ to build (concatenate) the password string.

CONCATENATION???
WEBSTERS
RELAX, PAL,
IT MEANS
ADD STRINGS.

Learned in Chapter 25

Statements	Functions	Miscellaneous
DEFSTR	LEN	Concatenation (+)

Chapter 26

VAL and STR$

The "hassle factor" can be very high when converting back and forth between strings and numerics.

By definition, if we convert a *numeric* variable (can hold only a number) to a *string* variable (can hold almost anything), the *contents* of that new string is still the original number. No letters or other characters were converted (except for a leading space) since they weren't in the numeric variable to start with.

Conversely, if we change a *string* variable to a *numeric* variable, we can't change any letters or other characters to numbers. Only the *numbers* in a string can be converted to a numeric variable. (Don't confuse this with ASCII conversions.)

If you'll keep the two previous paragraphs in mind, it'll save a lot of grief in dealing with strings.

VAL

Let's give string-to-numeric conversion a shot. The VAL function converts a *string* variable holding a *number* into a *number* if the number is at the beginning of the string. Try this VAL program:

```
1 CLS : PRINT
10 INPUT "ENTER A STRING ";A$
20 A = VAL(A$)
```

```
30 PRINT "THE NUMERIC VALUE OF ";A$;" IS";A
90 PRINT : GOTO 10
```

...and RUN

Try lots of different INPUTs such as:

```
12345
ASDF
123ASD
ASD123
1,2,3
A,B,C
```

and the same ones over again, but enclosed in quotes.

The screen tells all.

Break out of the program, then take the $ out of Lines 10, 20, and 30 and RUN, INPUTting both numbers and letters.

What you're seeing is typical of the frustrations that bedevil string users who don't follow the rules. VAL only evaluates STRINGs, and we've put A, a numeric value, in where a string belongs. Does this remind you of the problems in the last Chapter with LEN?

Let's put that A in quotes and see what happens.

```
20 A = VAL("A")
```

...and RUN.

No help at all! The rule remains unchanged.

Properly used, VAL converts a *string* holding a *number* into that *number* when the *number* is the first character in the *string*. Otherwise VAL interprets the first character as a letter and returns a 0.

OH, COME, NOW—YOU CAN GET VAL and STR$! SAY TO YOURSELF, "I WILL!"
CHOKE!

Looking at the screen you can see all the other uses we are finding for VAL are just not in the cards. Remember this irritating frustration and "The Rule" when you get in the thick of debugging a string-loaded program.

STR$

Now let's try the opposite, converting a *numeric* variable to a *string* variable. Change the program to read:

```
1 CLS : PRINT
10 INPUT "NUMBER TO CONVERT TO STRING";A
20 A$ = STR$(A)
30 PRINT "THE STRING VALUE OF";A;"IS";A$
90 PRINT : GOTO 10
```

...and RUN using the same INPUTs we used when wringing out VAL.

There it is. A short but very important Chapter. Spend as much time on this one as any other Chapter. The time spent learning to avoid the pitfalls surrounding these powerful two functions will come back manyfold in future debugging time. VAL and STR$ have very specific but narrow abilities.

> **EXERCISE 26-1:** INPUT your street address (e.g. 2423 LA PALMA). Use VAL to extract the street number. Add the number 4 to the street number and report this new number as your neighbor's street number.

> **EXERCISE 26-2:** Write a program using STR$ to PRINT the following 20 store item stock numbers: 101WT, 102WT, 103WT,...120WT. Hint: Looks like a natural for a FOR-NEXT loop.

Learned in Chapter 26

Functions

VAL
STR$

Chapter 27

Having a Ball with String

LEFT$, RIGHT$, MID$

Three different, yet very similar, functions are used for doing powerful things with strings. They are LEFT$, RIGHT$ and MID$. Let's start with this program:

```
10 CLS : PRINT
20 S$ = "KILROY WAS HERE"
50 PRINT LEFT$(S$,6),
60 PRINT MID$(S$,8,3),
70 PRINT RIGHT$(S$,4)
90 PRINT : LIST
```

...and RUN.

The screen says:

```
KILROY          WAS             HERE
```

(How about that one, nostalgia buffs?)

Learning to use these string functions is exceedingly simple. Study the program slowly and carefully as we go through what happened.

> LEFT$ PRINTed the LEFTmost 6 characters in the string, S$.
>
> MID$ PRINTed 3 characters in the string, S$, starting with the 8th character from the left. (Count 'em.)
>
> RIGHT$ PRINTed the 4 RIGHTmost characters in the string, S$.

The commas after Lines 5Ø and 6Ø cause everything to PRINT on the same Line.

SAVE this program as KILROY, then let's move some Lines around to exercise our new-found power. Move Line 6Ø to Line 4Ø:

```
4Ø PRINT MID$(S$,8,3),
```

RUN ... and we get:

```
WAS                 KILROY              HERE
```

Now move Line 7Ø to Line 3Ø and add a trailing comma.

```
3Ø PRINT RIGHT$(S$,4),
```

RUN ... and we get:

```
.HERE               WAS                 KILROY
```

These 3 functions can really do wonders with strings. Type in this NEW program, and examine each one in more detail:

```
1Ø CLS
2Ø S$ = "KILROY WAS HERE"
3Ø FOR N = 1 TO 15
```

```
40  PRINT "N =";N,
50  PRINT LEFT$(S$,N)
90 NEXT : PRINT : LIST
```

...and RUN.

The picture tells it faster than words. LEFT$ picks off "N" letters from the LEFT side of S string. See how this string function could be used to strip off only the first 3 digits of a phone number or the first letter of a name when searching and sorting?

Change Line 30 to read:

```
30 FOR N = 1 TO 20
```

SAVE as LEFT ... and RUN.

Even though there are only 15 characters in the string, the overrun is ignored. Change Line 30 back to `N = 1 TO 15.`

RIGHT$ works the same way, but from the RIGHT:

Change Line 50 to read:

```
50 PRINT RIGHT$(S$,N)
```

SAVE as RIGHT ... and RUN.

It's the mirror image of LEFT$.

Now let's exercise MID$ and see where it goes. Change Line 50 to:

```
50 PRINT MID$(S$,N,1)
```

SAVE as MID ... and RUN.

It very methodically scanned the string, from left to right, picking out and PRINTing one letter at a time. Slow it down with a delay loop if the action is too fast to follow.

27 CHAPTERS and ALL YOU CAN DISPLAY IS, "KILROY WAS HERE"?
AW, WE WERE JUST FOOLIN' AROUND!

With only a slight change, MID$ can act like LEFT$. Change Line 50 to:

```
50 PRINT MID$(S$,1,N)
```

...and RUN.

It PRINTed N characters counting from number 1 on the left.

MID$ can also simulate RIGHT$. Change Line 50:

```
50 PRINT MID$(S$,16-N,N)
```

...and RUN.

Would you believe RIGHT$ backwards, one at a time?

```
50 PRINT MID$(S$,16-N,1)
```

...and RUN.

How about a sort of "histogram" type graph:

```
50 PRINT MID$(S$,N,N)
```

...and RUN.

MID$ can also be used as a statement. Delete Lines 40 and 50 and change these lines:

```
30 MID$(S$,1,6) = "JACKIE" : PRINT S$
90 PRINT : LIST
```

...and RUN.

Sort of a BASIC "word processor." This statement replaces a portion of the original string with a new string. In our program, the MID$ statement replaced 6 characters beginning with the 1st position in the original string.

Make notes for future reference. If all these examples don't spark some ideas for your future use, I give up.

Suppose we want to PRINT the character in a specific position in the string. Make the program read:

```
10 CLS
20 S$ = "KILROY WAS HERE"
30 INPUT "CHARACTER # TO PRINT";N
40 PRINT MID$(S$,N,1)
90 PRINT : LIST
```

...and RUN.

If it's not obvious, we can assign any of these statements to a variable. That variable can in turn be used in tests against other variables. Change:

```
40 V$ = MID$(S$,N,1)
50 PRINT V$
```

...and RUN.

A short book could be written about these three powerful functions, but I think the point's been made. They are used **very** frequently in complex sort and select routines. If we dissect them into these simple components, they are easy to keep track of. The next section has some good examples.

EXERCISE 27-1: Write a program that asks the question "ISN'T THIS A SMART COMPUTER". Input a YES or NO answer. If the first character in the answer is a Y, PRINT "AFFIRMATIVE". If the first character is an N, PRINT "NEGATIVE". Otherwise PRINT "THIS IS A YES OR NO QUESTION," and send control back to the INPUT statement.

EXERCISE 27-2: READ in the following part numbers: N106WT, A208FM, and Z154DX. Use MID$ to find the numbers. PRINT the number with the largest value.

Searching with INSTR

INSTR (pronounced "In-string") is a function that can be of value when searching for a needle in a haystack. It compares one string against another to see if they have anything in common.

Suppose we have a list of names and want to see if another name (or part of that name) is in our list. It's the "part of" which makes this operation very different from a straight comparison of name-against-name which we already know how to do using ordinary string-against-string comparisons. Here we learn how to locate a name (and similar names) by asking for just a small part of it.

Start the NEW program by entering this list of names:

```
10000 DATA SMITH, JONES, FAHRQUART, BROWN
10010 DATA JOHNSON, SCHWARTZ, FINKELSTEIN
10020 DATA BAILEY, SNEED, JOE BFTSPLK, *
```

That was the easy part.

How do we READ these names, one at a time, and compare them, or parts of them, with the name or part of a name which we INPUT? Add these Lines:

```
10 CLS
20 INPUT "WHAT LETTER(S) IS WANTED";N$
30 PRINT
40 READ D$
50 IF D$ = "*" THEN GOTO 99
60 IF INSTR(1,D$,N$) = 0 THEN 40
70 PRINT ,N$;" IS PART OF ";D$
80 GOTO 40
99 PRINT : PRINT "END OF SEARCH" : END
```

SAVE this program as INSTR. We'll be needing it later.

Now this takes a bit of explaining:

Line 10	CLears the Screen.
Line 20	INPUTs the name or part of the name we are trying to locate.
Line 30	PRINTs a blank space for easier reading to help give this program some class.
Line 40	READs a single name from the DATA file.
Line 50	tests to see if D$ is READing the last item in the DATA file; IF so, execution branches to Line 99.
Line 60	uses INSTR to do all the searching. INSTR looks at D$, starting with the 1st character, to see if the characters INPUT in N$ match characters in D$. If INSTR returns the value of 0, it means there is no match and the program should READ the next piece of DATA. If there is a match, INSTR returns a number which is the number of characters it counted in N$ before a match was found. Since this number is not 0, execution drops to:
Line 70	which PRINTs both what we're looking for and the match.
Line 80	starts the process over again.

RUN trying various letters, names, and parts of names to get the hang of what's going on. It's pretty impressive!

Now that wasn't too bad, was it? It doesn't matter how hard a program seems; when broken down to its individual parts, it isn't very hard. As we've pointed out before, "The BASICs Are Everything."

These changes will show the inner machinations of INSTR.

```
60 L = INSTR(1,D$,N$)
65 IF L = 0 THEN 40
```

```
70 PRINT ,N$;" IS CHARACTER#";L;"IN ";D$
```

RUN it through a number of times trying different letters. It really does make sense!

To see the effect the starting number following INSTR has on our program, change Line 60 to:

```
60 L = INSTR(2,D$,N$)
```

INSTR now looks at D$ starting with the 2nd character.

RUN and type in the letter S. See how it skipped SMITH, SCHWARTZ and SNEED? Play around with the starting number in INSTR until you have a good handle on what it does.

EXERCISE 27-3: ReLOAD the INSTR program and change the DATA Lines to:

```
10000 DATA P-RUTH, OF-MANTLE, SB-MORGAN
10010 DATA SS-LEOTHELIP, P-KOUFAX
10020 DATA C-CAMPANELLA, P-FELLER,*
```

What string would we enter to LIST the pitchers only?

A. P
B. PITCHER
C. P-
D. None of the above

SAVE as BASEBALL and RUN. Practice sorting by team positions.

Snarled STRING

In the last Chapter we learned about STR$ which lets us convert a numeric variable to a string variable. For the purpose of confusion (no doubt), there is another "string-string" that does something completely different. Fortunately, it is written differently.

STRING$(N,A) is a specialized PRINT *modifier* which allows us to PRINT a single ASCII character, represented by A, a total of N times. Quite simple, really, and very useful.

Type:

```
NEW
10 PRINT STRING$(32,42);
20 PRINT "STRING$ FUNCTION";
30 PRINT STRING$(32,42)
```

...and RUN.

That really moved. It PRINTed ASCII character 42, which is a *, 32 times, then PRINTed the phrase STRING$ FUNCTION, and then PRINTed * 32 more times. This just has to have some good applications.

Suppose we need to type a "header" across the top of a report -- let's say the first Line of it is to be solid dashes. What is the ASCII code for a dash? Forgot? Me too. Everybody back to Appendix A to find the code number.

45 it is. We want to PRINT, 80 times, the character represented by ASCII code 45. That's the full width of a Line on our screen. The NEW program should look something like:

```
20 PRINT STRING$(80,45)
```

...RUN it.

An even easier way to use STRING$ is to replace the ASCII code of the character we wish to PRINT with the actual character itself. (It must be enclosed in quotes.) This works fine with characters that may be typed, such as letters, numbers and punctuation marks. Change Line 20 so the program reads:

```
20 PRINT STRING$(80,"-")
```

...and RUN.

Works nice, doesn't it, and we didn't have to look up the ASCII code.

We can bring in a single string character via a string variable. This simple NEW program shows a variation on the theme and may trigger some ideas:

```
10 INPUT "ANY LETTER, NUMBER OR SYMBOL";A$
20 PRINT STRING$(80,A$)
30 PRINT : GOTO 10
```

Play around with STRING$ awhile. It's really very helpful when needed, particularly for giving display PRINTouts some class. An obvious advantage is its ability to do a lot of PRINTing with very little programming.

> **EXERCISE 27-4:** Print a string of 30 asterisks centered at the top of the screen.

SPACE$ and SPC

The SPACE$ allows us to PRINT from 0 to 255 blank spaces. For example:

```
PRINT "A";SPACE$(20);"B"
```

will PRINT A and B with 20 spaces between them.

SPC is almost the same function as SPACE$, but it doesn't use string space. Example:

```
PRINT "A";SPC(25);"B"
```

PRINTs 25 blank spaces between A and B.

On the Lighter Side

The specialized string functions enable us to do all sorts of exotic things. Here is the beginning of a simple but fun NEW program which uses LEN and MID$. You can easily figure it out, especially after you've seen it RUN.

Enter:

```
10 REM  * TIMES SQUARE BILLBOARD *
20 CLS : N=0 : READ A$
30 L=LEN(A$) : F=1
40  IF L>N THEN L=N+2
50 B$ = MID$(A$,F,L)
60 PRINT TAB(78-N);B$
70 FOR T=1 TO 20 : NEXT T
80  IF N=75 GOTO 100
90 N=N+1 : IF N<75 GOTO 120
100 L=L-1 : F=F+1 : IF L<0 THEN L=0
110  IF L=40 GOTO 20
120 CLS : GOTO 40
500 DATA"LUCKY LINDY HAS LANDED IN PARIS. . ."
510 DATA". . .MET BY CROWD AT LEBOURGET AIRPORT."
```

...and RUN.

Your assignment, if you choose to accept it, is to complete the program so it repeats, ends, or otherwise does not crash.
Good luck!.

.

.

.

.

.

...................Fsssss!

Learned in Chapter 27

Functions

LEFT$
MID$
RIGHT$
INSTR
STRING$
SPACE$
SPC(N)

Miscellaneous

INSTRing routine
Cursor OFF and ON

Chapter 28

TIME$ and DATE$

How about a short and simple Chapter?

Remember when we first turned on the Computer, and it asked us to type in the *date* and *time?* Wouldn't it be nice to be able to use this information in a BASIC program? We can, and it's as easy as A$, B$, C$,...

All we have to do is type:

```
PRINT TIME$        ENTER
```

and TIME is displayed. The time shown is how long the Computer has run since it was last turned on or the current time if you set the clock when you turned on the Computer or if you have an internal clock.

The DATE can also be displayed by typing:

```
PRINT DATE$        ENTER
```

Setting the Clock and Calendar

The DATE is set from BASIC by typing:

```
DATE$ = "12/12/87"
```

The Computer places the date into the operating system. Verify it by typing:

```
PRINT DATE$        ENTER
12-12-1987
```

To set the time from BASIC, type:

```
TIME$ = "19:06:30"        ENTER
```

All of the string operators we learned about in the previous Chapters can be used to manipulate these two strings. For example, to PRINT only the day and month from DATE$, use:

```
10 DAY$ = MID$(DATE$,4,2)
20 MONTH$ = LEFT$(DATE$,2)
30 PRINT "THIS IS DAY #";DAY$;
40 PRINT " IN MONTH #";MONTH$
```

SAVE as DATE

...and RUN.

Note carefully that DATE$ and TIME$ are built into the Computer, but DAY$ and MONTH$ are simply string variables we created.

Type in this NEW program:

```
10 PRINT DATE$, TIME$
20 GOTO 10
```

...and RUN.

How's that for cheap and dirty? There are an endless number of much more sophisticated ways to display time and date. Any ideas?

> **EXERCISE 28-1:** Write a program which continuously displays the time and date neatly on the screen.

Just a Little More Time

BASIC has a feature that allows us to see, at a glance, how many seconds it has been since the Computer was turned on or since midnight, whichever happened last. This feature is called TIMER. To retrieve this value, simply type:

```
PRINT TIMER    ENTER
```

The only way we can set the value of TIMER is to set the time to 00:00:00 (midnight) or turn off the Computer and start over.

Try this program and RUN it against a stopwatch.

```
10 REM * TIMER PROGRAM *
20 CLS : INPUT "PRESS 'ENTER' TO START THE TIMER";A$
30 TIME$ = "00:00:00"
40 PRINT : PRINT "THE TIMER IS RUNNING"
50 INPUT "PRESS 'ENTER' TO STOP IT";A$
60 PRINT : PRINT "TIMER =";TIMER;"SECONDS"
```

Keyboard Buffer

You may have noticed that the Computer seems to remember what we have typed on the keyboard even when it is busy performing some other task.

An area in memory is set aside to be a Keyboard Buffer. This buffer stores our keystrokes until the Computer is ready to accept them. We can easily "type ahead" of the Computer while it is busy performing such tasks as reading a directory with the FILES command, printing information on the screen or printer, performing large calculations, executing FOR-NEXT loops, backing up a diskette, etc.

The Keyboard Buffer can store up to 15 key strokes. The Computer beeps when we try to enter more than 15 characters before it's had a chance to clear

YOU'RE OFF 30 SEC!
...and YOU'VE GOT A CHEAP WATCH.

the buffer. The buffer will even store characters created by holding down the key as it does under normal keyboard repeat operation.

On a 2000 with 256K, the buffer can store more than 150 strokes.

Enter this delay loop program.

```
10 CLS
20 FOR N = 1 TO 5000 : NEXT
```

As soon as you RUN the program, type:

```
LIST        ENTER
```

and wait. When the program execution is finished, the program is LISTed.

For fast typists this is a real time-saver.

Learned in Chapter 28

Statements	Miscellaneous
TIME$	Keyboard Buffer
DATE$	
TIMER	

PART 4

VARIABLE PRECISION AND MATH

Chapter 29

What Price Precision?

Unless told otherwise, the BASIC on Tandy Computers stores numeric variables with an accuracy of 7 digits and PRINTs them out to 7 though only 6 will be accurate. This is called *single precision* accuracy and is more than adequate for most applications.

The old slide rule was only accurate to 3 digits.

For large businesses or special scientific applications, however, greater accuracy is needed, and we have a capability called "double precision." Telling the Computer to go "double precision" will cause it to store numbers accurate to 17 digits and PRINT them out accurate to 16. However, we pay a price for this precision both in the additional memory it takes to store and process long numbers and in the extra time required to process them.

Type in this NEW program:

```
10 CLS : PRINT
20 X = 1234567890987654321          (Check 'em.)
30 Y = .0000000001234567 89          (Check 'em.)
40 Z = X * Y
```

```
50 PRINT X;"TIMES";Y;"EQUALS";Z

90 PRINT : LIST
```

...and RUN.

Ummm-hmmm. A very large number times a very small number and the answer -- all expressed in Exponential notation (that's what the "E's" in the answer stand for) and clipped to 7 significant digits.

```
1.234568E+18 TIMES 1.234568E-10 EQUALS

1.524158E+08
```

The number values in Lines 20 and 30 have been converted to Exponential Double Precision. That's what the "D" in those lines stands for.

DouBLe Precision

We can easily convert storage, processing, and PRINTing of X, Y and Z to DouBLe precision.

```
15 DEFDBL A-Z
```

DEFDBL stands for "DEFine as DouBLe precision," and A-Z means "every variable from A through Z."

Add the Line and RUN.

```
1.2345678909876540+18 TIMES 1.23456789D-10

EQUALS 152415787.6238378
```

Quite a difference, eh? Those lost digits in the answer came back from the hinterland and expanded our PRINTout from 7 significant places to 16.

Such precision is usually wasteful of memory space and time except in short programs; but fortunately only a few variables ever need to be so precise.

Since the letters X, Y and Z are in sequence, we could tell the Computer to process only those 3 variables in double precision and leave all other variables (of which there are none, right now) in single precision. Change Line 15 to:

```
15 DEFDBL X-Z
```

...and RUN.

Same results.

Overruled!

There is a way to *override* the DEFDBL declaration. Suppose we wanted Z to be PRINTed as just single precision? We can override part of the Line 15 declaration by changing each Line which contains Z, as follows:

```
40 Z! = X * Y
50 PRINT X;"TIMES";Y;"EQUALS";Z!
```

...and RUN.

```
1.2345678909876540+18 TIMES 1.234567890-10
EQUALS 1.524158E+08
```

The "raw" data and the calculating were held at double precision, but the final answer is PRINTed with only single-precision accuracy. A *specific* declaration (like the ! which stands for single precision), always takes precedence over a *global* declaration like Line 15 DEFDBL X-Z. (Global means "valid for the entire program" not just one variable or one Line.)

DouBLe Precision -- Simplified

There's another way to calculate with high precision but PRINT the answer in single precision. Since single precision is the *default* mode, we can simply not include Z in Line 15.

Change Lines 15, 40 and 50 and RUN.

```
15 DEFDBL X-Y        (or DEFDBL X,Y)
```

```
40 Z = X * Y
50 PRINT X;"TIMES";Y;"EQUALS";Z
```

...and RUN.

Same results, again.

Global Override

It is also possible to override the global DEFDBL declaration with a global Single Precision declaration. **Single takes precedence over double!** DEFSNG changes all numbers back to single precision. Let's try it by adding:

```
60 DEFSNG X-Y
70 PRINT X;"TIMES";Y;"EQUALS";Z
```

...and RUN.

Good Grief -- our "redeclared" DEFSNG X and Y numbers turned to zeros, but the Z answer is correct!

Well, it turns out that X *DouBLe precision* is a completely separate variable from X *SiNGle precision*. It's as different from X as is Y, or any other variable. If we want to use X and Y again as single-precision numbers, we have to go back and assign them values **after** declaring them to be single precision. Hmmmm. This is getting complicated.

A cheap and dirty way to show the point is to change Line 70 to:

```
70 GOTO 20
```

...and RUN very briefly -- hitting CTRL BREAK after both DouBLe and SiNGle precision versions are PRINTed by Line 50. Compare the top 2 display lines.

Line 60 reDEFined X and Y as SiNGle precision, then execution went back to Line 20 and performed the calculations again. (Fortunately, there is rarely reason to *redefine* a variable within a program.)

DouBLe Precision, Another Way

Instead of a global declaration of accuracy, we can do it one variable at a time. Change the resident program (very carefully!) to read:

```
10 CLS : PRINT
20 X# = 12345678909876540+18
30 Y# = 1.23456789D-10
40 Z# = X# * Y#
50 PRINT X#;"TIMES";Y#;"EQUALS";Z#
90 PRINT : LIST
```

...and RUN.

Same results as before. The # sign declared that the variable letter preceding it was to be handled as DouBLe precision overriding the normal presumption that it is SiNGle precision.

Remember, X# is not the same as X -- it is an entirely different variable. Same with Y# and Z#. To nail this point down, add:

```
15 X = 4.321
60 PRINT "X =";X
```

...and RUN.

The values of X and X# stayed completely separate, didn't they?

INTeger Precision

In those frequent cases where the numbers used are INTegers (and in the range between -32768 and +32767), execution can be speeded up by declaring them to be INTegers by using the % sign or the DEFINT statement. Enter this NEW program:

```
20 FOR N = 1 TO 6800
30 NEXT N
90 PRINT : LIST
```

1000 SX users, substitute 8200 for the 6800 in Line 20.

2000 users, substitute 20000.

On the 3000s, use 28000.

Use a stopwatch or clock with a second hand and measure the time it takes for the 6800 passes through the FOR-NEXT loop. Should be around 10 seconds.

...and RUN.

Now, let's declare N to be an INTeger, (which is all the accuracy we need) and time it again ... Add:

```
10 DEFINT N
```

...and RUN.

Aha! It took only about 7 seconds. A very significant difference.

We can accomplish the same thing using *specific* INTeger declarations. Delete Line 10, and add the % character to the N's in Lines 20 and 30.

Now RUN, and time it.

One More Way

The conversion functions CSNG(#), CDBL(#) and CINT(#) provide 3 additional ways to declare numbers as SiNGle, DouBLe or INTeger precision. Enter this NEW test program:

```
10 CLS
20 X = 12345.67898
30 PRINT X
40 PRINT CSNG(X)
50 PRINT CDBL(X)
60 PRINT CINT(X)
```

6,800 PASSES THRU
THE FOR-NEXT LOOP
IN 10 SECONDS!!
INCREDIBLE!
YOU SHOULD'VE
SEEN ME AT
THE OLYMPICS!

```
90 PRINT : LIST
```

...and RUN.

It tells the whole sordid story:

```
12345.68

12345.68

12345.6787109375

12346
```

Line 20	changed to 20 X = 12345.67898# indicating the number was so long that it could not be held in single precision.
Line 30	PRINTed the value of X accurate to 7 digits.
Line 40	PRINTed the SiNGle precision value of X -- the same value as printed by Line 30.
Line 50	PRINTed the DouBLe precision value of X, but it sure isn't a duplicate of what we specified as X in Line 20! The problem is, we only INPUT the number in Single Precision (by default). PRINTing it out in Double Precision requires the Computer to just "make up" numbers to fill out the places. Don't try to be more accurate than what you begin with. It's the programmer who's supposed to be creative, not the Computer!
Line 60	PRINTed the INTeger value of X. This works slightly differently than INT(X). CINT(X) "rounds off" the fractional part.

Make the value of X negative and see what happens. Change Line 20 to:

```
20 X = -12345.67890
```

...and RUN.

No surprises. CINT acted just like INT does, rounding downward to arrive at −12346.

DouBLe the Trouble -- DouBLe the Fun

Now let's go back and declare the value of X to be DouBle precision, change it to a positive number, and do all our PRINTing in DouBLe precision. The EDITed program reads:

```
10 CLS
20 X# = 12345.67898
30 PRINT X#
40 PRINT CSNG(X#)
50 PRINT CDBL(X#)
60 PRINT CINT(X#)
90 PRINT : LIST
```

...then RUN.

The display reads:

```
12345.67898
12345.68
12345.67898
12346
```

It makes sense and was quite predictable, wasn't it? Even CDBL behaved.

What do you think will happen if we again change the value of X to a negative number? Think it through; then change it and RUN.

In Memoriam

This is really a very important Chapter. Most readers find it necessary to study it more than once. Degrees of precision may not be the most inspiring subject, but if we have command of this Chapter, we'll not be caught off guard or be deceived by numbers that never were.

Learned in Chapter 29

Statements	Functions	Miscellaneous
DEFDBL	CDBL	DouBLe Precision (#)
DEFSNG	CSNG	SiNGle Precision (!)
DEFINT	CINT	INTeger Precision (%)

Chapter 30

Intrinsic Math Functions

The BASIC language includes a number of **mathematical** functions. These math functions are all very straightforward and easy to use, but if your math skills are a bit rusty, you will want to refresh them to fully understand what we're doing. We'll keep everything here at the 9th-grade Algebra level, so there's no need to panic (unless maybe you're in the 6th grade ... but even so, just hang on and you'll be OK).

INT(N)

We have studied the INTeger function in some detail in earlier Chapters so we won't cover that ground again. INT stores and executes numbers in single precision.

FIX(N)

FIX is just like INT, but instead of rounding negative numbers downward, it simply chops off everything to the right of the decimal point.

Try this simple test at the command level:

```
PRINT INT(-12345.67)
```

produces -12346

```
PRINT FIX(-12345.67)
```

produces -12345

The one we use depends on what we want.

SQR(N)

The SQuare Root function is simple to use.

Type this:

```
10 INPUT "THE SQUARE ROOT OF";N
20 PRINT "IS";SQR(N)
30 PRINT : GOTO 10
```

...and RUN some familiar numbers.

Math types can add:

```
25 PRINT CHR$(251); N; "="; SQR(N)
```

to take advantage of some of our special characters.

Another way to find the square (or any) root of a number is by the use of the ^ (caret). It means "raised to the power." Finding the square root of a number is the same as raising it to the 1/2 power. Delete Line 25 and change Line 20 to:

```
20 PRINT "IS ";N^(1/2)
```

...and RUN some familiar numbers.

The same logic which allows us to find the *square* root with the ^ will let us find any **other** root. Out of the sheer arrogance of power, let's find the

21st root of any number. Change the first two Lines:

```
10 INPUT "THE TWENTY-FIRST ROOT OF";N
20 PRINT "IS ";N^(1/21)
```

...and RUN.

Now there is real horsepower! Problem is, how are we sure that the answers are right? Well, it's easy enough to add a few lines that will take the root and raise it back to the 21st power to find out. Let's change the program to make it read:

```
10 INPUT "THE TWENTY-FIRST ROOT OF";N
20 R=N^(1/21)
30 PRINT "IS";R
40 PRINT
50 PRINT R;"TO THE 21ST POWER =";R^21
60 PRINT : GOTO 10
```

...and RUN.

The INPUT and output numbers check out pretty close, don't they? This "proof" process might not stand up under rigorous scrutiny, but the answers are correct.

EXERCISE 30-1: Pythagoras discovered that the sides of a right triangle always obey the rule:

$$C^2 = A^2 + B^2$$

where C is the longest side (hypotenuse). Stated another way: "The length of side C equals the square root of the sum of the squares of sides A and B" ($C = \sqrt{A^2 + B^2}$).

If side A = 5 and side B = 12, write a program to calculate the length of side C.

ABS(N)

ABSolute value has a lot to do with signs, or without them. The absolute value of any number is that number **without** a sign. If you've forgotten, this program will quickly refresh the memory:

```
10 INPUT "ENTER ANY NUMBER";N
20 PRINT : A = ABS(N)
30 PRINT A
40 PRINT : GOTO 10
```

...and RUN.

Respond with various large and small, positive and negative numbers, and zero.

They all come out as they went in, didn't they, except for the missing sign?

MOD

MOD isn't really a math function, but more of a math operator. MOD returns the remainder when one number is divided into another number. For example:

```
PRINT 17 MOD 4
```

returns a 1 since 17/4 is 4 with a remainder of 1.

Other examples to try:

8 or 16 or 24 MOD 8 each equals 0. (There's 0 remainder when any of them are divided by 8.)

9 or 17 or 25 MOD 8 each equals 1. (There's 1 remainder after any of them are divided by 8.)

10 or 18 or 26 MOD 8 each equals 2. (There's 2 remainder after any of them are divided by 8.)

15 or 23 or 31 MOD 8 each equals 7. (There's 7 remainder after any of them are divided by 8.)

LOG(N)

No, a LOG isn't what they build cabins with, but even the swiftest among us have to refresh our memory from time to time to keep the details straight.

A LOG (logarithm) is an *exponent*. Exponent of what? The exponent of a *base*. What's a *base?* A *base* is the number that a given number *system* is built on. Aren't all number systems built on 10? 'Fraid not.

$10^3 = 1000$

10 is the BASE.

3 is the LOG(exponent), and

1000 is the answer.

As if life isn't complicated enough, the LOGarithm system is centered around what are called *natural* logs. Exactly what that means is the subject of another discussion, but we're stuck with it anyway. Natural logs use the number 2.718282 as their base. (Really makes your day, doesn't it!) Some BASIC interpreters provide a second LOG option using 10 as the base, as in our decimal system, but making the conversion isn't too bad -- and we do have to live with it.

Type this NEW program:

```
10 INPUT "ENTER ANY POSITIVE NUMBER";N
20 PRINT : L = LOG(N)
30 PRINT ,"THE LOG OF";N;
40 PRINT "TO THE NATURAL BASE =";L
50 PRINT : GOTO 10
```

The LOG function is not valid for negative numbers or zero.

...and RUN.

LET ME GUESS –
NEW COMPUTER?
New Math

Ummm Hmmm. Can't relate to the conclusion? Respond with the number 100, and you should get the answer 4.60517. What that means is 2.718282 to the 4.60517 power = 100.

Let's jack this thing around to where the vast majority of us who have to work with LOGs can use it -- into the decimal system.

Decimal-based LOGs are called *common*, or *base 10* logs. Add these lines:

```
45 PRINT ,"THE LOG OF";N;
47 PRINT "TO THE BASE 10 =";L*.4342945
```

...and RUN using 100 as the number.

That's more like it. We can all see that 10 to the 2nd power equals 100. It's good to be back on **relatively** solid ground.

The magic conversion rules are:

> *To convert a natural log to a common log, multiply the natural log by .4342945.*
>
> *To convert a common log to a natural log, multiply the common log by 2.3026.*

This final NEW program scoops it up and spreads it out:

```
10 REM   * LOGARITHM DEMO *
20 CLS : PRINT
30 INPUT "ENTER A POSITIVE NUMBER";N
40 PRINT
50 PRINT "THE NUMBER","NATURAL LOG",
60 PRINT "COMMON LOG"
70 PRINT N,LOG(N),LOG(N)*.4342945
80 PRINT : GOTO 30
```

Wring it out until you're comfortable with the concept.

EXP(N)

EXP is sort of the opposite of LOG. EXP computes the value of the answer, given the EXPonent of a *natural* log. (Another winner.)

2.718282 raised to the EXP power = the answer.

Type in this NEW program:

```
10 INPUT "ENTER A NUMBER";N
20 A = EXP(N)
30 PRINT "2.718282 RAISED TO THE";N;
40 PRINT "POWER =";A
50 PRINT : GOTO 10
```

...and RUN.

We're entering the EXPonent now, so it's easy to INPUT a number that is too big for the Computer and will cause it to *overflow*.

As a benchmark against which to test the program, enter this number:

```
4.60517
```

The *base* of the natural log system raised to this power should equal 100 (or very close).

Being this far into logs, you can create your own advanced test programs, and check the results against a LOG table.

> **EXERCISE 30-2: (For math fans only)** Convince yourself that LOG and EXP functions are inverses of each other (hint: LOG(EXP(N)) = N). Try putting the two functions together in the opposite order using both positive and negative values for N. Why do the negative values create havoc?

Learned in Chapter 30

Functions

INT
FIX
SQR
ABS
MOD
LOG
EXP

Miscellaneous

Natural Logs
Common Logs

Chapter 31

The Trigonometric Functions

Since this is about as deep as we'll get into mathematics, I have to assume you know something about elementary trig.

Trigonometry, of course, deals with triangles, their angles, and the ratios between the lengths of their sides. In the triangle below, the Sine (abbreviated SIN) of angle A is defined as the *ratio* (what we get after dividing) of the *length* of side a to the *length* of side c. COSine and TANgent are defined similarly:

SIN A=a/c

COS A=b/c

TAN A=a/b

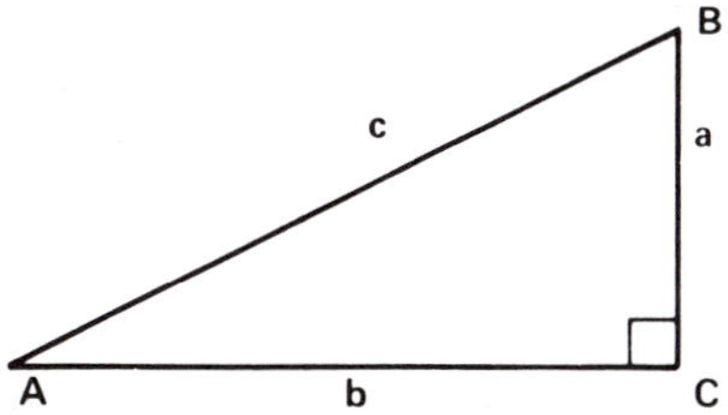

From these relationships, we can find any ratio if we know the corresponding angle. Let's try this simple NEW program:

```
10 INPUT "ENTER AN ANGLE (0-90 DEGREES)";A
20 S = SIN(A*.0174533)
30 PRINT "THE SIN OF A";A;"DEGREE ANGLE IS";S
40 PRINT : GOTO 10
```

...and RUN.

It really works! Try the old standard angles like 45°, 30°, 60°, 90°, 0°, etc.

Unless you're right up to snuff on trig, Line 20 undoubtedly looks strange. Well, it turns out that most computers think in radians, not degrees (always has to be some nasty twist, doesn't there...!) A *radian* is a unit of measurement equal to approximately 57 degrees. In order to convert from degrees (which most of us use) to radians, we changed the INPUT from degrees to radians. The SIN function will not work correctly without this conversion.

To convert angles from degrees to radians, multiply the degrees by 0.0174533.

To convert angles from radians to degrees, multiply the radians by 57.29578.

Failure to make these conversions correctly is by far the biggest source of computer users' problems with the trig functions.

COSine and TANgent work the same way. Change the resident program to:

```
10 INPUT "ENTER AN ANGLE (0-90 DEGREES)";A
20 C = COS(A*.0174533)
30 PRINT "THE COS OF A";A;"DEGREE ANGLE IS";C
40 PRINT : GOTO 10
```

...and RUN.

We know that COS(90°) should be 0. Unfortunately, the Computer is slightly off because it calculates these functions by approximation. It's doing the best that it can ... honest!

For TANgent, RUN this program:

```
10 INPUT "ENTER AN ANGLE (0-90 DEGREES)";A
20 T = TAN(A*.0174533)
30 PRINT "TAN OF A";A;"DEGREE ANGLE IS";T
40 PRINT : GOTO 10
```

NO, NO! COSine HASN'T ANYTHING TO DO WITH BANKING- GO BACK TO SQUARE 1!
SOMETIMES I COULD KICK 'IM RIGHT IN HIS 'OL ASTERISK!

The TAN function is not even defined for 90°, though the Computer will *try* to calculate it.

This next NEW program displays all 3 major trig functions at the same time. Note that in Line 30 we **divide** our incoming angle by 57.29578 instead of multiplying it by 0.0174533. The results are the same.

```
10 CLS : PRINT
20 INPUT "ENTER AN ANGLE (0-90 DEGREES)";A
30 A = A/57.29578 : PRINT
40 PRINT "ANGLE","SIN","COS","TAN"
50 PRINT A*57.29578,SIN(A),COS(A),TAN(A)
```

Inverse Trig Functions

The opposite of finding a *ratio* between two sides of a triangle when an *angle* is known is finding an *angle* when the *ratio* of two sides is known. There are 3 trig functions available to do it, but most computers only make provisions for one called ATN (Arc of the TaNgent).

The following simple program takes the angle we INPUT, converts it to radians, computes and PRINTs its TANgent. Then, as a "proof check," it takes that TANgent value and reverses the process by computing its arc (angle). The letter "I" is used in the program since the arctangent is also known as the "Inverse" (sort of the "opposite") of the TANgent.

```
10 REM  * ATN DEMO *
20 CLS : PRINT
30 INPUT "ENTER AN ANGLE (0-90 DEGREES)";A
40 T = TAN(A/57.29578) : PRINT
50 PRINT "TANGENT =";T,
60 I = ATN(T) * 57.29578
70 PRINT "ARC OF THE TANGENT =";I
```

If you're one of those rare types who is very familiar with trig, you can probably throw numbers around in such a fashion that the other 2 "inverse" trig functions, ARCSIN and ARCCOS, are not needed. But for those of us who get confused when we run out of fingers, the last 2 functions are built into this simple NEW program by way of special routines. The accuracy is "close enough for government" work. Give it a try:

```
10 REM  * INVERSE FUNCTION ROUTINES DEMO *
20 INPUT "ENTER THE RATIO OF 2 SIDES";R
30 CLS : PRINT
40 AS=2*ATN(R/(1+SQR(ABS(1-R*R)))) * 57.29578
50 AC=90 - AS : PRINT
60 PRINT "RATIO","ARCSIN","ARCCOS","ARCTAN"
70 PRINT "(NUMBER)","(DEGREES)","(DEGREES)",
80 PRINT "(DEGREES)" : IF ABS(R)>1 THEN 110
90 PRINT R,AS,AC,ATN(R)*57.29578
100 PRINT : GOTO 20
110 PRINT R,"U","U",ATN(R)*57.29578
120 PRINT : GOTO 20
```

Remember, while the TANgent can be any number, when our ratio moves outside the range of −1 to 1, SIN and COS are both mathematically "Undefined." Also, ARCTAN and ARCSIN produce angle measures between −90 and 90 degrees, but ARCCOS has a range between 0 and 180 degrees.

Learned in Chapter 31

Functions	Miscellaneous
SIN	Degrees
COS	Radians
TAN	
ATN	

Chapter 32

DEFined FuNctions

This Chapter is for advanced math types. If that isn't your bag, skim it lightly and move on to the next Chapter.

In addition to its *intrinsic* (built-in) functions, our BASIC allows us to define **our own** functions.

In what kind of situation would we want to do that? Formulas and simple operations that are used repeatedly can be greatly shortened by building a custom function. They won't operate as fast as factory-built-in functions, but, like subroutines, they greatly simplify BASIC programming.

The format for defining a function is:

DEF FN name(v1,v2,...) = formula

where:

name is the function name, and

v1, v2, ... are dummy variables that represent the values the function will act on. *Name* and *v1, v2 ...* can be any valid variable names.

Formula is the expression where the calculations are carried out.

Let's create a function to do MODular arithmetic. MOD is one of our math operators, but we'll use it to demonstrate the technique DEFined FuNction. Try this on for size:

```
10 CLS : PRINT
20 INPUT "ENTER X";X
30 INPUT "ENTER Y";Y
40 DEF FNC(X,Y) = INT(X-Y * INT(X/Y))
50 REM C = FUNCTION NAME/X,Y = THE NUMBERS
60 PRINT X;"MOD";Y;"=";FNC(X,Y)
```

...and RUN.

The variables X and Y used in defining the function in Line 40 are really "dummy arguments." They only show the Computer **how** to perform the calculations. Change Line 40 to:

```
40 DEF FNC(A,B) = INT(A-B * INT(A/B))
```

...and RUN.

Same results? You betcha. In fact, we could even use A and B elsewhere in the program; Line 40 won't affect their values at all.

The FuNction variable can be INTeger, Single, or Double precision or even a string variable. The value returned to the program is determined by the type of variable. Try this NEW sample with a string:

```
10 DEF FNZ$(A$) = "-" + A$ + "-"
20 PRINT FNZ$("FUNCTION")
```

...and RUN.

Functions are very powerful when used for repetitive calculations. How about

OKAY, OKAY, I'M SORRY I SOUNDED OFF - GIVE THE CHAPTER A SHOT!
DIPLOMA
ADVANCED MATH

the distance between two coordinate points in a plane, (X1,Y1) and (X2,Y2)? Use:

```
10 DEF FND#(X1,Y1,X2,Y2) = SQR((X1-X2)*(X1-X2)
   + (Y1-Y2)*(Y1-Y2))
20 PRINT "DISTANCE IS"; FND#(-1,3,2,7)
```

Note: Line 10 is shown on two Lines to fit the book. The Computer displays it on one Line.

...and RUN.

Note that D# is a double precision variable.

And it is even possible to come up with a function that uses no variables at all:

```
10 RANDOMIZE
20 DEF FNA = 1 + INT(RND*5)
30 PRINT FNA
```

Learned in Chapter 32

Statements

DEF FN

PART 5

DISPLAY FORMATTING

Chapter 33

Formatting with LOCATE

The LOCATE statement allows PRINTing to **begin** anywhere on the screen by first positioning the cursor. Type:

```
10 CLS
20 LOCATE 12,30
30 PRINT "HELLO THERE 12,30!"
```

...and RUN.

The first number is the row, and the second number is the column. There are 25 rows and 80 columns.

Refer to the Video Display Worksheet.

The LOCATE locations start at 1,1 in the upper-left hand corner and go through 1,80 in the first line. They pick up on the second line with 2,1 and continue through 25,80 (the lower-right hand corner).

LOCATE can directly address any of the 2000 PRINT locations. It can be used in the immediate print mode although it's a bit cumbersome. Type:

```
LOCATE 6,30 : PRINT "HERE I AM"        ENTER
```

Video Display Worksheet

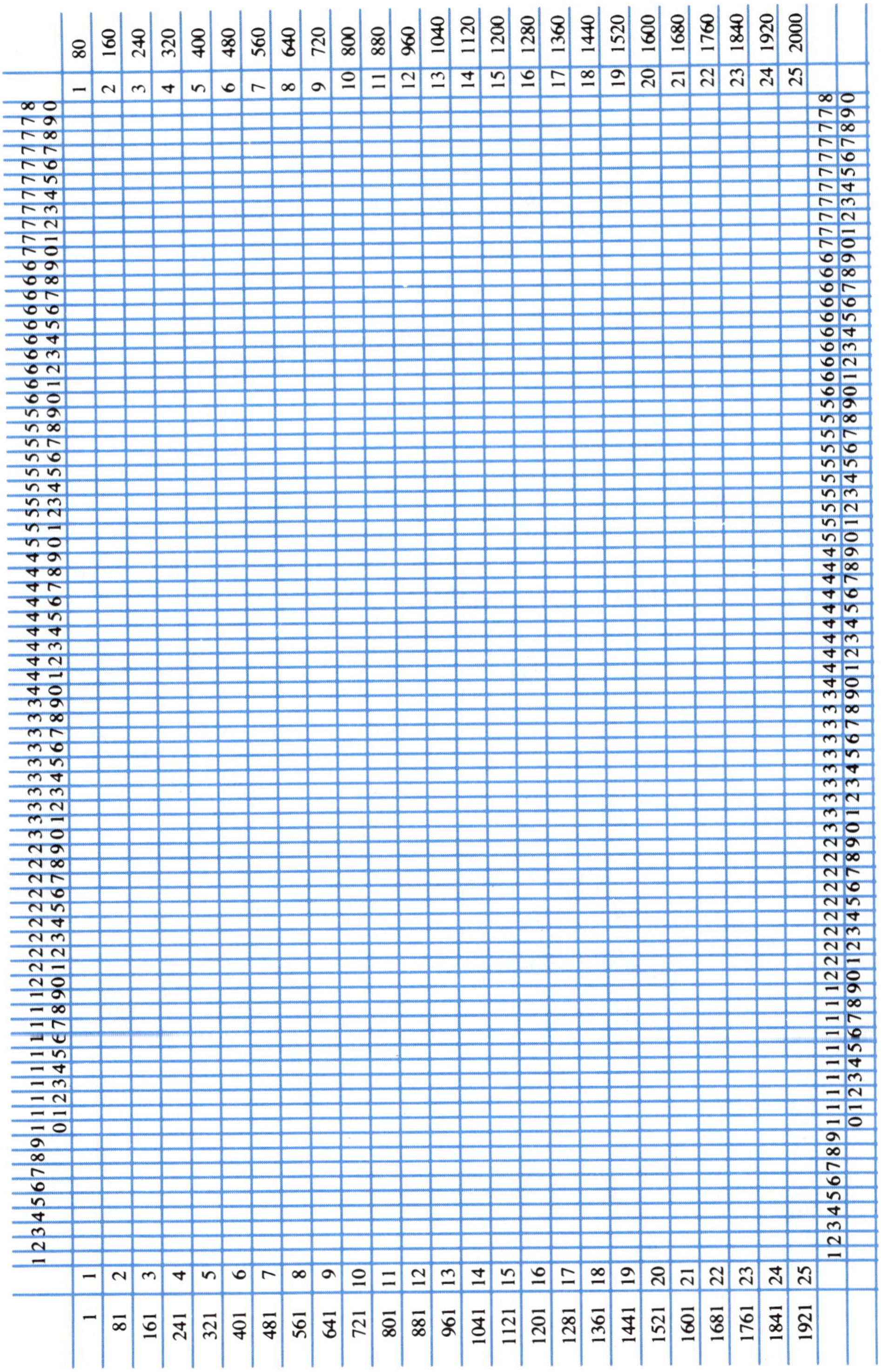

If we want to PRINT on Line 25, we must first turn off the soft key display by typing:

```
KEY OFF
```

or else we'll get an "Illegal function call" error notice.

Typing:

```
KEY ON
```

will turn the display back on.

It's That Time Already?

Let's create a 24-hour clock. That sounds like more fun than digging through this obscure PRINT statement mapping. Type:

```
10 CLS
20 LOCATE 12,35
30 PRINT "H    M    S"
40 FOR H=0 TO 23
50   FOR M=0 TO 59
60    FOR S=0 TO 59
70      LOCATE 13,34
80      PRINT H;":";M;":";S
90       FOR N=1 TO 680 : NEXT N
100    NEXT S
110   NEXT M
120 NEXT H
130 GOTO 10
```

Change Line 90 depending on your computer:

1000 SX: `FOR N = 1 TO 820`

2000: `FOR N = 1 TO 2000`

3000s: `FOR N = 1 TO 2800`

SAVE as TIMER ... and RUN.

"Hello? Bureau of Standards?"

Of course, the accuracy of this timer depends on how closely we calibrate it. The Tandy 1000 will execute somewhere around 680 simple FOR-NEXT loops per second when written as shown in Line 90 -- a multiple statement Line. If we really get carried away with this program, it can be calibrated against a precision timepiece, increasing or decreasing the "680" as needed, or better yet, just use our TIME$ statement along with LOCATE. However, over the short run, it is quite a good timer. Note that we are not triggering this with the power line frequency or a crystal oscillator, but relying solely on the amount of time required to execute FOR-NEXT loops. (It's not nearly as accurate as the Real Time Clock built into the Computer).

Oh, Yes...LOCATE

Anyway -- let's not lose sight of the forest for the trees (or is it trees for the forest?). The purpose of this little program is to demonstrate the LOCATE statement. We used it twice. With blazing speed, the HMS (Hours, Minutes and Seconds), are PRINTed -- and the HM&S are updated each second.

The real clock nut should see Section C for a better clock program.

LOCATEing the Cursor

The LOCATE statement has 3 more variable parts which determine the characteristics of the cursor. Type:

```
NEW

10 CLS
```

BUREAU OF STANDARDS?
I WANT YOU TO KNOW
YOU'RE OFF BY 2 SEC.
ACCORDING TO MY 1000!
TELL 'EM,
M' BOY!

```
20 LOCATE 5,40,0
30 PRINT "THIS IS 5,40"
40 FOR X=1 TO 6000 : NEXT X
60 PRINT : LIST
```

...and RUN.

Where's the cursor? The first 2 numbers determine the position on the screen. The 0 in the third position means "Make the cursor invisible," but it's only invisible when the computer is printing or "doing its own thing." Once program execution is completed, the cursor returns. A 1 makes it visible again if you need the cursor "on" during a program.

Tandy 2000 users can skip down to POS(N) and CSRLIN.

Delete Line 40, change Line 20 to:

```
20 LOCATE 5,40,1,0,7
```

...and RUN.

The cursor is now a block character! The 0 and the 7 determine the start and end *Scan Lines* for the cursor, in other words, how big the cursor will be. Each character on the display has 8 horizontal scan lines. They are numbered 0 through 7 with 0 being on the top. The last 2 numbers in LOCATE control which of the 8 scan lines in the cursor will be "lit."

This time change Line 20 to:

```
20 LOCATE 5,40,1,0,3
```

...and RUN.

Now the cursor is a small block, at the top of a Line. The 0,3 did it. We "turn on" the cursor starting at its top Line (Line 0), and "turn it off" on Line 3. The cursor is, therefore, 4 scan lines long which is half the size of a character.

What if we wanted to make the cursor a single Line? Change Line 20 to:

```
20 LOCATE 5,40,1,3,3
```

Special Effects Dept.

Now let's try for some special effects. If we start the cursor scan towards the bottom and end it at the top, it will "wrap around" and create a 2-part cursor. How about trying to surround a Line of type with the cursor? Change Line 20 to:

```
20 LOCATE 5,40,1,5,1
```

On the 3000s, if the start Scan Line number is smaller than the end Scan Line number (see Line 20 above), the cursor disappears.

This will make the cursor have four Lines on the bottom (5,6,7, and 8) and two Lines on the top (0 and 1). Move the cursor up a couple Lines and then to the right. We really know what letter is inside.

We can only make the cursor invisible at certain times. For example, we can't during an INPUT. To prove it, type:

```
50 INPUT "INPUT HERE"; A$
```

and change the 3rd number in Line 20 to a 0:

```
20 LOCATE 5,40,0,5,1
```

...and RUN.

Nope. The cursor won't disappear.

Now change the 3rd number in the LOCATE statement to a 1 and RUN it to see that the cursor is there. If any of the quantities are deleted, they take on their previous values. For example, to get the cursor back to normal, type:

```
LOCATE ,,,7,7
```

To summarize, the LOCATE statement looks like this:

```
LOCATE A, B, C, D, E
```

A is the ROW, 1-25

B is the COLUMN, 1-80

C determines if the cursor is ON or OFF. Valid numbers are Ø and 1. Ø = OFF; 1 = ON. The default value is Ø (OFF).

D is the starting scan line for the cursor, Ø-7. The default is 7.

E is the end Line for the cursor, Ø-7. The default value is 7.

A 9th scan line, below line 7, will appear whenever the cursor "wraps" from the bottom to the top. This line will not appear when the number D is less than E.

POS(N) and CSRLIN

An additional and sometimes useful function allows the Computer to report the horizontal POSition of the cursor. This simple NEW program exercises the POS function.

```
10 CLS : PRINT
20 INPUT "A NUMBER BETWEEN -9 AND 69";A
30 PRINT TAB(10+A);"X";
40 P = POS(0)
50 PRINT "MARKS THE #";P-1;"PRINT POSITION"
```

```
60 PRINT : LIST
```

...and RUN.

Line 40, containing POS, is the key. The 0 inside the parentheses is just a "dummy." Most any other number or variable would work as well -- but something has to be placed there. POS reports back any cursor POSition on the screen up thru 80 on any 80 column Line. Numbers above 80 start over again with 1.

To help locate the cursor, we can add these Lines to the resident program:

```
53 L = CSRLIN
57 PRINT "AND IS LOCATED IN LINE";L
```

CSRLIN tells us the CuRSor LINe (Row) number from 1-25 that the cursor was on at the time CSRLIN is encountered. Before CSRLIN can be used in Row 25, the function key line must be turned off with `KEY OFF`.

Remember, CSRLIN returns the CuRSor LINe (Row), 1-25, and POS(0) returns the column, 1-80.

WRITEing to the Screen

The WRITE statement allows us to PRINT on the screen. It is similar to PRINT, but the WRITE statement automatically *inserts a comma* between each item the Computer WRITEs on the screen. It also places quotes around all strings. Try this NEW program:

```
10 CLS : PRINT
20 READ A,B,C,D$
30 PRINT A;B;C;D$
40 DATA 100,200,300, ...ETC
50 PRINT : LIST
```

...and RUN.

Nothing new there. Now change Line 30 to:

```
30 WRITE A;B;C;D$
```

RUN, and see:

```
100,200,300," ...ETC"
```

Variables in Line 30 can be separated by semicolons or commas. The Computer will treat them the same.

We already know that BASIC is unable to READ a string from the DATA Line if it contains quotes within quotes. By using WRITE, we can READ a string and let the Computer insert the quotes.

Screen WIDTH Control

When the Computer enters BASIC, the screen width is set at 80 column width. This "normal" screen width can be changed to 40 column by typing:

```
WIDTH 40        ENTER
```

Try it and type a Line containing more than 40 characters. Notice how the Computer displays each character twice the width as in the 80-column mode. When more than 40 characters are entered on a line, the remaining characters fold over to the next line.

The effect of `WIDTH 40` may vary depending upon the video display board and the monitor being used. In some cases, typing `WIDTH 40` will not change the character size, but will cause line wrap to begin at mid line, (position 40).

Reset the WIDTH to 80 column by typing:

```
WIDTH 80        ENTER
```

Learned in Chapter 33

Functions	Statements	Miscellaneous
POS(N)	LOCATE	Video Display Worksheet
KEY OFF/ON	WRITE	Cursor OFF and ON
CSRLIN	WIDTH	

Chapter 34

INKEY$ and INPUT$

The INKEY$ (pronounced Inkey-string) function is a powerful one which enables us to INPUT information from the keyboard without having to use the ENTER key.

Enter this NEW program:

```
10 CLS : PRINT
20 IF INKEY$="T" THEN 40
30 GOTO 20
40 PRINT "YOU HIT THE LETTER 'T'"
50 GOTO 20
```

...and RUN.

Press a variety of individual alpha and numeric keys but not CTRL BREAK (or HOLD). Try the function keys too. Notice that when the function name contains a T, as in LIST, pressing that function key prints the message on the screen.

The keyboard seems to be dead until we hit the T key. Why?

The test in Line 20 then passes, execution moves to Line 40, and a message is PRINTed. Then the process starts over. Hit T again. Hold it down.

The way INKEY$ works is clever if somewhat subtle, so pay close attention.

The keyboard is constantly scanned by the Computer checking to see if any key is pressed. If a key is pressed before the Computer encounters INKEY$, the character that key represents is stored in the INKEY$ storage, or buffer area. The buffer can hold only one character at a time so when a new key is pressed, that new character replaces whatever preceeded it in the buffer, if anything. INKEY$ automatically assumes the string value of whatever character is in its buffer.

Since INKEY$ can only "photograph" one letter or number at a time, if we want to test for more than one character, we have to write the program to test for each one in sequence. In so doing, however, we must be careful or INKEY$ will trip us up.

Add these Lines to the program:

```
25 IF INKEY$="P" THEN 60
60 PRINT "YOU HIT THE LETTER 'P'"
70 GOTO 20
```

...and RUN again.

As you can see, we no longer get an instant response each time **T** or **P** are pressed. This distressing condition exists because the INKEY$ buffer is cleared and reset to a null string **each** time INKEY$ is hit. **CTRL** **BREAK** and LIST so we can take a good look at the program and see how this clearing of the buffer results in the "loss" of a keystroke.

Suppose the operator presses the **T** key just as Line 25 begins execution. Where does the "T" go? Into the INKEY$ buffer, of course. There it sits until another key is pressed, or INKEY$ is "called."

When Line 25 is executed, INKEY$ "reads" the buffer. The buffer's current value ("T") is compared to Line 25's "P." Since the two strings are not equal, control passes to the next Line, then back to Line 20. In Line 20, INKEY$ is called again, but when it checks the buffer this time, "T" is gone. What happened to the "T"?

Let's replay that last sequence, and zoom in for a closeup on the INKEY$ buffer. As the operator hits the T key, we see the "T" stored in the buffer. As the INKEY$ Function in Line 25 is executed, the buffer suddenly goes blank. Thank heavens for instant replay. It's now obvious that each time INKEY$ is called, its buffer is cleared, whether or not it meets the string test in the Line calling it. If we want to preserve the value of "T," we'll need to store it elsewhere, maybe in a temporary string variable.

Change Lines 2Ø and 25 to:

```
20 A$=INKEY$ : IF A$="T" THEN 40
25 IF A$="P" THEN 60
```

...and RUN.

Now we're getting somewhere. Give it the ultimate test -- alternate pressing T and P as quickly as possible.

By setting a "regular" string variable equal to INKEY$ and having T and P checked against the variable instead of against the INKEY$ buffer, we store its value for as long as needed and process it much more efficiently and predictably.

Rapid Scanner

If INKEY$ scans the buffer and does not find a key pressed (the usual case), it is said to read a *null string*. INKEY$ is a string function, and null means **nothing**. A null string is represented by two quote marks with nothing between them, thus:

```
""
```

The ASCII code for null is Ø.

To see how fast we can scan for INPUT with INKEY$, try this NEW program:

```
10 K$ = INKEY$
```

I NEVER REALIZED HOW MESSY COMPUTERS ARE. FIRST, THEIR CURSORS OVER-FLOW, NOW IT'S FULL OF INKEY STRINGS!
?

```
20 IF K$ ="" THEN PRINT "NO KEYBOARD INPUT"
30 PRINT ,,K$ : GOTO 10
```

...and RUN.

Type in random characters and words, and see them break the scan.

Get the general idea how to use INKEY$? So simple, yet the possibilities are enormous. Only a lot of experimenting will make you comfortable with it, but INKEY$ will keep you awake nights staring at the ceiling thinking of ways to put it to work.

Out of the Blue of the Western Sky...

While chasing the solitude needed to write computer books, your author piloted a heavily loaded private plane, packed with computers, ham radio and other goodies, into a medium sized city airport. Transferring this freight to a rental car turned out to be a big deal since security wouldn't let a car on the apron to unload the plane. (You're supposed to drop it by parachute?)

After some cajoling (and a gratuity) it was agreed that my car could be driven up **near** the apron, and an "officially approved" car would haul the goodies from the plane to the car.

Anyway, to get my car through the security fence, it was necessary to drive to an electrically-operated gate. A secret code was punched into a numeric keypad for some sort of computer to analyze. It controlled the motorized gate. *The secret code number was 1930.*

Needless to say, as soon as the computer was set up, I wrote a BASIC program to do everything but actually open the gate. It provides a good example of a real-life application of INKEY$ and is offered here for your careful study.

```
10 CLS : LOCATE 17,30 : PRINT "TYPE THE COMBINATION"
20 LOCATE 18,30 : PRINT "FOLLOWED BY AN ASTERISK"
30 LOCATE 2,27 : PRINT "THE ELECTRIC GATE IS CLOSED"
40 K$ = INKEY$ : IF K$ = "" GOTO 40
50 READ D$ : IF D$ = "*" GOTO 80
```

```
60 IF D$ = K$ THEN 40
70 RESTORE : GOTO 40
80 CLS : LOCATE 2,31 : PRINT "YOU MAY ENTER NOW";
90 LOCATE 4,27 : PRINT "WAIT FOR THE GATE TO OPEN"
100 FOR T=1 TO 3000 : NEXT T
110 RESTORE : GOTO 10
1000 DATA 1,9,3,0,*
```

SAVE as GATE and RUN. Try the combination.

The password (1930 followed by an asterisk) is imbedded, a character at a time, in DATA Line 1000. The commas only separate the characters and should not be typed in as part of the password.

Line 40	holds the magic. It stores the buffer contents in K$ and checks K$ for something besides a null string. If it finds a key was pressed, execution drops to Line 50.
Line 50	READs a piece of DATA. If it happens to be an asterisk (which can only be READ from DATA after all of the other code characters have been READ), execution moves to Line 80 where the gate is OPENed. If, however, the test in Line 50 does not find an asterisk, execution defaults to the next test, in Line 60.
Line 60	checks to see if the keyboard character matches up with the character READ from DATA. If so, the first hurdle has been passed and execution returns to Line 40 for INKEY$ to await another keyboard character. If the keyboard and DATA characters don't match, the test fails and execution drops to Line 70.
Line 70	RESTOREs the DATA pointer back to its beginning and returns execution to Line 40 to start scanning all over again. The keypad puncher sees none of this and has no idea if he is making progress towards cracking the code.
Line 100	merely allows the gate a brief time to open and close (and us to read the screen), then...

Line 110 RESTOREs the DATA and starts the program over from the beginning.

The password can be changed to any combination of characters by changing Line 1000. If we wanted it to be "TANDY" for example:

```
1000 DATA T,A,N,D,Y,*
```

Or, "OPENSESAME"

```
1000 DATA O,P,E,N,S,E,S,A,M,E,*
```

Don't forget that last piece of DATA, the asterisk. By changing Line 50, of course, we could change the asterisk to any other character we wanted.

INPUT$

INPUT$ can be thought of as a *multi-character* INKEY$. It allows us to INPUT a certain number of characters from the keyboard without printing them on the screen. It's great for entering passwords.

Delete Line 20, and make the following changes:

```
40 RESTORE : READ PASSWORD$
50 L = LEN(PASSWORD$)
60 K$ = INPUT$(L)
70 IF K$ = PASSWORD$ THEN 80 ELSE 40
1000 DATA TANDY
```

...and RUN.

Very carefully, type TANDY (no **ENTER**).

This change has a disadvantage in that once you start typing there's no way to start over if you make a mistake. With more elaborate programming, a "reset" could automatically take place after a period of time.

I hope you enjoyed this Chapter as much as I did creating it.

Learned in Chapter 34

Functions	Miscellaneous
INKEY$	INKEY$ Buffer
INPUT$	Null String

Chapter 35

PRINT USING

Of all the ways we have to PRINT, the most powerful (and most complex) is one called PRINT USING. The name PRINT USING implies that we PRINT by USING something else. That implication is correct.

As originally developed for use on large computers, PRINT USING consists of two parts -- PRINT and USING. PRINT prints USING the format (called the *image*) found in **another** Line. The Tandy Computers' PRINT USING feature is similar but does not always require a second Line for the image … as we will see.

PRINT USING with Numbers

Type in this NEW program:

```
10 CLS : PRINT
20 A = 123.456789
50 U$ = "###.##"
60 PRINT USING U$;A
90 PRINT : LIST
```

...and RUN.

The answer is:

```
123.46
```

It was rounded **up** and PRINTed to an accuracy of 2 *decimal* places following the same format as Line 5Ø, the *image Line*.

Add:

```
3Ø B = 1.6
7Ø PRINT USING U$;B
```

...and RUN.

The display shows:

```
123.46
  1.6Ø
```

Notice that we called upon Line 5Ø, the image Line, twice -- once in Line 6Ø and again in Line 7Ø. Also, note that the answers appear with their decimal points lined up. Last, see that a Ø has been added to the 1.6 to make it read 1.6Ø. These latter 2 points are important when PRINTing out financial reports.

One more addition:

```
4Ø C = 9876.54321
8Ø PRINT USING U$;C
```

... and RUN, produces:

```
123.46
  1.6Ø
%9876.54
```

Oh-oh! Vas ist los?

Well, the % sign means we have overrun our image Line's capacity to PRINT digits to the **left** of the decimal point, but it PRINTs them anyway. Better to lose the decimal point lineup than important numbers, but it does call our attention to a programming problem.

Let's add another # sign to make room for that extra digit left of the decimal point. (We are adding another *element* to the *field* in the image Line. Got that?)

```
50 U$ = "####.##"
```

Line 5Ø now has 4 elements in "left field" and 2 in "right field." The decimal point is the dividing point.

...and RUN.

That's better -- but the overrun message would appear again if we tried to PRINT a number with more than 4 digits on the left.

This PRINT USING business looks like it might have some potential, lining up decimal points like it does. We don't have any other reasonable, straightforward way to accomplish that, and it's essential for PRINTing dollars and cents. Wonder how we can PRINT a dollar sign?

Change the *image Line* to:

```
50 U$ = "$####.##"
```

(Check 'em carefully.)

...and RUN.

Nice, eh? The dollar signs all line up in a row:

```
$ 123.46
$    1.60
$9876.54
```

But suppose we want the dollar signs to snug right up against each dollar amount? Make 5Ø read:

```
50 U$ = "$$###.##"
```

...and RUN.

```
 $123.46
   $1.60
$9876.54
```

Not an especially attractive format, but taken singly, as when writing checks, it's almost essential.

The lessons so far are:

1. PRINT USING with # lines up the decimal points.

2. It rounds off the cents (the numbers to the right of the decimal point) to the number of elements specified. It does not round off dollars (left of the decimal point) but sends up an error flag (%), PRINTs all dollars, and slips the printout to the right if the field isn't large enough.

3. If a single $ is added to left field, dollar signs are PRINTed and lined up in a column like decimal points. This single $ does not expand the field.

4. If two $'s are placed on the left, one $ will be PRINTed on each Line immediately in front of the first dollar digit. One of these $'s can be used to replace one # in the field, thereby not expanding it.

We've covered a lot in a very small program but have a long ways to go.

Printing Checks

When using a printer for writing checks, it's usually wise to take extra precautions against "alterations." This is easily accomplished by changing Line 5Ø to read:

```
5Ø U$ = "*****.##"
```

(Count 'em.)

...and RUN.

The display reads:

```
**123.46
****1.6Ø
*9876.54
```

Well, it filled up the unused space alright, but there's no dollar sign. Okay, replace the first # sign with a dollar sign, like so:

```
5Ø U$ = "**$##.##"
```

Aren't you glad we have an Editor for all these changes?

And we get:

```
*$123.46
***$1.6Ø
$9876.54
```

just like they do it uptown! Only 1 $ was needed when using leading *'s, compared to $$ without them.

If we really want to impress others with the size numbers we usually deal in, add lots more # signs to the image Line, thus:

```
5Ø U$ = "**$################.##"
```

and our checks read:

```
**************$123.46
****************$1.60
*************$9876.54
```

...very impressive.

An Illegal funcion call error will occur if more than 24 characters are assigned to a PRINT USING variable.

Since we're obviously big time operators, it's getting hard to keep track of the big numbers. How about some commas to break them apart? (Knock out those extra #'s first. Too hard to count them.)

```
50 U$ = "**$,##.##"
```

(Look closely.)

...and RUN.

```
**$123.46
****$1.60
$9,876.54
```

Only one of our numbers has more than 3 digits in left field, but a comma separated its 9 and 8 for easier readability. In the image field, the comma can be placed **anywhere** between the $ and the decimal point, and only **one** comma is required to automatically insert commas to the left of every 3rd digit left of the decimal point. (You really big-time operators who deal in the millions will have to wait 'til the next Chapter to see how to go "double precision" to avoid losing the loose change.)

NOTE: The comma does **not** serve as a field element.

Stringing It Out

Let's rework the resident program to show some other PRINT USING capabilities:

```
10 CLS : PRINT
20 A = 123.456789
30 B = 1.6
40 C = 9876.54321
50 U$ = "####.##     ####.##     ####.##"
60 PRINT USING U$;A,B,C
90 PRINT : LIST
```

(5 spaces between each field in Line 50)

...and RUN.

The PRINT USING statement will reuse its image Line until all the fields are PRINTed.

Shorten Line 50 to:

```
50 U$ = "####.##     "
```

(5 spaces)

...and RUN again, with the same effect.

See how numbers can be displayed horizontally instead of vertically? Line 60 determines **where** the fields are PRINTed.

```
123.46        1.60     9876.54
```

(8 spaces, 5 spaces)

EXERCISE 35-1: Write the various forms Line 50 must take to PRINT these formats:

```
A) 123.46          1.60          9876.54
B) $ 123.46        $    1.60     $9876.54
C) $123.46         $1.60         $9876.54
D) $123.46         $1.60         $9,876.54
```

and finally

```
E) ***$123.46      *****$1.60      *$9,876.54
```

PRINT USING with Strings

Type in this NEW program:

```
10 CLS : PRINT
20 A$ = "THE"
30 B$ = "QUICK"
40 C$ = "BROWN"
50 D$ = "FOX"
60 U$ = "\\"
70 PRINT USING U$;A$
90 PRINT : LIST
```

...and RUN.

The only thing different about this program are the back slashes in Line 60. The \ is a symbol in PRINT USING which is to strings something like what the # is to numbers.

The \\ reserved 2 spaces for strings. Only TH was PRINTed. Unlike #, however, to reserve more spaces in a *string field*, we add spaces between the \ signs. Change Line 60 to:

```
60 U$ ="\ 1\"
```

(The small 1 is just for us.)

...and RUN.

From now on, the small number between the backslashes will tell us the number of spaces to leave between them.

3 spaces are set aside, and THE is PRINTed without clipping.

Let's make room for PRINTing another string on the same Line.

```
60 U$ = "\ 1\\  3 \"
```

HE'S EXPLAINING HOW HE PROGRAMMED "THE QUICK BROWN FOX" INTO HIS COMPUTER...
I THINK HE'S RUNNIN' A QUART LOW!

```
70 PRINT USING U$;A$,B$
```

...and RUN.

Oops! We ran:

```
THEQUICK
```

together.

To space them apart we have to put an actual space in the image field just as we did earlier when PRINTing numbers.

```
60 U$ = "\1\1\ 3 \"
```

...and RUN.

That's more like it.

Now it's your turn. Complete Lines 60 and 70 to print `THE QUICK BROWN FOX` all on one line.

Answer:

```
60 U$ = "\1\1\ 3 \1\ 3 \1\1\
70 PRINT USING U$;A$,B$,C$,D$
```

If you have trouble counting the spaces in PRINT USING, add an adjacent *measuring line* like this to help in both the LISTing and PRINTout.

```
59 PRINT "123456789012345678901234567890"
```

It's time to quit playing around and get down to business! Change our program to print some typical report headings.

```
10 CLS : PRINT
20 A$ = "PART NUMBER"
```

```
30 B$ = "DATE PURCHASED"

40 C$ = "DESCRIPTION"

50 D$ = "COST"

60     (Figure out this one yourself)

70 PRINT USING U$;A$,B$,C$,D$

90 PRINT : LIST
```

Assignment: Design the image needed in Line 60.

Answer:

```
60 U$ = "\   9 spaces   \  4  \        12        \  4  \
      9      \  4  \ 2 \"
```

> **EXERCISE 35-2:** Duplicate the following statement. Use PRINT USING for all but the column headings.
>
> ```
>                            CREDITS       TAX      TOTAL
> ASTRAL COMPUTER             18.30        .70      19.00
> BIOFEEDBACK ADAPTER          1.80        .00       1.80
> PERSONALITY MODULE           7.20        .30       7.50
>                                         DUE:      28.30
> ```

Learned in Chapter 35

Statements

PRINT USING

Miscellaneous

Image Line
PRINT USING Symbols
. $ * , \

Chapter 36

PRINT USING -- Round 2

In the previous Chapter we learned almost everything really needed to put PRINT USING to work. Here are a few other "tricks" that some will find helpful.

When PRINTing big bucks (over 9,999,999 dollars), it is necessary to use double-precision or we lose the loose change. Type in this NEW program:

```
10 CLS : PRINT
20 A$ = "$$#######,###.##"          (Count 'em.)
30 D = 123456789.01
40 PRINT USING A$;D
90 PRINT : LIST
```

...and RUN.

Sure enough, it rounds to $123,456,800.00. Granted, it's only a few seconds interest on the national debt, but for businesses doing the tax**paying**, the accuracy can be easily improved by simply switching to double-precision.

Change Lines 30 and 40 to:

```
30 D# = 123456789.01
```

```
40 PRINT USING A$;D#
```

...and RUN.

There it is -- $123,456,789.01. Notice that the image Line didn't have to change? All we did was use the double-precision techniques we learned earlier.

If the 17-place accuracy of double-precision isn't adequate to keep track of the Krugerrands in your mattress, you and Scrooge can probably afford to spring for a bigger computer.

Profit or Loss?

Was that last number this quarter's PROFIT or was it a LOSS? We can make the image Line PRINT either one. Change it to read:

```
20 A$ = "+$$######,###.##"
```

...and RUN.

Very nice. Wonder what would happen if D was a negative number?

```
30 D# = -123456789.01
```

...and RUN.

So far, so good. Suppose we take the + out of the image Line. Wonder if it will PRINT the minus sign anyway? Use the EDITor, and remove it from Line 20.

Then RUN.

Oh, oh! It goofed up. Negative numbers require one more field element than positive numbers, and the extra $ doesn't do the job. The + did count as an element, so let's put the + sign back in, this time at the *end* of the image.

```
20 A$ = "$$######,###.##+"
```

...and RUN.

Mmmmm. That's nice. The sign is PRINTed at the end. Let's change D back to a **positive** number and see what happens.

```
30 D# = 123456789.01
```

...and RUN.

Very nice. Looks better to have the signs at the end, not interfering with the dollar sign, don't you think?

Most printers don't PRINT deficits in red. How can we tag them so it's harder for the project manager to slip them by us? (We'll just take all + numbers for granted.) Let's try changing the image + to a minus and see what happens.

```
20 A$ = "$$#######,###,##-"
```

...and RUN.

Seems normal. How about when it's hit with a negative number.

```
30 D# = -123456789.01
```

...and RUN.

AHA! Sticks out like a sore thumb. Now about this little deficit here, Smythe...

EXERCISE 36-1: Duplicate this simplified ledger using PRINT USING:

```
    REVENUES      EXPENSES          ASSETS
1,203,104.22          0.00  1,203,104.22
        0.00    560,143.80     560,143.80-
```

More on Strings

There are three more PRINT USING characters that have real value. Like so many exotic upgrades of BASIC, it does nothing that can't be achieved using other BASIC words but does it easier. Enter this NEW program:

```
1Ø CLS : PRINT
2Ø X$ = "ALEXANDER"
3Ø Y$ = "GRAHAM"
4Ø Z$ = "BELL"
5Ø A$ = "!1!1\ 2 \"
6Ø PRINT USING A$;X$,Y$,Z$
9Ø PRINT : LIST
```

...and RUN.

Who should appear before our very eyes but:

```
A G BELL
```

Each ! reserves an element in the field for the *first letter* of the string assigned to it. Very handy when we want to PRINT the initials and last names of a list of people.

The Second Short Cut

Change Line 5Ø to:

```
5Ø A$ = "&1!1&"
```

and RUN to get:

```
ALEXANDER G BELL
```

The & PRINTs an entire string without any changes and relieves you of the need to PRINT adjacent "measuring" lines. As with the backslash, we have to put actual spaces in the image field to space the strings apart.

Change Line 50 one more time:

```
50 A$ = "&1&1&"
```

and RUN.

And the Third Short Cut

An area of PRINT USING worthy of examination is incorporation of the image Line into the PRINT USING Line. It requires some care and has value primarily when only a few variables are to be PRINTed or only PRINTed once. In more practial applications, the image Line is referenced many times during a RUN, frequently by different PRINT USING Lines.

Make a few changes in the resident program so it looks like this:

```
10 CLS : PRINT
20 X$ = "ALEXANDER"
30 Y$ = "GRAHAM"
40 Z$ = "BELL"
60 PRINT USING "!1!1\ 2 \";X$,Y$,Z$
90 PRINT : LIST
```

...and RUN.

We simply did away with A$ and incorporated its elements into a combination PRINT and image Line separated by a semicolon. It does save space, and for short and uncomplicated PRINT USING applications, has great value. For the long and complicated ones, it's better to keep the image and PRINT USING Lines separate.

INPUTting the Image

We move deeper into the woods as we make BASIC's PRINT formatting capabilities resemble the superior (and far more complicated) ones of the FORTRAN language from which it is derived. We can even INPUT the image Line since it is a string. An easy way to see this is by using our resident program but change:

```
50 INPUT A$
60 PRINT USING A$;X$,Y$,Z$
```

...and RUN.

We now have to respond by typing in the image Line. (Seems like they're hard enough to create without INPUTting.) The safest one to use is old Line 5Ø, so respond to the question mark with:

```
? !1!1\ 2 \          ENTER
```

and see:

```
A G BELL
```

appear again.

RUN again, this time responding with:

```
? \    7    \1\  4   \1\ 2 \
```

and we should see:

```
ALEXANDER GRAHAM BELL
```

Try some other INPUTs and see how fast we get into trouble with "Illegal function call" errors. The down-to-earth value of this particular capability is a little elusive.

Let's experiment with the & introduced earlier. RUN the program again, and when it asks for an INPUT, type:

```
&
```

This character allows the use of variable length strings. The three names are concatenated and PRINTed. This use of & is a little strange because it defeats the purpose of PRINT USING since there's no way to control column placement. However, when the right application pops up, it's there to use.

What's the Bottom Line?

Inserting an underscore into a PRINT USING Line causes the next character to be displayed as shown in the image Line.

Delete Line 50 from our resident program, and change Line 60 to:

```
60 PRINT USING "_!1!1\ 2 \";X$,Z$
```

(_ is SHIFT -.)

...and RUN.

You should have gotten:

```
! A BELL
```

Now for a quick analysis:

The underscore caused the ! to be printed.

The single space caused a space to be printed.

The second ! (with no underscore) did what it always does, print the first letter of the string, ALEXANDER.

The second single space printed the space **after** the A.

The \ 2 \ printed the 4 characters of the second string.

Any questions?

Scientific Forms of PRINT USING

Would you believe a double-precision number, clipped and expressed via PRINT USING in double-precision Exponential notation? The technical types among us with mismatched socks and a rope for a belt will salivate at that one. We aren't going to bore the business types with gory details except for a quick intro.

Change or add these Lines:

```
10 CLS : PRINT
20 A$ = "##################^^^^"
```

(18 + 4)

WOULD YOU BELIEVE A DOUBLE-PRECISION NUMBER, CLIPPED and EXPRESSED IN DOUBLE-PRECISION EXPONENTIAL NOTATION, IN PRINT USING ?...
Z

```
30 D# = 12345678909876543 21
```

```
30 D# = 1234567890987654321
40 D = 1234567890987654321
50 PRINT USING A$;D#
60 PRINT USING A$;D
90 PRINT : LIST
```

...and RUN.

What we see is what we get, both in double and single precision. Using the Editor, move the block of 4 carets to the left, one position at a time, filling in with #'s.

Try:

```
20 A$ = "#################^^^^#"
20 A$ = "################^^^^##"
20 A$ = "###############^^^^###"
```

etc.

Have fun!

Bring on the Money Changers

Here is a straightforward user program which uses PRINT USING in a practical way. One would be hard pressed to get the same results in so short a program without using it.

If you're not in the international currency biz, just type in the first half-dozen or so DATA Lines, plus Line 1500 to get a feel for what PRINT USING can do. See how \ and # can be mixed with blank spaces on the same image Line?

Remember, DATA items are easy to change. If you want to use the current rate of exchange, just enter them in place of these.

Count spaces in Line 90 **very carefully!** Add measuring Line 89 if necessary.

```
1 CLS
10 REM  * INTERNATIONAL MONEY CHANGER *
20 REM  * RATES AS OF APRIL 1985 *
30 KEY OFF : RESTORE : LOCATE 25,15
40 PRINT "HOW MANY U.S. DOLLARS";
50 INPUT" DO YOU WISH TO EXCHANGE ";D: CLS
60 PRINT TAB(26); "AT TODAY'S RATE YOU WILL GET"
70 PRINT
80 READ A$,A,B$,B : IF A$ = "END" THEN 30
90 P$ = "\        (16 spaces)      \  3  ########.##  4  "
100 PRINT USING P$; A$; D/A; B$; D/B
110  GOTO 80
1000 DATA ARGENTINE PESO, .002553
1010 DATA AUSTRALIAN DOLLAR, .6360
1020 DATA AUSTRIAN SCHILLING, .04746
1030 DATA BELGIAN FRANC, .01645
1040 DATA BRAZILIAN CRUZEIRO, .0002128
1050 DATA BRITISH POUND, 1.279
1060 DATA CANADIAN DOLLAR, .7407
1070 DATA CHINESE YUAN, .3550
1080 DATA COLOMBIAN PESO, .007741
1090 DATA DANISH KRONE, .09272
1100 DATA DUTCH GUILDER, .2935
1110 DATA ECUADORIAN SUCRE, .01489
1120 DATA FINNISH MARKKA, .1587
1130 DATA FRENCH FRANC, .1087
1140 DATA GREEK DRACHMA, .007692
1150 DATA HONG KONG DOLLAR, .1285
1160 DATA INDIAN RUPEE, .0197
```

```
1170 DATA INDONESIAN RUPIAH, .0009042
1180 DATA IRISH PUNT, 1.0475
1190 DATA ISRAELI SHEKEL, .001090
1200 DATA ITALIAN LIRA, .0005214
1210 DATA JAPANESE YEN, .004027
1220 DATA LEBANESE POUND, .05714
1230 DATA MALAYSIAN RINGGIT, .4060
1240 DATA MEXICAN PESO, .004098
1250 DATA NEW ZEALAND DOLLAR, .4590
1260 DATA NORWEGIAN KRONE, .1147
1270 DATA PAKISTANI RUPEE, .06389
1280 DATA PERUVIAN SOL, .0001151
1290 DATA PHILLIPPINE PESO, .05426
1300 DATA PORTUGUESE ESCUDO, .005952
1310 DATA SAUDI ARABIAN RIYAL, .2771
1320 DATA SINGAPORE DOLLAR, .4541
1330 DATA SOUTH AFRICAN RAND, .5230
1340 DATA SPANISH PESETA, .005952
1350 DATA SWEDISH KRONA, .1139
1360 DATA SWISS FRANC, .4016
1370 DATA TAIWANESE DOLLAR, .02524
1380 DATA THAI BAHT, .03674
1390 DATA URUGUAY NEW PESO, .01040
1400 DATA VENEZUELAN BOLIVAR, .1333
1410 DATA WEST GERMAN MARK, .3323
1500 DATA END, 0, END, 0
```

Learned in Chapter 36

Miscellaneous

PRINT USING Symbols
+ − ^ ! & (ampersand) _ (underline)

Chapter 37

Coloring in Text Mode

COLOR statement? I thought we couldn't use COLOR with the Monochrome Monitor? Well you're **right**. COLOR is mostly used with the High Resolution Color Monitor to choose the COLOR we want to draw in. However, we **can** use the COLOR statement on the Monochrome Monitor for some nice effects. You **do not** need a color monitor or any other special hardware to use this Chapter. With a monochrome, we simply get different shades.

NOTE: Monochrome Monitors first came only in black and white (black background, white characters). Now the text, or characters, can be green, amber, or even blue.

Back in Chapter 33, when we talked about LOCATE, we said that to PRINT on the bottom line of the video display, the function key display has to be turned off. What if we turn OFF the keys, set a **new** color, and then turn the keys back ON? Let's try it. Type in and RUN this NEW program:

```
10 CLS
20 KEY OFF
30 COLOR 31,0,0
40 KEY ON
50 COLOR 7,0,0
```

Here's what took place:

Line 10	CLeared the Screen.
Line 20	turned OFF the function key display.
Line 30	set the video to display all characters in high intensity white and flashing.
Line 40	turned ON the function key display.
Line 50	set the display to its normal color.

Press CTRL HOME to bring the entire display back to normal.

O.K. So we changed the color of the function key display, but how did it work?

The format for COLOR is:

```
COLOR text, background, border
```

`text` can be a number from 0 to 31 and sets the color of the foreground characters (text). 0 to 7 are all different colors. 8-15 are the same colors as 0 to 7, but in a "high intensity" mode. Adding 16 to any number causes it to blink, so 16 through 23 are the original colors, but blinking. 24 through 31 are intense and blinking.

`background` can be a number from 0 to 7 and sets the background color.

`border` is a number from 0 to 15 which sets the color of the border around the screen.

To display something in a new color, the color must first be changed. Everything printed after the change is printed in the new color; anything printed before the color change remains the same. That's why we turned off the function key display, changed the color, then turned it back on.

Here's what each of the COLOR numbers mean:

1000 Series/3000 Series

NUMBER	RESULT
0	Black
1	Blue
2	Green
3	Cyan
4	Red
5	Magenta
6	Brown
7	White (Normal)
8	Gray
9	Light Blue
10	Light Green
11	Light Cyan
12	Light Red
13	Light Purple
14	Light Yellow
15	White (High intensity)

Tandy 2000

NUMBER	RESULT
0	Black
1	Underline
2-7	White (Normal)
10-15	High intensity white
16 or 24	Black blinking
17	Underline white blinking
18-23	Blinking
25	High intensity white underlined blinking
26-31	High intensity blinking

These color codes even work with a Monochrome Monitor. The characters are just printed in shades of green and black. (The 2000 doesn't print in shades of color, just green or black.)

Try this NEW program:

```
10 CLS
20 COLOR 23,0,0
30 PRINT "THIS IS BLINKING"
40 COLOR 0,7,0
50 PRINT "THIS IS INVERSE"
60 COLOR 7,0,0
70 PRINT "BACK TO NORMAL"
```

...and RUN.

Let's look at each of the three COLOR statements separately to see why they changed the data displayed.

`THIS IS BLINKING` is blinking in white so the original color was 7 (the color code for white). Adding 16 to any number causes it to blink (7+16=23). The second number is 0, the code for black, and is the background color. The last 0 represents the border color, which also remains black.

`THIS IS INVERSE` shows up as inverse because the text color is 0 (black) and the background color is 7 (white), which is the opposite, or inverse, of what they normally are.

`BACK TO NORMAL` is printed in normal mode. The text color is white (code 7) and the background color is black.

Let's try doing a screen "White Out." By putting the screen in reverse mode and clearing everything with CLS, we can fill the screen with the reversed background color which is "white" (looks green to me). Try:

```
COLOR 0,7,0 : CLS
```

and the screen changes COLOR. Type:

```
COLOR 7,0,0 : CLS
```

to go back to normal.

Type in this command to see the border feature:

```
COLOR 7,0,1
```

To return to normal, just type:

```
COLOR 7,0,0
```

The following program demonstrates the COLOR capabilities of the Tandy 1000 and 3000 Personal Computers when using the Monochrome Monitor. Study the program and results carefully.

```
10 CLS
20 COLOR 7,0,0                  'NORMAL DISPLAY
```

```
30 PRINT "C";
40 COLOR 1,Ø,Ø              'DARK VALUE
50 PRINT "O";
60 COLOR 1Ø,Ø,Ø             'LIGHT VALUE
70 PRINT "M";
80 COLOR 15,Ø,Ø             'HIGH VALUE INTENSITY
90 PRINT "P";
100 COLOR 7 + 16,Ø,Ø        'NORMAL BLINKING
110 PRINT "U";
120 COLOR 1 + 16,Ø,Ø        'DARK VALUE BLINKING
130 PRINT "T";
140 COLOR 1Ø + 16,Ø,Ø       'LIGHT VALUE BLINKING
150 PRINT "E";
160 COLOR 15 + 16,Ø,Ø       'HIGH INTENSITY WHITE BLINKING
170 PRINT "R";
200 COLOR 7,Ø,Ø             'NORMAL DISPLAY
220 PRINT : LIST
```

SAVE as COLOR

...and RUN.

For a demonstration of the 2000's COLOR capabilities, enter the following NEW program. SAVE it as COLOR and RUN.

```
10 CLS
20 COLOR 7,Ø,Ø              'NORMAL DISPLAY
30 PRINT "C";
40 COLOR 1,Ø,Ø              'UNDERLINED NORMAL
50 PRINT "O";
60 COLOR Ø,7,Ø              'INVERSE
```

```
70 PRINT "L";
80 COLOR 7 + 16,0,0          'INVERSE BLINKING
90 PRINT "O";
100 COLOR 15 + 16,0,0        'HIGH INTENSITY BLINKING
110 PRINT "R"
120 COLOR 7,0,0              'BACK TO NORMAL
130 PRINT : LIST
```

Now we'll PRINT in reversed mode. Just add or change the following Lines:

```
120 COLOR 0,7,0
130 PRINT " COMPUTER"
140 COLOR 7,0,0
150 LIST
```

SAVE this program as COLOR2.

The use of reverse letters adds considerable impact to visual displays. Type in this NEW program:

```
10 REM  * ON BASE OF STATUE OF LIBERTY *
20 REM  * LARGEST STATUE EVER ERECTED *
30 CLS : KEY OFF : COLOR 0,7,0
40 LOCATE 10,10 : PRINT "KEEP, ANCIENT LANDS,"
50 LOCATE 12,12 : PRINT "YOUR STORIED POMP!"
60 FOR T = 1 TO 3000 : NEXT
70 COLOR 7,0,0 : CLS : COLOR 0,7,0
80 LOCATE 3,1 : PRINT "GIVE ME YOUR TIRED, YOUR POOR,"
90 FOR T = 1 TO 2000 : NEXT
```

OKAY, SO YOU ACED THE CHAPTER-THAT DOESN'T NECESSARILY MAKE YOU A COLOR WHEEL!

```
100 LOCATE 7,1 : PRINT "YOUR HUDDLED MASSES YEARNING TO"
110 LOCATE 8,5 : PRINT "BREATHE FREE,"
120 FOR T = 1 TO 2700 : NEXT
130 LOCATE 12,1 : PRINT "THE WRETCHED REFUSE OF YOUR"
140 LOCATE 13,5 : PRINT "TEEMING SHORE."
150 FOR T = 1 TO 3000 : NEXT
160 LOCATE 17,1 : PRINT "SEND THESE, THE HOMELESS,"
170 LOCATE 18,5 : PRINT "TEMPEST-TOSSED TO ME,"
180 FOR T = 1 TO 3200 : NEXT
190 LOCATE 22,1 : PRINT "I LIFT MY LAMP BESIDE THE GOLDEN"
200 LOCATE 23,5 : PRINT "DOOR!"
210 FOR X=1 TO 8000 : NEXT
220 COLOR 7,0,0 : KEY ON : END
```

...and RUN.

Since we only use the left half of the screen, let's create something on the right side of the display.

Add the following Lines to the resident program:

```
35 GOSUB 1000
75 GOSUB 1000
1000 REM  * SUBROUTINE TO PRINT GRAPHICS CHARACTERS *
1010 RESTORE : COLOR 7,0,0
1020 FOR I = 1 TO 3           ' 3 LETTERS
1030  PRINT : PRINT
1040  FOR J = 1 TO 5          ' 5 LINES PER LETTER
1050   PRINT : PRINT TAB(72)
1060   FOR K = 1 TO 4         ' 4 CHARACTERS PER LINE
1070    READ Y
```

```
1080     PRINT CHR$(Y);
1090    NEXT K
1100   NEXT J
1110 NEXT I
1120 COLOR 0,7,0
1130 RETURN
1200 DATA 186,32,32,186,186,32,32,186,186,32,32,186
1210 DATA 186,32,32,186,200,205,205,188
1220 DATA 201,205,205,205,186,32,32,32,200,205,205,187
1230 DATA 32,32,32,186,205,205,205,188
1240 DATA 201,205,205,187,186,32,32,186,204,205,205,185
1250 DATA 186,32,32,186,186,32,32,186
```

...and RUN.

This one gives us a chance to flex our muscles with the *Line graphics* characters.

Learned in Chapter 37

Statements

COLOR

Chapter 38

Using a Printer

Ready to learn something that's very simple?

LPRINT and LLIST

These BASIC commands/statements are almost too easy.

We have learned a lot of ways to PRINT, but they have all been on the video screen. Now we'll learn how to PRINT to a Computer printer. If you don't have a printer yet, at least skim this Chapter before proceeding.

Hook up and turn on the printer. Then type this new one-Line program:

```
10 LPRINT "THE PRINTER WORKS!!!"
```

Notice that the first word is LPRINT, not PRINT. Note also that L? will not work for LPRINT. RUN the program.

Did it print? If your printer did nothing, check the connections again. Make sure the printer is *on* and *on-line*. Try RUNning the one-Line program again.

NOTE: There is much widespread misuse of the language when it comes to naming printers. Here are some definitions:

PRINTer = a device which converts computer talk to *hard copy*.

Dot Matrix Printer = a printer such as the DMP 120 which creates characters by printing clusters of dots which resemble letters and numbers.

Character Printer = a printer that, like most typewriters, prints complete pre-formed characters.

Line Printer = a very large "hi-speed" printer which literally "sets" and then prints an entire LINE of print at one time.

There is much misnaming of printers. Very few are true "Line Printers," though many are sold under that name. True Line Printers are very expensive and can print over 1000 Lines of type per minute.

It is from the name Line Printer that the "L" in LPRINT was derived.

LLISTing the Program

LLIST is typed at the command level when we want a LISTing of a program sent to the PRINTer.

Both LPRINT and LLIST can be used either as statements or commands. If you want to PRINT both on the screen and on paper, use duplicate program Lines, with PRINT for the screen and LPRINT for the PRINTer.

Enter any program of your choice, and convert it to LPRINT the results on your PRINTer. Make a hard copy by LLISTing it.

To LIST a program on the printer, you can also use:

```
LIST, "LPT1:"
```

The program will be LISTed on PrinTer #1.

If we accidentally precede either PRINT or LIST with the letter L and don't have a PRINTer connected, there may be trouble. It's especially easy to have a simple LIST turn into LLIST. If there is no PRINTer hooked up or it's turned off, we will get a "Device Unavailable" error after a delay of about 20 seconds. If the PRINTer is hooked up but Off Line, after about 15 seconds, we will get a "Device Timeout" error.

To temporarily halt the PRINTer, hit **HOLD**. Hit **HOLD** a second time to continue PRINTing. (On the 3000, use **Ctrl** **Num Lock**.)

The Tandy Computers have a special screen dump key directly below the **INSERT** key. Press **SHIFT** **PRINT** (or **Shift** **Prt Sc**) to send all the characters on the screen to the PRINTer. Unprintable characters are printed as blanks.

LPRINT TAB

The TAB function can handle numbers up through 32767 (255 on Tandy 2000). This has little value in displays PRINTed on the Computer, but on big PRINTers, it is common to PRINT Lines up to 132 characters long.

LPRINT Spaces

We recall that PRINT STRING$ is used to repeat a number of characters or actions. We can use it to sneak around the above rule by having it repeat a number of spaces. For example:

```
10 LPRINT STRING$(95,32);X
```

will "PRINT" 95 blank spaces before PRINTing the value of X (which should be Ø). "32" is the ASCII code for a space. On an 80 column width, Ø will be printed in position 15 on the second line.

The WIDTH statement can be used to tell the Computer that the PRINTer is wider than 80 columns. Use:

```
WIDTH LPRINT 255
```

at the beginning of programs that need to use more than 80-column width.

Formatting

Now, let's see how to PRINT with a nice format. Type:

```
10 FOR X=1 TO 100
20  LPRINT X,
30 NEXT X
```

...RUN it.

See how the printer will format the PRINTing into neat little columns? The comma with LPRINT works the same as it does with PRINT, except there may be a different number of columns on your printer. (The number of columns depends on which PRINTer you have.)

Try using a semicolon in Line 20 rather than a comma. Type:

```
20 LPRINT X;
```

...and RUN. The semicolon works the same on the PRINTer as it does on the video screen. Let's see how TAB works. Type this simple NEW program:

```
10 LPRINT TAB(25); "TELEPHONE LIST"
20 LPRINT
30 LPRINT TAB(15); "NAME";
40 LPRINT TAB(45); "TELEPHONE NUMBER"
50 LPRINT
60 INPUT "TYPE A FRIEND'S NAME";A$
70 INPUT "PHONE NUMBER";B$
80 PRINT "THANK YOU"
90 LPRINT TAB(15); A$;TAB(45); B$
100 INPUT "IS THERE ANOTHER FRIEND (Y/N)";Q$
110 IF Q$="Y" THEN 60
```

If your paper size is larger or smaller than 8 1/2 by 11 inches, you'll want to use different TAB settings.

...and RUN.

YOU'D BETTER
HIT HOLD BEFORE
WE BOTH GET
BURIED!

LPOS

LPOS(1) is a statement used for locating the printer head position in the printer buffer for LPT1:. If you place a 0 in the parentheses, the current position of the printer head in the printer buffer of line printer 0 will be returned. This statement is used for column formatting various length words or numbers. Try the following program:

```
10 FOR I = 1 TO 81
20  LPRINT "*";
30  IF LPOS(1) > 70 THEN LPRINT
40 NEXT
50 LPRINT
```

Be sure to include Line 50. It causes the printer buffer to be emptied.

LPRINT USING

In the last Chapter we saw how PRINT USING can format our PRINT outputs on the screen. Those same features can be applied to the printer by using LPRINT USING. Incorporate LPRINT USING in one of the simple programs from the last Chapter.

```
10 X$ = "ALEXANDER"
20 Y$ = "GRAHAM"
30 Z$ = "BELL"
60 LPRINT USING "!1!1\ 2 \";X$;Y$;Z$
```

...and RUN.

Advanced LPRINT Capabilities

4 different ASCII codes are set aside for use with PRINTers. Since different PRINTers respond differently, we can only talk here in general terms and learn how to test our own PRINTer to see how it responds. The 4 codes are:

9	Tab
10	Line feed
12	Form feed
13	Carriage return and line feed

To see what this all means, enter this program:

```
10 CLS : PRINT
20 INPUT "ENTER A CODE NUMBER";N
30 LPRINT CHR$(N)
90 PRINT : LIST
```

...and RUN.

Try each of the codes and see what happens. Some codes may do nothing. Your PRINTer's manual may have additional (or replacement) codes.

There are no universal rules. Keep your test program simple, and be aware that LPRINT with CHR$ is not always predictable when mixed on the same program Line.

The "top of form," or "top of next sheet," feature is a necessary one for preparing PRINTed statements or PRINTing information which must always start at the top of a page.

When your Computer is turned on, if it is going to do any PRINTing, it automatically assumes it will be PRINTing 6 Lines per inch on sheets of paper 11 inches long; that's 66 Lines per page.

With a little experimenting, your PRINTer will be doing what you paid to have it do.

Learned in Chapter 38

Statements

LPRINT
LLIST
LPOS

Miscellaneous

Trailing semicolon
SHIFT PRINT
or Shift Prt Sc

PART 6

ARRAYS

Chapter 39

Arrays

We know we can use combinations of the 26 letters of the alphabet, digits 0-9 and periods to create variable names. We've also discovered that very few of our programs have required anywhere near that many variables. There are times, however, when we need more variables -- sometimes **hundreds** or even **thousands** of them.

The way we control and keep track of that many variables is by holding them in an ARRAY. Array is just another word for "lineup," "arrangement," or "series of things."

Let's organize a collection, arrangement, or lineup (array) of autos, each of which has a different I.D. (address) number.

We line up 10 cars, as in an *array*. They are all the same except for their engine size -- and each has a different I.D. or license number. Let's say the I.D. numbers range from 1 to 10, and we want to use the Computer to quickly spit out the engine size when we identify a car by its I.D. number. This might not seem like a real heavyweight problem -- but, as before, we discover the full potential of these things by learning little steps at a time.

The I.D. numbers and engine sizes are as follows:

CAR #	ENGINE
1	300
2	200
3	500

CAR #	ENGINE
4	300
5	200
6	300
7	400
8	400
9	300
10	500

We could give each of these cars a different letter name, using the variables A through J, but what a waste -- and what will we do when there are a thousand cars not just ten?

Setting Up Arrays

Our BASIC allows any valid variable name to be used as an array name. An *Array* named "A" is not the same as the *Numeric* variable "A," and neither is it the same as *string* variable A$. It is a totally separate "A" used to identify a *Numeric array*. We call it A-sub(something), and it can only hold numbers. We will name the cars A(1) through A(10), pronounced "A sub 1" through "A sub 10." Get the idea?

What's that -- you don't believe there can be 3 separate variables all named "A"? Ok, in immediate mode type:

```
A = 12          ENTER
A$ = "(Type in your name)"          ENTER
A(1) = 999          ENTER
```

then: `PRINT A,A$,A(1)` ENTER

Does that make you a believer?

Let's store the car engine sizes in DATA statements. Type in:

```
500 DATA 300,200,500,300,200
510 DATA 300,400,400,300,500
```

Notice how carefully we kept the DATA elements in order from 1 to 10 so the first car's engine size is found in the first DATA location and the 10th one's in the 10th location.

We now have to "spin up" an array inside the Computer's memory to make these data elements *immediately addressable*.

Big words meaning "so we can find a car fast."

Think how difficult it would be to try to address the 7th engine (or the 7 thousandth!) for example, using only what we've learned so far. It **can** be done using only DATA, READ and RESTORE statements, but that would be very messy and slow.

The easy way to create the array is to type in:

```
30 FOR L = 1 TO 10
40  READ A(L)
50 NEXT L
```

...and RUN.

Nothing happen? Yes, it did. We simply didn't display what happened.

The FOR-NEXT loop READ 10 pieces of DATA and named the elements (or "cells") in which they're stored A(1) through A(10). To PRINT out the values in those array elements, type:

```
105 FOR N = 1 TO 10
110  PRINT A(N)
120 NEXT N
```

...and RUN.

It worked! We READ the DATA elements into an array called A(L), but PRINTed them out of an array called A(N). Why the difference? Nothing significant.

The array's *name* is "A." The *location* of each data element within that array is identified by the number we place inside the parentheses. That number can be brought inside the parentheses by using any numeric variable and can even do some simple arithmetic inside the parentheses, if necessary. We arbitrarily used L to READ them in and N to PRINT them out.

Remember, the array we are using is named "A." Its elements are numbered and called A-sub(number).

Some pure mathematicians might insist on calling A(X) "A OF X." We don't need that added confusion, but best you know, just in case.

Let's work some more on the program.

Type:

```
10 CLS
90 PRINT
100 PRINT "CAR#","ENGINE SIZE"
110 PRINT N,A(N)
```

...and RUN.

Now that's more like it. We have every I.D. number, every engine size, and we're not "using up" any of the "regular" alphabetic variables to store them. Having demonstrated that point, delete Lines 105 and 120, and type:

```
20 INPUT "WHICH CAR TO EXAMINE";W
110 PRINT W,A(W)
990 PRINT : LIST
```

...and RUN answering with a car #.

Get the idea? Can you see the crude beginning of a simple inventory system for a small business?

HEH, HEH, ALL I SAID WAS " I NEED ARRAYS TO FINISH MY PROGRAM"...
$

Let's go one small step further. Suppose we know the color of each of the 10 cars, and for simplicity, suppose the colors are coded 1, 2, 3 and 4. We might then have a master chart that looks like this:

CAR#	ENG. SIZE	COLOR
1	300	3
2	200	1
3	500	4
4	300	3
5	200	2
6	300	4
7	400	3
8	400	2
9	300	1
10	500	3

In the language of professional computer types, this is called a *matrix*. A *matrix* is just an array that has more than one dimension. (Our first array had the dimension of 1 by 10 -- 1 *column* by 10 *rows*.) This new array has a horizontal dimension of 2 and a vertical dimension of 10.

If we wanted to be terribly inefficient about the matter, we **could** say that this is a 3 by 10 array counting the I.D. number. If so, our first example would be called a 2 by 10 array -- but who needs it? As long as we keep the I.D. numbers in a simple 1 to 10 FOR-NEXT loop and the DATA in proper sequence, the arrays will be simple and easier to handle.

Since we do not store the car number in the Computer, it is a "pointer," or an "index." That's why we don't consider it as another "DIMension" to the matrix.

How then can we label this 2 by 10 *matrix*? We have already used up our A array elements numbered 1 through 10.

Let's arbitrarily assign array locations 101 through 110 to hold the color code. We also have to put the color code info in the program using a DATA statement. From the table, type:

```
520 DATA 3,1,4,3,2,4,3,2,1,3
```

and:

```
60 FOR S = 101 TO 110
70  READ A(S)
80 NEXT S
```

These last Lines load the color code DATA into the array. Array element numbers 11 through 100 are not used, nor are those from 111 to the end of memory since they have not been formally assigned any values.

...RUN, and select any car number.

What is this "Subscript out of range" business? Well, since arrays take up a lot of memory space, the Computer automatically allows us to use up to only 11 array elements without question. (They can be numbered from 0 to 10.) Then our credit runs out. We earlier used elements numbered from 1 to 10 without any problem.

If we'd wanted to, we could have put at the beginning of our program:

```
5 OPTION BASE 1
```

This OPTION changes the lowest array element number to 1, instead of 0. 1 or 0 are the only numbers that can be used with the OPTION BASE statement.

To use array elements numbered beyond 10 in the array called "A," we have to "reDIMension" the available array space. Our highest number in Array "A" needs to be 110, so we'll add a program DIMension statement:

```
10 DIM A(110) : CLS
```

...and RUN again. That's better, but it's not PRINTing the color code.

To display all the information, change these Lines:

```
100 PRINT "CAR#","ENG. SIZE","COLOR"
110 PRINT W,A(W),A(W+100)
```

...then RUN.

Check your answers against the earlier master chart. SAVE the program as CARARRAY.

Let your imagination go. Can you envision entire charts and "look-up" tables stored in this way? Entire inventory lists? How about trying to *find* the car which has a certain size engine *and* a certain color? Hmmm. We will come back to the logic needed for that last one.

EXERCISE 39-1: Assume that your inventory of 10 cars includes 3 different body styles, coded 10, 20 and 30, as follows:

CAR#	BODY
1	20
2	20
3	10
4	20
5	30
6	20
7	30
8	10
9	20
10	20

Modify the resident program to PRINT the body style information along with the rest when the car is identified by I.D. number.

A Smith & Wesson Beats 4 Aces

If we want to create a computerized card game (they make good examples to show so many things), how can we program it so it draws the 52 or so (watch the dealer at all times) cards in a totally random way? **ANSWER:** Spin up the deck into a single-dimension array, and pick array elements using a random number generator. As each card is "drawn," set its array element value equal to zero, then test each card drawn to be sure it isn't zero. (Might want to read it once again, more slowly.)

We will now, a step at a time, write a program which will draw, at random, all 52 cards numbered from 1 through 52, and PRINT the card numbers on the screen as they are drawn. No card will be drawn more than once. When all cards have been drawn, it will PRINT "END OF DECK!"

You do a step first, then check against my example. Then change yours to match mine -- otherwise we might not end up at the same place at the same time.

STEP 1: Spin up all 52 cards into an array.

```
20 DIM A(52) : CLS
30 FOR C=1 TO 52 : READ A(C) : NEXT C
500 DATA 1,2,3,4,5,6,7,8,9,10,11,12,13
510 DATA 14,15,16,17,18,19,20,21,22,23
520 DATA 24,25,26,27,28,29,30,31,32,33
530 DATA 34,35,36,37,38,39,40,41,42,43
540 DATA 44,45,46,47,48,49,50,51,52
```

At this point, all we can tell when RUNning is that processing time is required since the OK doesn't come back right away.

Shhhh! I know there's a shorter way to program this special case, but it doesn't teach what's needed.

STEP 2: Draw 52 cards at random, PRINTing their values.

```
40 FOR N = 1 TO 52
50  V = 51 * RND + 1
60  PRINT A(V);
70 NEXT N
990 PRINT : LIST
```

...and RUN.

True, 52 card values are PRINTed on the screen, but if we look carefully, we'll find the same number more than once. This means that some "cells" are not being READ and some READ more than once.

STEP 3: When a card is drawn, set its array value equal to Ø. Test each card drawn to be sure it is not Ø. When 52 cards have been drawn and PRINTed, PRINT "END OF DECK!"

```
40 P = 52
55 IF A(V) = Ø GOTO 5Ø
7Ø A(V) = Ø : P = P - 1
8Ø IF P<>Ø GOTO 5Ø
9Ø PRINT : PRINT "END OF DECK!"
```

...and RUN.

Line 7Ø sets the value in cell A(V) equal to Ø only if Line 55 finds it *not* equal to Ø already, letting the program pointer fall through.

When a "fall through" occurs:

1. The card's value is PRINTed (Line 6Ø).
2. The number stored in that cell is set to Ø (Line 7Ø).
3. The second statement in Line 7Ø counts down the number of cards PRINTed. Line 4Ø initialized the number of PRINTs at 52.
4. The number of PRINTs is tested (Line 8Ø). When there are no more PRINTs to go, "END OF DECK!" is PRINTed (Line 9Ø).

Pretty slick -- and we don't have to watch the dealer (just the programmer).

But how do we really know that every card has been dealt? Write a quick addition to the program to "interrogate" each array cell and PRINT its contents.

```
100 FOR T = 1 TO 52
110  PRINT A(T);
120 NEXT T
```

RUN ... and every cell comes up zero. If you don't really trust all this, change Line 40 to read:

```
40 P = 50
```

...RUN and see what happens.

AHA! It flushed out those 2 cards up the sleeve, didn't it?

To add a final touch of "randomness" to the deal, add:

```
10 RANDOMIZE
```

Change P back to 52, Delete test program Lines 100, 110, and 120, and we end up with a good card-drawing routine. You might want to clean it up to your satisfaction and SAVE it as CARDDRAW for future projects.

Question: Why does the PRINTing of card numbers slow down to a near halt as those last few cards are being drawn. Is the dealer reluctant?

Answer: The random number generator has to keep drawing numbers until it hits one that is the array address of an element which has *not* been set to zero. Near the end of the deck, almost all elements have been set to zero. The random number generator has to draw numbers as fast as it can to find a "live" one.

Look again at the card numbers PRINTed. There will not be any duplication. No stray aces.

EXERCISE 39-2: Change the program so the original array can be loaded with the card numbers without having to READ them in from DATA Lines.

New Dimensions

We have already done some DIMensioning with single dimension *numeric* arrays. *String* arrays must also be DIMensioned.

Suppose we have a program like this: (Type it in.)

```
10 FOR N = 1 TO 15
20  READ A$(N)
30  PRINT A$(N),
40 NEXT N
90 PRINT : LIST
100 DATA ALPHA,BRAVO,CHARLIE,DELTA
110 DATA ECHO,FOXTROT,GOLF,HOTEL
120 DATA INDIA,JULIETTE,KILO,LIMA
130 DATA MIKE,NOVEMBER,OSCAR
```

...and RUN.

Oops. There's that same problem. "Subscript out of range in 2Ø" means "not enough space set aside for an array." Recall that only 11 elements *per array* (from 0-10) are set aside on power-up. We are trying to read in 15 of them, starting with 1. The solution:

```
5 DIM A$(15)
```

...and RUN.

DIMensioning a string array is just like dimensioning a numeric one -- simply call it by its name. In this case, its name is A$. You "high speed" types will want to know that to do "dynamic redimensioning" (that's doing it while a program is running) the program must first encounter a CLEAR.

All CLEAR

The CLEAR command simply CLEARs the memory of all meaningful information except the actual program. It makes **all** string variables and arrays contain nothing and sets **all** numeric variables to Ø. And anything we DEFined with a DEF FN statement will also be forgotten.

For example type:

```
CLEAR
```

and then:

```
PRINT A$(3)
```

Nothing. RUN the program again to reload the Array, then PRINT A$(3).

ERASE will null out the contents of a **specific** array variable.

For example, type:

```
ERASE B$
```

By telling the Computer to ERASE all data in the B$ array, we have not removed the data in A$ array. (Since we don't actually have a B$ array in our program, we'll get an "Illegal function call.") To prove this point type:

```
PRINT A$(3)
```

Now type:

```
ERASE A$
```

and

```
PRINT A$(3)
```

Try PRINTing other elements in A$ array. They have **all** been ERASEd.

Array Names

```
A(N)
BC(N)
```

```
D3(N)

E4$(N)

XY$(N)
```

are examples of legal array names. The last 2 are for "string arrays."

> **EXERCISE 39-3:** Study the User programs in Section C to better understand the use of arrays for storage and access purposes. Time spent studying programs written by others is wisely invested.

Learned in Chapter 39

Commands	Statements	Miscellaneous
CLEAR	DIM ERASE OPTION BASE	Arrays

Chapter 40

Search and Sort

One of the Computer's most powerful features is its ability to *search* through a pile of DATA and *sort* the findings into some order. Alphabetical, reverse alphabetical, numerical from smallest to largest, or the reverse are all common sorts. The *search/sort* feature is so important we will spend this entire Chapter learning how to use it.

Typical applications of *search* and *sort* include:

1. Arranging a list of customers' or prospects' names in **alphabetical** order.

2. Sorting names in **ZIP-code** order for lower-cost mailing.

3. Sorting the names of clients in telephone **area code** order.

While not really all that complicated, the sorting process is sufficiently rigorous that we are going to take it **very slowly** and examine each step. Once we get the hang of it, the Computer can blaze away without our considering the staggering number of steps it's going through.

A Problem of Sorts

Let's start with a problem. We have the names of 10 customers. (If that doesn't grab you, make it 10 million -- the process is identical.) We wish to arrange them in alphabetical order.

Start by storing their names in a DATA Line. Type in:

```
1000 DATA BRAVO,XRAY,ALPHA,ZULU,FOXTROT,TANGO,
     HOTEL,SIERRA,MIKE,JULIETTE
```

Since we are sorting by **name** rather than by number, we have to use *string* variables, *string* arrays, etc. They work equally well with numbers such as zip codes, while numeric variables and arrays work **only** with numbers.

The backbone of a *sort* routine is the array. Each name is to be READ from DATA into an array, so add:

```
10 REM  * ALPHA SORT OF STRINGS FROM DATA *
20 CLS : FOR D=1 TO 10 : READ A$(D) : N=N+1 :
   NEXT D
```

Line 10 is, of course, just the title.

Line 20 CLears the Screen, then "loads the array" by READing the 10 names into storage slots A$(1) to A$(10). N is simply a counter that will follow through the rest of the program. In this simple program we could have made N=10 since we know how many names we have. In the next sample program we won't know how many names there are, so let's leave N the way it's usually used.

Important to the sort routine are 2 nested FOR-NEXT loops.

1. The first one, F, controls the First name.
2. S, the Second one, controls the name to be compared against the first.

Names and words are compared as we learned in the Chapter on ASCII set, remember?

Let's establish the loops first, and fill in the guts later:

```
30 FOR F = 1 TO N-1       (F=First word to be compared)
40    FOR S = F+1 TO N    (S=Second word to be compared)
90    NEXT S                        (makes 9 passes)
100 NEXT F                          (makes 9 passes)
```

It may seem puzzling that F and S only have to make 9 passes when there are 10 names. Think of it this way. Whatever word **isn't** smaller (ASCII #) than the rest just ends up last. No need to test again to prove that.

The F loop READs array elements 1 through 9 (N - 1 = 9). The S loop READs array elements 2 through 10. This always provides **different** array elements to compare.

Now we'll jump to the end of the program and prepare it to PRINT out what will happen. Type:

```
110 FOR D = 1 TO N : PRINT A$(D), : NEXT D
990 PRINT : LIST
```

When the sorting is done, the contents of A$(1) to A$(10) will be the same names READ from DATA, but they will be in alphabetical order. We'll PRINT the array contents on the screen.

```
50    IF A$(F) <= A$(S) THEN 90   (tests for smaller ASCII#)
60    T$ = A$(F)              (First word to Temp storage)
70    A$(F) = A$(S)           (Copies Second word to First place)
80    A$(S) = T$              (Copies Temp word to Second place)
```

And there is the biggie! If you can understand the last 4 Lines, the rest is duck soup.

Line 50 — says, "If the First word is smaller than (or equal to) the Second word, leave well enough alone and bail out of this routine by going to Line 90, which will end this pass and READ another word to compare against F. If it is larger, drop to the next Line."

Line 60 says, "Oh, they weren't in the right order, eh? We'll just copy the First word in a Temporary storage location called T$ and store it there for future use. I'm sure we'll need it again."

Line 70 copies the name held in the Second cell into the First array cell. If the Second one had an earlier starting letter than the First one, we do want to do this, don't we?

Line 80 completes the switch by copying the name Temporarily stored in T$ into the Second array cell. The contents of A$(1) and A$(2) have now been exchanged with the aid of the Temporary holding pen, T$.

Us simple country boys find this one easy: *There are two brahma bulls in separate pens, A$(1) & A$(2), and we want to switch them around. Ain't no way we're going to put them in the same pen at the same time. (Not with me in there anyway. Already broken too many 2 by 4's between their horns and have some scars on the wrong end from escapes that were a hair too slow.) That's why we built a temporary holding pen called T$.* Got it?

If we did everything right, the program should:

RUN

and in a flash the names appear on the screen in alphabetical order:

```
ALPHA         BRAVO         FOXTROT       HOTEL         JULIETTE
MIKE          SIERRA        TANGO         XRAY          ZULU
```

Printing will be in standard 14 space tab zone format.

SAVE as SORT and RUN it to your heart's delight. This is one of the most powerful things a Computer can do, and it does it so well. The identical procedure is used to sort very long lists of names (or zip codes, or whatever), but we would, of course, have to reDIMension for a larger array.

To get a really good look at what's happening, it's necessary to slow the beast *way* down and insert a few extra PRINT Lines. They allow us to peer inside the program by watching the tube.

IF I'M GOING TO SWITCH 2 BULLS IN PENS, IT'S GOING TO BE "SORTing from the outside"!
OLÉ!

Add these temporaries:

```
45        PRINT F;A$(F),,S;A$(S)
55        PRINT TAB(10); "<<--<<   SWITCHEROO"
85        PRINT F;A$(F),,S;A$(S)
```

Allow three spaces after the arrow -- that way it will look nice on the screen when you RUN it.

...and RUN.

If that wasn't slow enough, add Line 47 and make the delay long enough so there is time to completely think through each step. Pretend you're the Computer, and make the decision that Line 50 has to make. Take it from the top -- very slowly!

```
47        FOR Z = 1 TO 1000 : NEXT Z
```

The Diagnosis

```
1 BRAVO                                    2 XRAY
```

means, "In cell #1 is the word BRAVO and in cell #2 is the word XRAY" just like they came from the DATA Line. Of those two words, BRAVO is the "smallest" (ASCII#), so it stays in number 1 place. On to the next pass of S.

```
1 BRAVO                                    3 ALPHA
```

Oops. BRAVO is in #1 and ALPHA is in #3, but ALPHA is smaller than BRAVO. We better switch them around. So

```
                 <<--<<   SWITCHEROO

1 ALPHA                                    3 BRAVO
```

Don't worry too much about what is happening in the second column. S is scanning through the array and its contents are always changing, testing against what's in the first. It's what **ends up** in the **first** column that counts -- and that list must be in increasing alphabetical order.

As the program RUNs, watch new words appear in S, loop and column, and compare them against what's in F. Try to guess what the Computer's going to do. Also keep an eye on the increasing numbers on the left. The **final word** assigned to a given number in the first column is what will appear in the final PRINTout.

RUN the program as many times as it takes (and at as many sessions as it takes) to completely understand what's happening. It's awfully clever, very important and absolutely fundamental. We carry this technique over to many useful programs in the future but only if we **really** understand it.

When you feel it's under control, add one more little item to the screen. What T$ is holding while all this sorting is going on is interesting. Add and change these Lines so they read:

```
45    PRINT F;A$(F),,S;A$(S),"T$ = ";T$
85    PRINT F;A$(F),,S;A$(S),"T$ = ";T$
```

...and RUN.

"T$ = " starts off empty since there is nothing in the holding pen. When BRAVO is replaced by ALPHA in the switching process, however, T$ holds it. When BRAVO replaces XRAY in the #2 position, T$ holds XRAY, etc.

On a clear head it's not hard to follow what's happening. If you're tired, it's hopeless. SAVE this program and review it as often as necessary for a deep understanding of the process.

The Big SWAP (An Easier Way)

Our BASIC has a unique statement called SWAP. To see what it does, type in this program:

```
10 A$ = "ORANGES"
```

```
20 B$ = "APPLES"
30 SWAP A$,B$
40 PRINT "LIKE COMPARING ";A$;" WITH ";B$
```

...and RUN.

Did you see what happened? Line 30 is the culprit. SWAP exchanged, or SWAPped, the contents of the two variables, A$ and B$. After the SWAP, what was in A$ ended up in B$ and what was in B$ ended up in A$.

SWAP eliminates the need for a temporary variable (like T$ in our SORT program) when sorting through an array. We could eliminate these lines from our array sort:

```
60 T$ = A$(F)
70 A$(F) = A$(S)
80 A$(S) = T$
```

and replace them with just:

```
70 SWAP A$(F),A$(S)
```

Go ahead; try it. Load the SORT program back in, and eliminate the temporary Lines (45, 47, 55, 85). Then make the above changes, and RUN. Same thing...only shorter, sweeter, and so much more sensible!

SORTing from the Outside

We don't really have to keep all our names, numbers or other information in DATA Lines. It can be INPUT from the keyboard or from disk. The following program is quite similar to the resident one, and the logic is identical. Change and add these Lines:

```
10 REM  * ALPHA SORT OF NAMES VIA INPUT *
20 INPUT"NEXT NAME";N$ : IF N$="END" GOTO 30
25 N=N+1 : A$(N) = N$ : GOTO 20
```

Delete Line 1000.

...and RUN.

INPUT 6 or 8 random names, and when finished, INPUT the word "END". The sort process is identical to what we used before.

Can you see the potential for all this?

> **EXERCISE 40-1:** Change Line 50 of the SORT program to list the names in reverse alphabetical order.

Learned in Chapter 40

Statements	Miscellaneous
SWAP	Sorting

Chapter 41

Multi-DIMension Arrays

We have learned that an array is nothing more than a temporary parking area for lots of numbers or characters, or both. In addition, we learned that it is a straight-forward procedure to compare values of variables outside the matrix (or array) with those inside it.

An array which only has one DIMension, that is, just one long line-up of parking places, is sometimes called a *vector*. We can take that one-dimensional array, cut it into perhaps four equal chunks and position those chunks side by side. We then call it a two-dimensional array -- since the parking places are lined up in *rows* and *columns* (or streets and avenues). Its DATA holding or processing abilities are not changed. Only the *addresses* of the parking places (or elements or memory cells) have changed.

Type in this NEW program:

```
10 DIM M(50)
20 FOR V = 1 TO 50
30  PRINT V,M(V)
40 NEXT V
```

Remember, any array with more than 11 elements (counting 0) must be DIMensioned.

...and RUN.

The RUN simply shows the addresses (numbers) of 50 storage positions and their contents. Since they are all lined up in a single row, it is a vector array.

Why are the cell contents always 0? Because every cell value is initialized at zero upon entering BASIC or whenever we RUN, just like all other numeric and string variables. Line 30 shows how easy it is to specify the *address* and read the *contents* of each memory cell.

Side by Side

Let's cut our 50 cell array into 5 equal strips and line them up side by side. That would make 10 *rows* each containing 5 cells ... right? Or 5 *columns* each containing 10 cells. "Multi-dimensional arrays" always have *rows* and *columns*.

Start over with this NEW program:

```
10 DIM M(10,5)          (10 rows by 5 columns)
20 FOR R=1 TO 10
30  FOR C=1 TO 5
40   PRINT R;C,
50  NEXT C : PRINT
60 NEXT R
```

SAVE as MATADR and RUN.

The *addresses* of all 50 cells displayed on the screen at the same time but not their contents. Nothing was changed from the earlier vector array containing the same 50 cells. We just rearranged the furniture and gave it different addresses. They read:

`1 1` meaning "first row, first column"

`8 3` meaning "8th row, 3rd column"

etc.

To view the *contents* of each of these cells, change Line 4Ø:

```
40    PRINT M(R,C),
```

...and RUN.

See, the contents remain unchanged. They are still at their initialized value of Ø, since we made no arrangement to store information in them. (The *addresses* are no longer displayed.) Isn't this easy (...so far)?

Memory cells, like any other variables, have to be "loaded" with values to be useful. This can be done by READing in DATA from DATA Lines, by INPUTting it via the keyboard or from a previously recorded DATA disk. We will load our matrix from DATA Lines imbedded in the program.

Add these Lines:

```
100 DATA 1,2,3,4,5,6,7,8,9,10,11 etc. to 26
110 DATA 27,28,29,30,31,32,33,34,35 etc. to 5Ø
```

and this Line to READ the DATA into matrix cells:

```
35   READ M(R,C)
```

SAVE as MATCONT and RUN.

The DATA is nicely arranged in the matrix, and each matrix position has its original specific address. Again, that address is not displayed -- just the contents. Let's stay in the command mode for a minute and "poll" or "interrogate," several matrix positions to see what they are holding. Ask:

```
PRINT M(2,3)        ENTER
```

Write down 8, the answer. We'll RUN the program again later and check it.

```
PRINT M(9,4)        ENTER
```

says that cell holds the number 44.

```
PRINT M(3,6)          ENTER
```

"Subscript out of range?" Why did we get that? Oh, there is no column 6? No wonder.

RUN the program again and check the screen counting down the rows and over the columns to see if the answers match up.

Mine did -- how about yours?

Row 2, Column 3 = 8.
Row 9, Column 4 = 44.

As an aside, type:

```
ERASE M          ENTER
```

then, at the command level, check any matrix memory spot again.

```
PRINT M(2,2)          ENTER
```

and get 0. ERASE M re-initialized **all** cells of array M to zero. We can, of course, reload them by:

...RUN

and verify the results by:

```
PRINT M(2,2)          ENTER
```

Row 2, Column 2 = 7.

We must ERASE an array before reDIMensioning it, or we'll get a "Duplicate Definition" error. It isn't often necessary to reDIMension.

Okay, Now What Do We Do with It?

Good question. Everything we learned in the last Chapter on Arrays applies.

We've only rearranged the deck chairs on this Titanic -- the end result is unaffected.

At this point, what we've learned is best utilized for calling up and loading relatively unchanging DATA. It is placed in a matrix so it can be accessed and compared, processed or otherwise put to work. Typical applications are:

1. Technical Tables: Instead of looking up the same information in tables, store the tables in DATA Lines and let the Computer look them up and do any needed calculations. The time saved may quickly pay for the Computer.

2. Price Quotes: I saw this approach used by a lumber yard to furnish fast quotes on building materials, and by a printing shop for fast quoting of all sorts of printed matter. The programs are so easy to use that customers just belly up to the counter, answer the computer's questions, and get their quote right on the screen and printer.

   The latest prices on paper products and printing costs are held in DATA Lines and "spun up" into the matrix at the beginning of the day. The customer responds to a "Menu" on the screen, then answers some questions on quantity and quality. The quote is calculated and PRINTed.

DATA is loaded in externally, either via the keyboard or disk. We obviously don't want to have to go through that loading process **each time** we want an answer. It's important, therefore, to never let execution END. Always have it come back to a screen "Menu" of choices, or at least, a simple INPUT statement. If an END is hit, the matrix crashes and the DATA has to be reRUN to reload it.

String Matrices

So far we have concentrated on *numeric* arrays. They can also be used to hold letters or words using the same rules learned in the Chapters on strings, including CLEARing enough string space.

String matrices need string names. Make these subtle changes in the resident program.

```
10 DIM M$(10,5)
```

IF THAT THING IS SO SMART WITH MENUS, HOW ABOUT ASKING IT WHAT WE SHOULD HAVE FOR DINNER?

```
35    READ M$(R,C)
40    PRINT M$(R,C),
```

...and RUN.

Absolutely no difference! We changed to a string matrix, but the data is all numeric. Strings handle numbers as well as letters but not vice-versa.

Let's change the DATA to words, and try it again. Change:

```
10 CLS : DIM M$(5,5)
20 FOR R=1 TO 5
100 DATA ALPHA,BRAVO,CHARLIE,DELTA,ECHO,FOXTROT,
    GOLF,HOTEL
110 DATA INDIA,JULIETTE,KILO,LIMA,MIKE,NOVEMBER,
    OSCAR,PAPA,QUEBEC
120 DATA ROMEO,SIERRA,TANGO,UNIFORM,VICTOR,
    WHISKEY,XRAY,YANKEE
```

SAVE as STRMAT and RUN.

Stop for a moment, and contemplate the string-comparing and string-handling techniques we learned a few Chapters ago. Your mind should be running flat out at this point considering the possibilities.

How About Mixing Strings and Numerics?

Funny you should ask. That's why we ran all numbers in a string matrix, then all words with that same program. They mix very well as long as the mixer is a string matrix and not a numeric one.

We have one final program. It is designed for demonstration only but could be expanded to INPUT the DATA from disk and be quite usable. It demonstrates some important possibilities and programming techniques.

The Objective

The objective of this demo program is to allow a church treasurer to keep track of who gave what, when. Could use the same program with a service club, bowling league, or any organization that has a membership and dues. We want to be able to access every member's record by name and get a readout on his status.

Let's start with the DATA. Type this in the NEW program:

```
1000 REM  * DATA FILE *
1010 DATA 07.0187,JONES,15
1020 DATA 07.0187,SMITH,87
1030 DATA 07.0187,BROWN,24
1040 DATA 07.0187,JOHNSON,53
1050 DATA 07.0187,ANDERSON,42
```

The first number in each DATA Line employs *data compression*, that is, *encoding* several pieces of information into one number. This number contains the Month, Date and Year in one 6 digit number. (Using string techniques, we could easily strip them apart again, if we wished, for special reports.) Single precision will hold the 6 digits accurately.

The second thing we've done with this first number is protect the leading 0. Since months below October are identified by only one digit, the leading 0 would be lost in these months and the number changed to only 5 digits. There are other ways to get around that problem, but we put in a decimal point just to act as an unmovable reference.

The second element in each DATA Line is the name. We could put in the full name and if we used a comma would, of course, have to enclose the name in quotes.

The third element in each DATA Line holds the amount of money tendered on that date.

Obviously, a full DATA set would contain many entries for each week and many weeks in a row. We don't need to enter that much DATA to demonstrate the principles involved and want to keep it short and to the point.

This DATA must now be READ into a string matrix (displaying it as we go). Add:

```
10 CLS : PRINT
20 PRINT "ENTRY #","DATE","NAME","AMT $" : PRINT
30 FOR E = 1 TO 5 : PRINT E,   'LOAD 5 ENTRIES
40  FOR D = 1 TO 3             'LOAD DATE, NAME AMT
50   READ R$(E,D)
60   PRINT R$(E,D),            'TEMP ARRAY PRINTOUT
70  NEXT D
80  PRINT
90 NEXT E
```

SAVE as RECORDS1 and RUN.

Very good. The matrix is loaded, and its accuracy confirmed on the screen. We see the first 5 bookkeeping entries from July 1, 1987.

Now that we know it loads OK, we can remove some of the test software. Change this Line:

```
30 FOR E = 1 TO 5            'LOAD 5 ENTRIES
```

Delete Lines 60 and 80

...and RUN.

Good. We still get the heading, but the matrix contents display is gone. Now, how can we interrogate the matrix to pull an individual member's record? Guess we first have to ask a question. Type:

```
100 INPUT "WHOSE RECORD ARE YOU SEEKING";N$
```

Then we have to write the program to scan the matrix and compare N$, the name we INPUT, with each element, R$(E,D), until we find a match. This means setting up the FOR-NEXT loops again and scanning every element. Add:

```
110 FOR E = 1 TO 5
120  IF R$(E,2) = N$ THEN 160
130 NEXT E
140 PRINT N$, "IS NOT IN THE FILE."
150   PRINT : GOTO 100
160 PRINT E,R$(E,1),R$(E,2),R$(E,3)
170   PRINT : GOTO 100
```

SAVE as RECORDS2 and RUN.

Answer with names that are in the DATA Lines and those that are not. Lines 150 and 170 have built-in defaults back to the question.

The key Line is #160. It PRINTs 4 things:

E	The entry number on that date
R$(E,1)	The date in the memory cell just **preceding** the one containing the member's name
R$(E,2)	The name
R$(E,3)	The amount

If you have trouble visualizing what Line 160 is doing, add this temporary Line. It PRINTs the *address* of each DATA element just below it and is very helpful:

```
165 PRINT E, E;1, E;2, E;3
```

...and RUN.

Again, the preceding program was not written to be a model of programming style and efficiency -- but to teach the basics of loading and retrieving "record-keeping" type information from a matrix.

EXERCISE 41-1: Write a program that fills a two dimension string array with:

JONES, C.	10439	100.00
ROTH,J.	10023	87.24
BAKER,H.	12936	398.34
HARMON,D.	10422	23.17

EXERCISE 41-2: Sort the names of the array in Exercise 41-1 alphabetically. Don't forget to keep the rest of the information on each row with the original name. This Exercise will be a challenge. Think it through carefully.

EXERCISE 41-3: If you survived Exercise 41-2, try sorting the array in increasing order by the numbers in Column 3.

Learned in Chapter 41

Statements	Miscellaneous
ERASE	Multi-Dimension Arrays
	String Arrays
	Data compression

PART 7

SOUND

Chapter 42

A Cheap Buzz

Type:

```
BEEP        ENTER
```

Sorry if that scared the dog! Just couldn't resist it. It is widely incorporated in programs as an alarm to indicate something.

Sure...do it again. We'll wait.

Since our Computer has a Real Time Clock, we can use it as a "time is up" alarm. Just include BEEP in the program. It also makes a great audio prompter telling the operator it's time to do something. The applications are virtually endless.

The BEEP is just a simplified form of:

```
PRINT CHR$(7)        ENTER
```

Try it.

Technically, what we heard is called the BELL, and ASCII 7 makes it ring. Buzzers have pretty well replaced bells, so we'll usually refer to it as a buzzer, alarm, or something more contemporary.

SORRY OL' BOY...
OUR MASTER WAS
JUST PLAYING WITH
SOUND...
GRRRRR

Type in this NEW program:

```
10 CLS : PRINT
20 INPUT "ENTER A NUMBER TO DIVIDE INTO 100";X
30 IF X <> 0 THEN 60
40 BEEP : PRINT "I CAN'T DIVIDE BY ZERO!"
50 GOTO 20
60 PRINT "100 /";X;"=";100/X
70 PRINT : GOTO 20
```

...and RUN.

SAVE as ERROR0

Enter some familiar numbers and try 0. The Computer tells all. The noise can be interpreted as a chastisement for trying to divide by 0. Your imagination can take it from there.

Here's another program using BEEP, LOCATE, POS, CSRLIN, INKEY$ and the Print Screen button (**SHIFT** **PRINT** or **Shift** **Prt Sc** .)

```
10 CLS : KEY OFF
20 READ A$
30 X=POS(0) : Y=CSRLIN
40 LOCATE 25,1
50 IF A$ = "END" THEN 120
60 BEEP
70 PRINT " INSERT ";A$;" DISK AND STRIKE A KEY          ";
80 IF INKEY$=""THEN 80
90 LOCATE Y,X
100 PRINT TAB(32);A$
110 FILES : PRINT : PRINT : GOTO 20
120 PRINT "THAT'S ALL THE DISKS.  PRESS ";
```

```
130 COLOR 0,7 : PRINT " SHIFT "; : COLOR 7,0 :
    PRINT " "; : COLOR 0,7 : PRINT " PRINT "; :
    COLOR 7,0
140 PRINT " WHEN PRINTER IS READY";
150 IF INKEY$<>"F" THEN 150
160 KEY ON : CLS : END
170 DATA GAMES,SYSTEM MASTER,VISICALC,GRAPHICS
180 DATA END
```

SAVE as DIRS.

Change the DATA, Line 170, to suit your own needs.

This one allows us to get a hard copy LISTing of the DIRectories of our disks. In Line 20 we READ the name of a disk. The Computer then instructs us, with the help of BEEP, to insert that disk in the default drive and uses FILES to put the directory on the screen. We then loop back to READ another DATA item. After all the disks have been READ, the Computer tells us to press **SHIFT** **PRINT**. After the dump is finished, hit **F** to end. Because **SHIFT** **PRINT** (or **Shift** **Prt Sc**) prints only what's on the screen, it's best to do a screen dump each time the screen is full.

The point of this is that the BEEP statement is used mostly to alert the user about something. It may tell us to do something, alert us we've made an error, or that we just zapped a Klingon.

However (as we segue into the next Chapter), remember BEEP is pretty limited as far as Music is concerned...

Learned in Chapter 42

Functions

BEEP

Chapter 43

The SOUND of Music

Fortunately, our use of sound isn't limited to the single tone of the BEEP statement. The full range of frequencies audible to most human ears is available to create our concertos with. Move over, Beethoven!

For example, type:

```
SOUND 440,18          ENTER
```

We hear a perfect concert pitch A of 440 cycles per second for about 1 second.

In the last Chapter, we used BEEP as a prompt. Now type:

```
SOUND 800,4
```

Sound familiar? It is the frequency used by the BEEP statement, and it sounded for 4 internal "clock ticks" or about 4/18 = .22 seconds.

The SOUND statement plays a specific frequency for a specific duration, and we do the specifying. The first number is the frequency in cycles per second, or Hz. The second number is the duration in clock ticks. The clock ticks about 18 times per second.

If you happen to have an acoustic Modem for communicating over the phone line, put it in originate Mode and type:

```
SOUND 1830, 25
```

By using the chart below, we can determine the frequency of the note we want to play. Let's listen to the range of sounds we can use. Type in this program:

```
10 FOR X=110 TO 200 STEP 10
20  SOUND X, 10
30  PRINT X,
40 NEXT X
50 CLS : PRINT "SECOND LOOP"
60 FOR X=200 TO 2000 STEP 25
70  SOUND X,5
80  PRINT X,
90 NEXT X
```

SAVE as RANGE

...and RUN.

Middle C	= 523
C# or Db	= 555
D	= 587
D# or Eb	= 623
E	= 659
F	= 698
F# or Gb	= 741
G	= 784
G# or Ab	= 832.
A	= 880
A# or Bb	= 934
B	= 988

To move up an octave, double the number; to move down an octave, halve the number.

I DON'T THINK HE LIKES A PERFECT CONCERT PITCH A!

It sounds terrible because we're going up the musical scale without regard to musical "intervals." We must choose the notes more "chromatically." Try this NEW program:

```
10 SOUND 523,7
20 SOUND 880,7
30 SOUND 698,7
```

...and RUN.

We could use a different statement for each note, as above, but we're into advanced stuff now so let's cut down the programming by using READ-DATA statements. Type NEW, and then we'll start over again:

```
10 CLS
20 READ N,L
30 IF N = 0 THEN END
40 PRINT N;L,
50 SOUND N,L
60 SOUND 32767,2
70 GOTO 20
500 DATA 523,7,523,7,784,7,784,7,880,7,880,7,784,16
599 DATA 0,0
```

...and RUN.

Yes, yes, I'm sick of Twinkle, Twinkle too, but now that we have it started, we might as well finish it:

```
510 DATA 698,7,698,7,659,7,659,7,587,7,587,7,523,16
520 DATA 784,7,784,7,698,7,698,7,659,7,659,7,587,16
530 DATA 784,7,784,7,698,7,698,7,659,7,659,7,587,16
540 DATA 523,7,523,7,784,7,784,7,880,7,880,7,784,16
550 DATA 698,7,698,7,659,7,659,7,587,7,784,7,1047,16
```

SAVE as TWINKLE

...and RUN.

We simply READ in a pair of numbers, the frequency and duration, and PLAY them in Line 50. A rest is needed between notes in our masterpiece. By selecting 32767 as the frequency in Line 60, the SOUND is out of the audible range, giving a note that only the dog will enjoy.

Now let's try for a song with a little more programming built in. Since we don't think in clock ticks, let's use timing numbers that make more sense, and let the program do the converting for us. How about 1 divided by the actual note length? Quarter notes would be 4, eighth notes would be 8, and whole notes would be 1.

Delete Lines 500-550, and change Line 50 to:

```
50 SOUND N,(1/L)*18
```

and let's put in some DATA:

```
500 DATA 659,1,587,4,523,8,659,4,587,8,523,2,1047,2,880,
     4,1047,1
```

...and RUN.

SAVE as SWANEE

...and RUN.

Hey, that doesn't SOUND too bad. Since this phrase is repeated, we can use the same DATA Line. We could retype them, but why not use the EDITor and change Line numbers? Type EDIT 500 and then type 520. Hit **ENTER** and do a LIST. Both Lines 500 and 520 are exactly the same.

We must be careful when doing this. It's very easy to get GOTOs or GOSUBs mixed up when just changing individual Line numbers like this. When we use the RENUM statement, all of that is taken care of for us.

Now add Lines 510 and 530:

```
510 DATA 784,1,659,2,523,2,587,,5
530 DATA 784,2,659,4,523,8,587,2,587,2,523,1
```

SAVE as SWANEE

...and RUN.

(Hey man, where's the gig?)

Learned in Chapter 43

Statements

SOUND

Chapter 44

A Tune or Two

Tandy BASIC users have the added capability of a musical "language" to make PLAYing songs much easier. By just saying PLAY "A," we can get the Computer to PLAY the note A. For example, type:

```
PLAY "CEG"          ENTER        (Major Key)
```

and those 3 notes, C, E, & G, are PLAYed. We'll use the upper registers now, and come back down later. Isn't that how Maynard started out? If we want to PLAY sharp or flat notes, we insert a # or + (sharp) or – (flat) after the name of the notes. For example:

```
PLAY "CE-G"    (Minor Key)
```

will PLAY the notes C, E flat, and G. Also:

```
PLAY "CEG#"    (or "CEG+")          (Augmented)
```

will PLAY the notes C, E and G sharp. Now you don't have to be a Bach or Beethoven to use music with your Tandy Computer. A good ear helps, however, and **real** talent is always in short supply.

In addition to the names of the notes, we can also specify the Length of a Note, Octave, Tempo, and style.

We have a full 7 octaves, numbered Ø-6. For example type:

```
10 REM  * CLOSE ENCOUNTERS  *
20 PLAY "MST120O3"
30 PLAY "L4CDO2B-O1B-O2L1F"
```

SAVE as ENCOUNTR

...and RUN.

Here's how it works.

Line 20: The MS says PLAY every note "Stacatto" (3/4 of the Length specified later). T120 specifies the Tempo as 120 beats per minute. O3 means use the notes in the 3rd Octave.

Line 30: L4 says, "Make the note Length 1/4 notes." (The actual note length is 1/n.) Placing a period after the note (L4C.) causes the note to play half again as long as the Length specified. More than one period can be used. Sixteenth notes are L16, half notes are L2, and a whole note is L1. We then start PLAYing the notes. First a C and a D, then we jump down to O2 (second octave) with a B flat, drop one more octave to O1 and PLAY another B flat, then back up to Octave 2 to PLAY a whole note F.

We also have 5 music string modifiers to change the way all the notes are PLAYed. We already talked about MS, Music Stacatto.

MN is Music Normal. Every note will be PLAYed 7/8 of the time specified by the Length statement. This is the default mode for MN, ML and MS.

ML is Music Legato. Every note will be PLAYed the full Length of what's specified.

MF is Music Foreground. The Computer waits until each note is played before continuing. This is the normal default mode for the Tandy 2000.

I THINK IT'S TIME WE GOT OFF THIS MUSIC KICK, MASTER. ...MASTER!

MB is Music Background. This is the normal default mode for the Tandy 1000. This places the string in a buffer so our program can continue execution while the music is being PLAYed. For example:

```
PLAY "MBO2CDEFGABO3CDEFGABO4CDEFGABL105C"
```

PLAYs 3 octaves of the musical scale.

There are also 3 more commands that are used by the PLAY statement. To PLAY a specific note (Ø through 84), we can use:

```
PLAY "N2Ø"
```

This will PLAY the 20th note, or G in Octave 1 (the second octave). NØ is a rest.

If we want a pause, we can use P in our music string:

```
PLAY "O2L4CP4DP4EP4FP4G"
```

The length of the pause is determined by the current value of L. The Pause can be lengthened by adding a period after the note as with the L option.

The X command eXecutes a certain string to be PLAYed. Type in this NEW program:

```
1Ø LAMB$ = "EDCDEEE"
3Ø PLAY "XLAMB$;"
```

...and RUN.

To PLAY it low and slow, add:

```
2Ø PLAY "O1T6Ø"
```

For a high and fast etude, try:

```
2Ø PLAY "O5T24Ø"
```

Now let's try a whole song. An old college fight song:

```
10 REM  * SAN DIEGO STATE FIGHT SONG  *
20 CLS : PRINT
30 INPUT"ENTER TEMPO (32-255)";Z
40 PLAY "T=Z;O3"
50 A$ = "B-2P4F4A2P4F4G2F2D1"
60 B$ = "D4D4C#4D4F4F4C#4D4A2A-4G1P4"
70 C$ = "C4C4O2B4O3C4E-2D4C4O2B-2O3D2F1E4E4F4F#4G4G4F#
        4G4A4P4G#4P4A4F4G4A4"
80 D$ = "D4D4C#4D4F2F#2G1P4G4F#4G4O4C2O3B-2F#2E-
        2D2F2A2G2B-4G4B-4G4B-2O4C2O3B-1"
90 REM *  BEGIN PLAYING  *
100 PLAY "MSMBF2"
110 PLAY "XA$;XB$;XC$;XA$;XD$;"
130 CLS
140 END
```

SAVE as FIGHT

...and RUN.

The four sections of the song are assigned to strings A$, B$, C$ and D$ in Lines 50-80. We then play the parts in Line 110. Notice section A is repeated after PLAYing section C.

We can execute a display subroutine while PLAYing background music. Type in the remainder of the program:

```
120 GOSUB 1000
1000 REM  * SUBROUTINE TO PRINT CHARACTERS  *
1010 COLOR 23,0
1020 FOR V = 1 TO 300
```

```
1030    E$ = CHR$(INT(RND*241+14))
1040    X = INT(RND*79)+1
1050    Y = INT(RND*24)+1
1060    LOCATE Y,X
1070    PRINT E$;
1080 NEXT V
1090 RETURN
```

SAVE again as FIGHT

...and RUN.

The entire song is played staccato in the background.

Hooray for our team!

NOISE (Tandy 1000 only)

The NOISE command consists of three parts: source, volume and duration. The source can be a number from 0 to 7. 0 to 3 is periodic noise (like a broken record), and 4 to 7 is white noise (like static on a radio). Volume has a range of 0 (low) to 15 (high). The duration, like SOUND, is in clock ticks. It can be between 0 and 65535.

The format is:

```
NOISE source, volume, duration
```

This program demonstrates the various sounds that are generated with NOISE.

Remember to use a SOUND ON statement, or an Illegal function call error may occur.

```
10 REM * NOISE GENERATOR *
20 SOUND ON
30 FOR N = 0 TO 7
```

```
40  FOR S = 0 TO 15
50   NOISE N,S,5
60   FOR D = 0 TO 250 : NEXT D
70  NEXT S
80 NEXT N
```

With everything we've learned about BEEP, SOUND, PLAY and NOISE, you could go on an develop your own Moog machine.

Learned in Chapter 44

Statements	Commands
PLAY	NOISE

PART 8

MISCELLANEOUS

Chapter 45

Introduction to Data Processing

Data Processing is an important computer application. An example of DP would be storing all the names in the telephone book, then recalling any name, address and phone number very quickly. Sorting, alphabetizing, adding and deleting vast quantities of data, or maintaining inventory (merchandise), general ledger (money), mailing lists (people), recipe files, or other records replace intricate and complex calculations as the computer's purpose. DP is not the same thing as programming but is simply an application which requires specialized programming with emphasis on disk files used for other than just SAVEing and LOADing the program itself.

At the heart of Data Processing is the accumulation of data in what is known as a DATA FILE. The DATA may be similar to the data we know how to store in DATA Lines, but the quantity is often so large the entire memory of the computer is not enough to hold it. Thus the need for "external storage," as on a disk.

Up to now we've relied on BASIC's numeric variables, string variables, and DATA Lines to store the data the programs need. This has 2 severe limitations:

1. The Computer's memory may not be large enough to hold all the data (for example, an inventory list).

2. When the Computer is turned off, the values of all variables are lost.

OOPS! THERE GOES
ALL MY VARIABLES and
HIS SACROILIAC!

Diskette data files solve both problems. Virtually endless quantities of information can be stored on an endless stack of disks and retrieved later at will, just as we now SAVE and reLOAD programs. Besides SAVE and LOAD, we need to learn more special statements.

OPEN the Door, Richard

The first is the OPEN statement. OPEN handles all the details of creating a new DATA file. It communicates 3 things to the system:

1. What we plan to **do** with the file, i.e., INPUT data from it or PRINT information into it

2. What *buffer number* (1-5) to assign to the file (More on that in a second ...)

3. The file's *name*

Type:

```
30 OPEN "TESTDATA" FOR OUTPUT AS 1
```

but don't RUN yet. OUTPUT means that we intend to OUTPUT information from the Computer to a data file on the disk named "TESTDATA." The program Line reads, "OPEN the data file named 'TESTDATA' FOR OUTPUTting to disk." If we wanted to INPUT information back from disk to memory, we will use INPUT instead of OUTPUT. We'll learn how to INPUT in a minute.

File Buffers

Line 30 assigns *buffer* number 1 to the file and names it TESTDATA. Any number from 1 to 5 may be used.

A file buffer is a small part of the computer's memory which is assigned to act as a Traffic Director for information traveling to and from the Computer and a disk file. Only 5 buffers are available at any one time, but they can control an unlimited number of files by being reassigned to different disk files as needed.

The OPEN statement is our written instruction to the Computer to OUTPUT its data to TESTDATA through buffer #1 until notified otherwise. In addition, the OPEN statement sets the file buffer size to 128 bytes.

OPEN simply assigns the data file TESTDATA a buffer number (1 in this case) and prepares TESTDATA for either OUTPUT (as in this case) or INPUT from disk to Computer memory. TESTDATA will stay on the disk indefinitely under that name, but its assignment of an exclusive buffer number ceases each time it is CLOSEd.

CLOSE the Barn Door

The opposite of OPENing a file is CLOSEing it. It's a good habit to CLOSE all files when they aren't being used. Better add:

```
50 CLOSE 1
```

Line 50 will CLOSE the file OPENed in Line 30. (Remember, don't RUN yet!)

CLOSE Options

The CLOSE statement severs the association of a file with its assigned buffer.

Without getting too far ahead of ourselves, it's worth noting that if any left-over or stray data is still in the file's buffer, that data is saved to disk when the file is CLOSEd. For example:

`CLOSE 1,3`	CLOSEs only files numbered 1 and 3 and saves to disk any data left in buffers 1 and 3.
`CLOSE N`	CLOSEs only file number N and saves to disk any data left in buffer N.
`CLOSE`	CLOSEs all files currently OPEN and saves any data left in all of the buffers to the correct disk file.

Most of the time, we will simply use:

```
CLOSE
```

since it CLOSEs everything in sight, secures all data from the file buffers, and writes it all to the disk. To fully understand the value of the CLOSE statement, we need to take a closer look at the way data is transferred to the disk.

To send data to a disk file, we need 2 additional BASIC statements:

PRINT

Our old friend PRINT directs output to the screen, and LPRINT directs it to the printer. The third member of the family is PRINT # which sends output to a disk file.

Remember the file buffer number that we assigned in the OPEN statement? It's used by the PRINT # statement to direct output to that buffer for transfer to the disk file. We assigned buffer #1 to the file TESTDATA, so we use:

```
PRINT #1
```

to send information to the TESTDATA file.

But what do we want to PRINT, and how do we do it?

Writing DATA into a "sequential file" is very similar to writing data to the screen. We can think of a sequential file as one

V....E....R....Y...

long stream of data.

Numbers, strings, and variables can be separated by commas or semicolons, and these "formatters" have precisely the same effect on the disk file as they do on the screen or printer output. If the formatting is unusually complex and we have enough disk space, we can even use PRINT USING just like we learned for the screen and printer. For example:

```
PRINT #1,USING "##.##";A
```

(See Chapters 35 and 36 for a review if your PRINT USING skills have grown dull.)

Add the following Lines, and RUN:

```
10 CLS : REM * SEQUENTIAL FILE PROGRAM *
20 A = 1 : B = 2 : C = 3
40 PRINT #1,A,B,C
990 PRINT : LIST
```

This is what happened:

Line 20	assigned values to variables A, B, and C.
Line 30	OPENed a file on disk named TESTDATA and assigned buffer #1 to OUTPUT data to that file.
Line 40	PRINTed the values in A, B, and C to buffer #1 (at this point it is still not on disk).
Line 50	transferred the data from buffer #1 to the TESTDATA file and CLOSEd it.

We now have a "permanent" record which can easily be read back into the Computer or any other computer which is compatible. Note that the variables A, B, and C were **not** written onto the disk -- just the *values* of those variables (in this case, 1, 2, and 3).

INPUT

The next step in this learning process is to INPUT that data from disk back into memory. After all, the only reason to store something on disk is so we can retrieve it later.

Once file buffer number 1 is CLOSEd in Line 50, it is no longer associated with disk file TESTDATA. It's free to be used with any file specified in a new OPEN statement. Add:

```
70 OPEN "TESTDATA" FOR INPUT AS 1
```

We are reOPENing the file TESTDATA using buffer number 1, but this time for INPUTing. (Any other valid buffer number will work as well.) It's important to remember with sequential files that we must first CLOSE the file, then reOPEN it when switching from reading to writing, and vice versa.

To read the contents of the sequential DATA file, add these Lines:

```
60 PRINT "THE NUMBERS";A;B;C;" ARE WRITTEN ON DISK."
80 INPUT #1,A,B,C
90 PRINT "THE DATA HAS BEEN READ FROM DISK."
```

```
100 PRINT "A =";A,"B =";B,"C =";C
110 CLOSE
```

...and RUN.

The Computer says:

```
THE NUMBERS 1 2 3 ARE WRITTEN ON DISK
THE DATA HAS BEEN READ FROM DISK.
A = 1          B = 2          C = 3
```

If yours doesn't look that way, here is a complete program listing:

```
10 CLS : REM * SEQUENTIAL FILE PROGRAM *
20 A = 1 : B = 2 : C = 3
30 OPEN "TESTDATA" FOR OUTPUT AS 1
40 PRINT #1,A,B,C
50 CLOSE 1
60 PRINT "THE NUMBERS";A;B;C;"ARE WRITTEN ON DISK."
70 OPEN "TESTDATA" FOR INPUT AS 1
80 INPUT #1,A,B,C
90 PRINT "THE DATA HAS BEEN READ FROM DISK."
100 PRINT "A =";A,"B =";B,"C =";C
110 CLOSE
990 PRINT : LIST
```

Here's what happened:

Line 70	OPENed the TESTDATA file for INPUT via buffer number 1.
Line 80	INPUT # the three numbers from disk into buffer number 1 where the values were assigned to variables A, B, and C.

Line 90 PRINTed a reassuring message.

Line 100 PRINTed the data values that were read from disk.

Line 110 CLOSEd file buffer number 1.

APPEND

APPEND allows us to OPEN a sequential file and add data to the end of it.

To APPEND more information, add these lines:

```
200 OPEN "TESTDATA" FOR APPEND AS 1
210 PRINT #1, "MORE INFO"
220 CLOSE 1
230 OPEN "TESTDATA" FOR INPUT AS 1
240 INPUT#1, A,B,C,D$
250 PRINT A,B,C,D$
260 CLOSE
```

Line 200 OPENs TESTDATA so something can be done to or with it and assigns it to buffer 1.

Line 210 PRINTs MORE INFO at the end of what's already in file TESTDATA.

Line 220 CLOSEs it again.

Line 230 reOPENs the TESTDATA file to INPUT the 4 pieces of data in it, and Line 250 PRINTs them. Note that since the new data is made up of letters, it is a string variable.

Line 260 CLOSEs the file for the last time.

EXERCISE 45-1: Write a program that stores a shopping list of five items on disk. The program should ask for each item and then write it to the disk. HINT: Use a FOR-NEXT loop. Be sure to CLOSE the file when you are through writing to it.

EXERCISE 45-2: Add a second part to Exercise 45-1 that reads the five items from the disk and displays them to the screen. SAVE the entire program (both output and input) as SHOPLIST.

EOF

Until now, we've been dealing with a precisely known quantity of data, but most of the time, the amount of data in the file is not known. How would we know where the end of the file is? The EOF, or End Of File, function is the answer.

Type in the following NEW program:

```
10 REM  * EOF DEMO *
20 CLS : RANDOMIZE
30 OPEN "UNKNOWN" FOR OUTPUT AS 1
40 FOR N = 1 TO INT(10*RND(1))
50  PRINT #1, "DATA";N
60 NEXT N : CLOSE
```

Note that Line 50 PRINTs 2 pieces of DATA to file, the word "DATA" and the value of N. Due to the deliberate use of the RND function in Line 40 to determine how many FOR-NEXT loops will be executed, we don't know how many data pairs will be written to the file named UNKNOWN.

To read the data back in from UNKNOWN into memory and to display it, add these lines. We'll use GOTO in Line 110 to keep reading in the DATA until it runs out. Since the information was written to disk in "data pairs," we INPUT # it back in with a single variable A$ in Line 90.

```
70.OPEN "UNKNOWN" FOR INPUT AS 1
80 REM
90 INPUT #1,A$
100 PRINT A$
110 GOTO 80
120 CLOSE
```

```
990 PRINT : LIST
```

RUN the program.

An error! BASIC won't allow us to just keep reading DATA from disk until it runs out, any more than it will permit us to do it from DATA Lines. The error message, "Input past end," tells the story. If we don't know the exact length of the file, we must test for the EOF condition.

EOF works this way. If we are at the end of file, the numeric value of EOF equals −1, paradoxically known as "true." If there's still more data to be read, EOF will equal 0, called "false." From these little truths, EOF can be used in a test, as follows:

Change Line 80 to:

```
80 IF EOF(1) THEN 120
```

The 1 in parentheses is the buffer number assigned to the file when it was OPENed. Line 80 reads, "If we have reached the End Of the File (EOF is true), then branch to Line 120." The EOF function can "look ahead" to signal when INPUT # is at the End Of the File.

Save this program as EOFTEST ... and RUN.

Nothing like a smooth running program to make your day!

> **EXERCISE 45-3:** Write a program that asks for the names and ages of several people. Use a GOTO loop to enter the data. After all the names are entered (signified by typing "DONE" or some other key word), CLOSE the file, then reOPEN it for INPUT to read the names and ages back into the Computer. Use EOF to avoid reading past the file's end.

For a sample program that demonstrates how to use a data file to create, process, and update an ongoing and ever-increasing list of data items, along with simple calculations to do something with it, see Appendix D.

Learned in Chapter 45

Statements	Miscellaneous
OPEN	Data files (Sequential)
CLOSE	File numbers
PRINT #	File buffers
PRINT #, USING	Output
INPUT #	Input
EOF (End Of File)	Append

Chapter 46

Advanced SAVEing, MERGEing and CHAINing

Everyone type in this NEW program:

```
10 REM LINE 10
20 REM LINE 20
40 REM LINE 40
```

We know this program is not destined for fame, but SAVE it on disk anyway. Each program SAVEd to disk becomes a FILE. Like any file, it is labeled with a file name. We will call this program FIRST. Type:

```
SAVE "FIRST"        ENTER
```

BASIC programs can be SAVEd on disk in either of 2 "formats." Unless we specify otherwise, the so-called *compressed format* is used.

1. In the *compressed format*, everything that can be abbreviated is stored in a shortened form. All numbers except those enclosed in quotes are stored in a minimum number of bytes, with BASIC keywords like PRINT and GOTO stored as special shorthand codes. This format is the one usually used and is fine for most purposes since it conserves disk space. This is all "invisible" to the user.

2. But there are times when we will sacrifice a little disk space for the luxury of saving a program or data on disk in the "character-for-character" format. It is called the *ASCII format*.

ASCII formatted files have several special purposes.

1. They can be loaded directly into word processing programs for easy editing. A word processor's *search and replace* capacity is a great way to make massive *global* changes in BASIC programs or other files.

2. Files in ASCII format can be sent over phone lines to other computers. Electronic mail is here!

3. The ASCII format can be used to MERGE two files -- either hook them end-to-end, overlay one on top of the other, or intermesh their Line numbers. Using ASCII format, we can MERGE a useful routine into several programs without retyping it. (Remember our SGN subroutine?)

MERGEing Files

Let's try a MERGEr right now. Type this NEW program:

```
30 REM THIS LINE GOES BEFORE LINE 40
40 REM THIS LINE REPLACES LINE 40
50 REM THIS LINE APPEARS AFTER LINE 40
```

and SAVE it:

```
SAVE "SECOND",A
```

(Look carefully!)

The ",A" causes it to be SAVEd in ASCII format.

Now we can MERGE the two programs. LOAD the original program back into memory:

```
LOAD "FIRST"
```

then:

```
LIST
```

to be sure only the FIRST program is in memory. Now bring in the next program by typing:

```
MERGE "SECOND"        ENTER
```

LIST to verify that programs were MERGEd.

```
10 REM LINE 10
20 REM LINE 20
30 REM THIS LINE GOES BEFORE LINE 40
40 REM THIS LINE REPLACES LINE 40
50 REM THIS LINE APPEARS AFTER LINE 40
```

Of course, it worked! Look very carefully. We have **new** Lines 30 and 50, and the original Line 40 was **replaced** by Line 40 from the incoming file.

Observe that the FIRST program did not have to be in ASCII format, only the second one drawn in for MERGEr. If we wish to MERGE 2 programs and their Line numbers conflict, RENUMber them first.

The combined program can be SAVEd as usual under any name. Let's use:

```
SAVE "MERGER"        ENTER
```

Removing Files from the Diskette

The 2 program files, FIRST and SECOND, are now combined into a MERGEd file, MERGER, and SAVEd on disk. They are no longer necessary. Right?

What's that about a safety copy of the program?

Yes, we **should** keep an extra copy of any important program, and right now FIRST and SECOND are the only protection we have if MERGER should somehow get zapped. What if we erased them, and a nasty electrical spike sizzled the MERGER file?

A safety backup copy is normally made on a different diskette. Since we are only risking 5 Lines of code at this point, we'll gamble with Murphy's law and make our safety copy of the MERGER program on the **same diskette**.

Since we can't SAVE the same program on the same diskette under the same name, we have to give it another name. Rather than have to remember an excessive number of names, just type:

```
SAVE "MERGER.BAK"
```

By appending the "." and the three letter extension "BAK", we create a second file with the same "first name" (MERGER) as our original. The extension "BAK" reminds us that the program is a safety BAcKup, and thus a duplicate, not a different program. .SAF for SAFety, .COP for COPy, .NO1 for Number 1 and other extensions will work as well.

KILL! KILL!

Now we can erase the 2 original files with a clear conscience. From BASIC, type:

```
KILL "FIRST.BAS"        ENTER
KILL "SECOND.BAS"       ENTER
```

Check the disk DIRectory by typing:

```
FILES       ENTER
```

to make sure FIRST and SECOND have disappeared.

The KILL instruction doesn't actually "erase" FIRST and SECOND from the diskette. It simply removes their names from the DIRectory. The result is the same, however; if they can't be found, they can't be used. (Sort of like having an unlisted telephone number.)

(To answer the question in some readers' minds, YES, with a special UTILITY program we could conceivably patch up the DIRectory and retrieve our "dead" files. Of course, if another new file is SAVEd first and it happens to use the same place on the disk, the file(s) is lost for good. For all intents and purposes, consider the files KILLed.)

MUST YOU YELL KILL! SO LOUD? THE NEIGH-BORS ARE BEGINNING TO WONDER...

We can also reNAME programs from BASIC. Suppose we want to change the name of the backup copy to NEWMERGE. No problem. Just type:

```
NAME "MERGER.BAK" AS "NEWMERGE"
```

Check the DIRectory with FILES to be sure that MERGER.BAK is gone and NEWMERGE took its place. Note that NEWMERGE has no .BAS or .BAK since none was specified.

CHAINing

The ability to CHAIN programs is very powerful. Not only can we RUN one program by calling it from another, but the values of the variables can be transferred from one program to the next without being reset to 0. Try this:

```
NEW
10 REM  * THIS IS THE FIRST PROGRAM
30 CLS : PRINT "PROGRAM ONE"
40 M$ = "TANDY"
50 A = 20
60 PRINT "M$ = ";M$
70 PRINT "A =";A
80 RUN "TWO"
```

SAVE as ONE, but **do not RUN it!** Type NEW and ENTER these Lines:

```
10 REM  * THIS IS THE SECOND PROGRAM
20 PRINT : PRINT "PROGRAM TWO"
30 PRINT "M$ = ";M$
40 PRINT "A =";A : PRINT
```

SAVE it as TWO, but **do not RUN**. Now, from the command level, type:

```
RUN "ONE"
```

Note very carefully that the string and numeric variables were **not** carried over from the first to the second program. We used a RUN statement to execute TWO. Remember RUN initializes all variables back to 0 or null. Now:

```
LOAD "ONE"
```

and change Line 80 to:

```
80 CHAIN "TWO",,ALL
```

SAVE as ONE

...and RUN.

Wow! The variables passed from ONE to TWO.

By adding the ALL option, program ONE passed ALL variable data to program TWO. Now let's see what gets placed between the two commas.

Add this Line to program TWO:

```
50 CHAIN "ONE",100,ALL
```

and SAVE as TWO. Line 50 will LOAD program ONE and begin execution at Line 100. If we don't specify a Line number, it would start ONE running at its first Line again, and we would be in an endless loop, or endless CHAIN. If the starting Line number is omitted, as it was in Line 80 of the ONE program, we still have to use the commas as place holders.

Now LOAD ONE back in. Change Line 80 to:

```
80 CHAIN "TWO"
```

and add the following:

```
20 COMMON M$
99 STOP
100 PRINT "WE ARE NOW BACK IN 'ONE'"
```

```
110 PRINT "M$ = ";M$
120 PRINT "A =";A
```

SAVE as ONE and RUN.

Here's what happened. Program ONE ran up through Line 8Ø where it CHAINed to program TWO. Only M$ was forwarded from ONE.

Since the ALL option was removed from Line 8Ø, all variables were not carried over to the CHAINed program. But, by adding Line 2Ø, we made M$ COMMON to both programs. Variable M$ was forwarded, but A was not. Program TWO ran through Line 5Ø where it CHAINed back to Line 1ØØ of ONE. ALL variables were forwarded, but A=Ø in TWO, so that's what was printed this second time by ONE.

The Line 99 STOP will never be executed and is not necessary. It was placed there as a reminder that program ONE in this case is really executed as 2 different programs under the same name.

The way to forward only selected variables without CHAINing them all is:

```
20 COMMON M$,A        (etc...)
```

Do it, SAVE as ONE and RUN again.

LOAD and LIST both ONE and TWO on the screen at the same time, and study them very carefully.

CHAINing and MERGEing have real programming value. What you have learned here will satisfy most programming needs. If you need to use more advanced CHAIN and MERGE features, refer to **The BASIC Handbook** by your favorite author.

Learned in Chapter 46

Statements	**Commands**
MERGE	KILL
CHAIN	
COMMON	
NAME	

Chapter 47

PEEK and POKE

PEEK and POKE are BASIC words that allow us to do "non-BASIC" things. They provide the means whereby we can PEEK into the innards of the Computer's memory, and if we wish, POKE in new information.

It is not our purpose here to become expert in machine language programming nor on how the Computer works. We have to approach this and related topics a little gingerly lest we fall over the edge into a Computer abyss.

We do know, however, that computers do their thing entirely by the manipulation of numbers. Therefore, when we PEEK at the contents of memory, guess what we'll find? Numbers? Very good!

Large chunks of the Computer's memory are reserved, or "mapped," for very specific uses. All numbers we talk about here are decimals, not hex, octal, or binary.

The range of the numbers we can PEEK or POKE is Ø to 65535 (64K). But that's just our Read/Write user memory. We obviously have **many** more addresses than Ø-65535. Our Tandy Computers allow us to use up to 640K of memory (if we have it installed), beyond the range of our usual PEEK and POKE. In order to access these additional memory addresses, we use the DEF SEG statement. This statement DEFines the SEGment of memory that we will PEEK or POKE at a given time.

But it isn't as easy as it sounds. We must give the DEF SEG statement the address of the segment we want, **divided** by 16. When the DEF SEG statement gets an address, **it** automatically multiplies it by 16.

Turn the Computer off to clear out memory, wait a minute, turn it back on, bring up BASIC, and type in this NEW program:

```
10 DEF SEG
20 FOR N = 0 TO 1100
30  PRINT N, PEEK(N), CHR$(PEEK(N))
40 NEXT N
```

Let's analyze the program before RUNning it.

Line 10 sets the SEGment of memory to the beginning of BASIC's data storage. The actual highest absolute address is (65536 * 16) − 1 = 1048575 (FFFFF Hex).

Line 30 PRINTs three things:

1. The address -- that is, the number of the byte at whose contents we are PEEKing.

2. The contents of that byte expressed as a decimal number between 0 and 255.

3. The contents of that address converted to its ASCII character. (Many of the ASCII characters are not PRINTable. Go back to the Chapter on ASCII if *your* memory has grown dim.)

OK, now RUN the program, but be ready to freeze it with **HOLD** or **Ctrl** **Num Lock** if you see something interesting. It can also be STOPped at any time with **CTRL** **BREAK**, and restarted with CONT **ENTER**, or **F5**, without having to start all over again. Did you see all the function key labels? How about the program? Did you see it fly by?

Change N to start at different places in memory and PEEK to your heart's delight. You can't goof up anything by just PEEKing. It's indiscriminate POKEing that gets one into trouble.

The command level is very handy for resetting the starting address. Change the value of N by just typing:

CTRL BREAK

```
N = 500
```
ENTER

for example, then:

```
CONT
```
ENTER (or F5)

instead of RUN.

When done PEEKing, and having seen far more information than can possibly be absorbed, rework Line 30 to read simply:

```
30 PRINT CHR$(PEEK(N));
```

...and RUN.

It PRINTs only the ASCII characters, horizontally, and is the ideal program to RUN when friends visit. Just act casual about the whole display and avoid any direct questions. Makes a great background piece for a science fiction movie.

When you find an interesting spot, hit CTRL BREAK, then:

```
PRINT N
```
ENTER

at the command level to find out where in memory we are PEEKing. (Don't you wish we could explore the corners of our minds as easily?)

CONTinue when ready.

Having degenerated from PEEKing to leering, we'd better move on.

Careless POKEing Can Leave Holes...

Before POKEing, we'd better see that we're not POKEing a stick into a hornets' nest. It's with the greatest of ease that we destroy a program in memory by POKEing around where we shouldn't.

Obviously there is no use POKEing the ROM area. Since ROM stands for Read Only Memory, it's not changeable. The rest of the "Memory mapped" area is reserved for specific things, so best not to POKE in there while we're just bungling around. Anything between 2000 and 65535 in the current DEF SEG should be available memory, unless taken up with our BASIC program or required for processing. With such a short program as ours we surely can't goof anything up? Can we?

Let's PEEK around the current memory segment and see if anything is going on. Change these 3 program Lines to:

```
10 DEF SEG
20 FOR N = 1200 TO 12000
30  PRINT N; PEEK(N),
```

...and RUN.

This default value of DEF SEG means, "Set the segment to the beginning of where BASIC stores its programs."

What we see are the address numbers and their contents, in easy-to-read parallel rows. Unless you've been messing around with other programs since power-up, you should see mostly nice rows of Ø's.

Great! Write a NEW program, POKE in some information, and do something with it. Make it read:

```
10 REM  * POKE PROGRAM *
20 DEF SEG
30 N = 7000
40 READ D
50 POKE N,D
```

HEE HEE
HO HO HA HEE
HEE HEE
THAT TICKLES!
JES' POKIN' FRIEND!

```
60 N = N + 1
70 IF N = 7011 THEN END
80 GOTO 40
100 DATA 80,69,69,75,45,65,45,66,79,79,33
```

Before RUNning, let's analyze it:

Line 20	sets the SEGment to the beginning of program storage.
Line 30	initializes the starting address at 7000.
Line 40	READs a number from the DATA Line.
Line 50	POKEs the DATA "D" into address "N."
Line 60	increments the address number by one.
Line 70	ENDs execution after we've POKEd in all 11 pieces of DATA.
Line 80	sends us back for more DATA.
Line 100	holds the DATA we are going to POKE into memory.

...now RUN.

Well, that was sure fast. I wonder what it did? How can we find out? Should we PEEK at it? Yes, but let's leave the old program in and just start a new one at 200.

```
200 REM * PEEK PROGRAM *
210 FOR N = 7000 TO 7010
220  PRINT N, PEEK(N)
230 NEXT N
```

...and RUN 200.

```
7000    80
7001    69
7002    69
7003    75
7004    45
7005    65
7006    45
7007    66
7008    79
7009    79
7010    33
```

How about that? We really **did** change the contents of those memory locations. We shot the numbers from our DATA Line right into memory. Now if we only knew what those numbers stood for. Wonder ... if we changed them to ASCII characters, would they tell us anything?

Add:

```
205 CLS
220  LOCATE 13,30 + N-7000
225  PRINT CHR$(PEEK(N));
```

to PRINT at a certain location on the screen

...and RUN 200.

That's how PEEK and POKE work.

Function Keys

Let's take one more look at our special function keys. Keys 1-5, 7 and 8 seem to be pretty useful so we'll leave them alone, but why don't we change the others? After all, this **is** a personal computer. Enter this NEW program:

```
10 KEY 6, "EDIT "
20 KEY 9, "AUTO" + CHR$(13)
30 KEY 10, "CLS" + CHR$(13)
```

...and RUN.

SAVE this program as KEYS. Notice the bottom row on the display with our new creations.

Perhaps the most used of these keys will be F10. When we get in the habit, it'll be so convenient to just hit a single key to CLear the Screen. We can't use F10 if there is anything on the screen on the same Line as the cursor or we'll get a Syntax error. Best in that case to use CTRL HOME instead.

Suppose we like this new soft key arrangement so much that we want the Computer to automatically power-up with it, instead of what comes with the Computer. MS-DOS has a beautiful feature called AUTOEXEC.BAT that bypasses typing in the DATE and TIME and AUTOmatically EXECutes a command, such as LOAD BASIC. So, let's add one more line before we go back to DOS:

```
50 KEY ON : NEW
```

Be sure to SAVE the program as KEYS **before** you RUN it.

We put in the NEW command so the program will erase itself after the keys are reprogrammed.

We include here the process without explanation for the thrill seekers among us who can't leave well enough alone. If you aren't a thrill seeker, skip the rest of this Chapter.

First return to DOS (SYSTEM) and make the prompt read:

```
A>_
```

Now (temporarily) take the write-protect tab off the **COPY** of the System Master disk you've been using, place it in the drive and type:

```
COPY CON: AUTOEXEC.BAT        ENTER
DATE        ENTER
B:          ENTER        (B: is for multiple drive users only.)
A:BASIC A:KEYS          ENTER    (The second A: is for multiple
                                  drive users only.)
```

Press F6 ENTER

And the display reads:

```
1 File(s) copied
```

The first instruction copies from the CONsole (keyboard) into the file AUTOEXEC.BAT. B: sets the default to Drive B for 2-disk users. BASIC KEYS loads BASIC and automatically RUNs our KEYS program. We could also make the last Line simply:

```
A:BASIC
```

That way we wouldn't have to RUN a program, just load BASIC. Replace the write-protect tab on the System Master disk. Reset the Computer by pressing the reset button or by simultaneously pressing the ALT CTRL and DELETE keys.

The Computer will AUTOmatically power-up with the soft keys programmed as before and will continue to do so each time the Computer is reset or turned on as long as we use the same System Master disk. Other disks could be prepared with other automatic soft key programming or a variety of BASIC programs could be held on 1 disk and called up for different purposes as needed.

To remove the auto-power-up feature, simply KILL "AUTOEXEC.BAT" from the disk.

Learned in Chapter 47

Statements

PEEK
POKE
DEF SEG

Miscellaneous

AUTOEXEC.BAT

Chapter 48

Logical Operators

In classical mathematics (fancy words for simple ideas), there exist what are known as the "logical AND," the "logical OR," and the "logical NOT."

So the One Cow Said to the Other Cow...

In Figure 48-1, if gate A AND gate B AND gate C are open, the cow can move from pasture #1 to pasture #2. If any gate is closed, the cow's path is blocked.

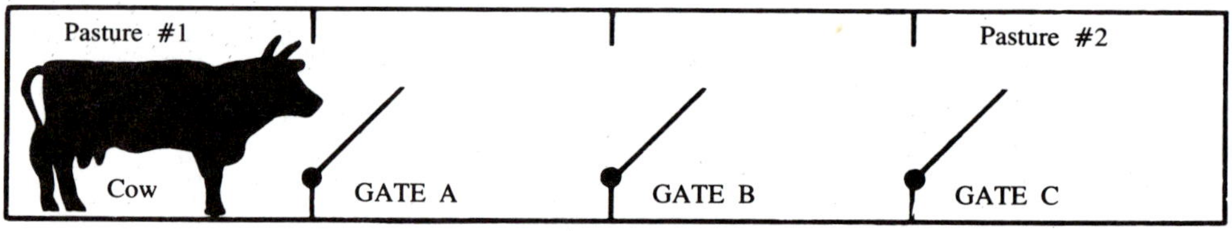

Figure 48-1

The principle is called "logical AND."

In Figure 48-2, if gate X OR gate Y OR gate Z are open, then old Bess can move from pasture #3 to #4. That principle is called "logical OR." These ideas are both pretty logical.

Using these ideas is very simple. Type this NEW program:

```
10 INPUT "IS GATE 'A' OPEN";A$
```

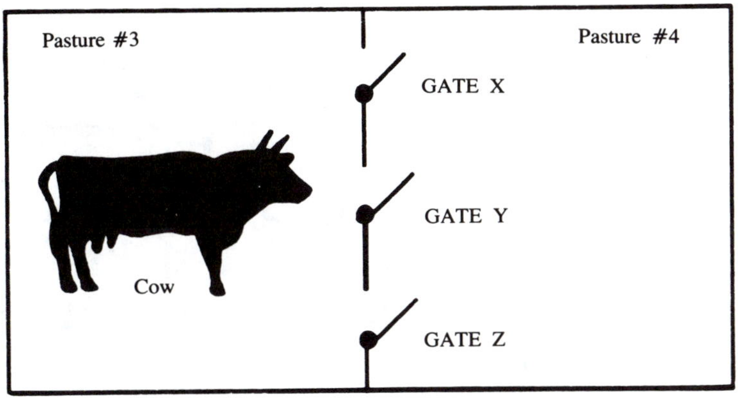

Figure 48-2

```
20 INPUT "IS GATE 'B' OPEN";B$
30 INPUT "IS GATE 'C' OPEN";C$
40 PRINT
50 IF A$="Y" AND B$="Y" AND C$="Y" THEN 80
60 PRINT "OLD BESSIE IS SECURE."
70 END
80 PRINT "ALL GATES ARE OPEN."
90 PRINT "OLD BESSIE IS FREE TO ROAM."
```

...and RUN.

Answer (Y/N) the questions differently during different RUNs to see how the logical AND works in Line 50.

Where Is the Logic in All This?

You should, by now, understand every part in the program except perhaps Line 50.

Lines 10, 20, 30	INPUT the gate positions as **open** (which we defined as equal to "Y") or **closed** (defined as "N"). We could have defined them the other way around and rewritten Line 50 to match, if we'd wanted to.

"ALL GATES ARE OPEN" and THE COW IS FREE TO ROAM?? JUST WHO'S GOING TO CLEAN UP THIS MESS IN HERE?

Line 5Ø is the key. It reads, literally, "If gate A is **open**, AND gate B is **open**, AND gate C is **open**, then go to Line 8Ø. If any one gate is closed, report that fact by defaulting to Line 6Ø."

Imagine how this simple logic could be used to create a super-simple "computer" consisting of only an electric switch on each gate. Add a battery and put a light bulb in the farmer's house. The bulb could indicate if any of the gates are open. Such a "gate-checking" computer would have only three memory cells -- the switches.

> **EXERCISE 48-1:** Using the above program as a model, and the "OR logic" seen in Figure 48-2, write a program that will report Bess' status as determined by the position of Gates X, Y and Z.

Teacher's Pet

Here is a simple program which uses > instead of the equals sign in a logical test. The student passes if he has a final grade over 60 OR a midterm grade over 70 AND a homework grade over 75. Enter this NEW program and RUN it a few times to see how efficiently the logical OR and logical AND tests work in the same program Line (4Ø).

```
10 INPUT "FINAL GRADE";F
20 INPUT "MIDTERM GRADE";M
30 INPUT "HOMEWORK GRADE";H
40 IF (F>60 OR M>70) AND H>75 THEN 70
50 PRINT "FAILED"
60 END
70 PRINT "PASSED"
```

Does this give some idea of the power and convenience of logical math? The actual "cut off" numbers could, of course, be set at any level.

Logical Variations

This next program example mixes equals, greater-than, and less-than signs in the same program. It determines and reports whether the two numbers we INPUT are both positive, both negative, or have different signs.

Analyze the program. Note the parentheses. Although they are not necessary, they tell us to shift our thinking to "logical." Type it in and RUN.

```
10 INPUT "FIRST NUMBER IS";F
20 INPUT "SECOND NUMBER IS";S
30 IF (F>=0) AND (S>=0) THEN 70
40 IF (F<0) AND (S<0) THEN 90
50 PRINT "OPPOSITE SIGNS"
60 END
70 PRINT "BOTH POSITIVE OR ZERO"
80 END
90 PRINT "BOTH NEGATIVE"
```

NOT

In addition to the logical AND and OR functions, we have what is called logical NOT. Here is how it can be used:

```
10 INPUT "ENTER A NUMBER";N
20 L = NOT(N>5)
30 IF L = 0 GOTO 60
40 PRINT "N WAS NOT GREATER THAN 5"
50 END
60 PRINT "N WAS GREATER THAN 5"
```

...and RUN.

Line 20, containing NOT, is obviously the key one. If the statement in Line 20 is **true** (namely, that N is NOT larger than 5), the Computer makes the value of L=-1. The test in Line 30 then fails.

If, on the other hand, N IS larger than 5, the statement is **false**,and the Computer makes the value of L = 0.

True = -1 and False = 0. (Time for the primal scream, again. All together, now...)

More Logical Operators

As if these 3 *logical operators* weren't enough, the Tandy Computers allow use of 3 more *logical* words. They are (in order of appearance):

EQV, XOR, and IMP.

To help see how these things work, let's write a "testbed" program into which we can install them.

```
10 INPUT "ENTER A VALUE FOR X";X
20 INPUT "ENTER A VALUE FOR Y";Y
30 IF (X<10) AND (Y>10) THEN 60
40 PRINT : PRINT "CONDITION WAS FALSE"
50 END
60 PRINT : PRINT "CONDITION WAS TRUE"
```

...and RUN.

INPUT the number 5 for X and 15 for Y. Both comparisons were true which made the AND condition true.

OR

Replace the AND in Line 30 with OR and RUN. Try different numbers to get a feel for the program.

EQV

There are several more "advanced" logical operators. EQV stands for EQuiValence. Replace the OR in Line 30 with the word EQV.

```
30 IF (X<10) EQV (Y>10) THEN 60
```

The condition in Line 30 will be true only if both arithmetical comparisons are the same. Only if X is less than 10 AND Y is greater than 10, OR if X is **not** less than 10 AND Y is **not** greater than 10.

Try the number 5 for X and 15 for Y. Both tests pass so the overall condition is true.

Try 15 for X and 5 for Y. Both conditions are false, but since they are **both** the same (false in this case), the overall condition is true and execution jumps to Line 60.

XOR

XOR stands for eXclusive OR. This means that if one **and only one** test passed, the overall condition will be true.

Replace the EQV in Line 30 with the word XOR. RUN with different numbers. Try 5 for X and 15 for Y. Execution falls through to Line 40 because **both** tests pass. Remember if we were using the regular OR, the overall condition would be true.

IMP

Our final operator is IMP which stands for IMPlication. This is probably the hardest to understand. The IMP condition will be **true** for all conditions except when the first test is **true** and the second test is **false.** The **overall condition** is then **false.** Replace the XOR with an IMP:

```
30 IF (X<10) IMP (Y>10) THEN 60
```

...and RUN.

Try 5 for both X and Y. These numbers give us a **false** condition. All other conditions are **true.**

Order of Operations

When trying to figure out which gets calculated first in the thick of a "humongous" equation, refer to this list of the pecking order:

Those operations buried deepest inside the parentheses get resolved first. The idea is to clear the parentheses as quickly as possible. When it all becomes a big tie, here's the order:

1. Exponentation -- a number raised to a power.
2. Negation -- a number having its sign changed. Typically, a number multiplied times -1.
3. Multiplication and division -- from left to right.
4. Addition and subtraction -- from left to right.
5. Less than, greater than, equals, less than or equal to, greater than or equal to, not equal to -- from left to right.
6. The logical NOT.
7. The logical AND.
8. The logical OR.
9. The logical XOR.
10. The logical EQV.
11. The logical IMP.

And in Conclusion

Logical math is worth the hassle. As one last fun program, enter and RUN this "Midnight Inspection." Line 100 checks each response for a NO answer (instead of a YES). Using logical OR, it branches to the "no-go" statement (Line 120) if any one of the tests is negative ("N").

```
10 CLS
20 PRINT "ANSWER WITH 'Y' OR 'N'."
30 PRINT
40 INPUT "HAS THE CAT BEEN PUT OUT";A$
```

```
50 INPUT "PORCH LIGHT TURNED OFF";B$
60 INPUT "ALL DOORS/WINDOWS LOCKED";C$
70 INPUT "IS THE T.V. TURNED OFF";D$
80 INPUT "THERMOSTAT TURNED DOWN";E$
90 PRINT:PRINT
100 IF A$="N" OR B$="N" OR C$="N" OR D$=
    "N" OR E$="N" THEN 120
110 PRINT "          GOODNIGHT":END
120 PRINT "SOMETHING HAS NOT BEEN DONE."
130 PRINT "DO NOT GO TO BED"
140 PRINT "UNTIL YOU FIND THE PROBLEM!"
150 GOTO 30
```

In most cases, AND and OR statements are interchangeable if other parts of a program are rewritten to accommodate the switch.

Learned in Chapter 48

Miscellaneous

Logical AND
Logical OR
Logical NOT
Logical EQV
Logical XOR
Logical IMP
Order of Operations

Chapter 49

A Study of Obscurities

Tandy Computers' BASIC has some features that are not used by most beginning programmers. Their use presumes special applications and requires knowledge which is really beyond the scope of this book. In the interest of completeness, however, abbreviated descriptions of what they are and how they are used are included in this Chapter.

USR

The USR function has a variety of uses, most of them having little to do with BASIC. It allows us to "call," or "gosub," a program written in Assembly language and "return" to the main BASIC program when it's finished. The benefit of USR is that the "wordy" type programming requiring PRINT, etc. can be done in BASIC while complex mathematical programming can be done in Assembler which executes extremely fast. To make much sense of USR, you'll need Assembly language skills -- a whole book in itself.

USR in Use

Without getting out too deep in the water, we must first DEFine the address that our Machine language routine starts at with the DEF USR statement. Up to 10 Machine language routines can be DEFined at once.

For example, if a program starts at 32000 (offset into the current SEGment), then try:

```
DEF USR3 = 32000
```

To CALL the non-existent machine language program at 32000 from BASIC we would say:

```
X = USR3(1)
```

Hmmm. We seemed to have lost control.

Press the reset button (or CTRL ALT DELETE), then return to BASIC.

There is no way to predict what may result from calling a non-existent USR program.

To get a little taste for Machine language let's try the classic example of a screen "white out". In order to get our Machine language routine ready, we will POKE the numbers (or the *object code*) into high memory. Type in:

```
10 REM 'USR' PROGRAM
20 DEF SEG
30 DEF USR = 10000
40 FOR X = 0 TO 13
50  READ P
60  POKE 10000+X,P
70 NEXT X
80 INPUT "HIT ENTER TO DO IT"; A$
90 X = USR(0)
100 FOR X = 1 TO 5000 : NEXT X : CLS
110 DATA 183, 112, 184, 0, 6, 185, 0, 0
120 DATA 186, 79, 24, 205, 16, 203
```

SAVE as GREENOUT **before** you RUN it. Double check the DATA to be sure it's correct. Remember, POKEing around with numbers in memory is the easiest way to lose a program or lock up the Computer.

...and RUN.

In Line 90 we tell the Computer to execute the program beginning at the address specified with the DEF USR statement (10000 in this example). Lines 110 and 120 contain the instructions to "green out" the screen.

The USR function should be used with BASIC programs containing DEF USR statements. Otherwise CALL is the recommended method for moving from a BASIC program to an Assembly language subroutine and back again.

CALL

The CALL function is a lot like USR. CALL allows us to set certain parameters for use in the Machine language program. A typical CALL statement might look like this:

```
CALL MEMLOC
```

This tells the Computer to execute the program beginning at the memory address specified by the variable MEMLOC.

Without getting out too deep in the water, there are storage areas called *registers* that hold information used by a Machine language subroutine. This information is passed through the registers to our program via CALL.

```
CALL MEMLOC (A,B,C$,D...etc.)
```

tells the Computer to execute the Machine language program at the address specified by MEMLOC and pass the data stored in A,B,C$,D...etc. to the Machine language program.

That's as far as we're going to press our luck on this one right now.

Machine and Assembly language programming books are readily available for that small percentage of readers who want to pursue the subject. You, at least, have a sufficient introduction to nod your head and smile knowingly when others try to impress you with their knowledge of these things.

INP (Tandy 2000 owners skim to WAIT)

The 1000 Series and 3000 Series Computers have 65536 "ports," or channels of communication with the "outside world." They are numbered from 0 to 65535. Because this subject is worthy of an entire book itself, we will only learn enough here to get an elementary "feel" for it.

?
I TOLD YOU, MASTER, THAT LINES 110 and 120 CONTAIN INSTRUCTIONS TO "BLACK OUT"!

Only one of these ports will be considered here. Port number 889 monitors the printer status if a printer is connected to your computer. Type NEW and enter the following program:

```
10 CLS
20 D = INP(889)
30 IF D = 223 THEN 60
40 LOCATE 12,30 : PRINT "PRINTER IS NOT READY",D
50 GOTO 20
60 LOCATE 12,30 : PRINT "PRINTER IS READY",D
70 GOTO 20
```

Now, connect a printer (if you have one) to the Computer and RUN.

Here's how it works:

Line 20	looks at port #889 and reads a coded message.
Line 30	tests that code number. If it is equal to 223, execution branches to Line 60. If not, it defaults to Line 40. Execution returns to Line 20 where we begin "polling" the port again.

Astute observers have probably noted that there is a definite pattern to the numbers displayed. The point is, DATA is entering port 889 from the printer indicating its status, and this is what INP reads and acts upon.

One more view of INP. Enter this NEW program, and RUN.

```
10 PRINT INP(1)
20 GOTO 10
```

This program monitors the first port in the Computer and gives us its status.

OUT (1000 Series only)

Let's see what OUT does. Put on your flying helmet, and type in this program:

```
10 FOR X = 0 TO 64
20  OUT 192,X
30 NEXT X
40 RUN
```

...and RUN.

Putt. Putt. Putt.

When we send data OUT of port 192, it goes to the Computer's Sound Generator. The rapid changing of values in the FOR-NEXT loop causes the "putting" noise you heard after your typed RUN. Press **CTRL** **BREAK** to stop the noise.

In addition to port 192, ports 193 to 199 are used in sound generation. Feel free to experiment on your own with these OUTports creating new sounds as you go. Pressing **CTRL** **BREAK** will stop any sounds that you may produce -- but bring along some cotton for your ears just in case.

WAIT

The WAIT statement ties right in with INP and OUT. It is used as a port monitor. When a program encounters the WAIT statement, it WAITs for a certain value to be INPUT from a port. For example:

```
WAIT 30,2,5
```

tells the Computer to WAIT until a non-zero value is produced when the byte value at port 30 is eXclusively ORed with the byte value of 5, and the result logically ANDed with the byte value of 2. When this condition is met, program execution continues at the next statement. If the last byte value (5 in the example above) is omitted from the WAIT statement, the Computer assumes its value to be 0.

In the above example, the byte value at port 30 must have its 2nd bit "turned on" before the Computer continues program execution as illustrated by this table.

	PORT VALUE		VALUE2				VALUE1		
	0		1		1		0		0
	1	X	0		1	A	1		1
BINARY	0		1		1		0		0
VALUES	0	O	0		0	N	0		0
	0		0	=	0		0	=	0
	0	R	0		0	D	0		0
	0		0		0		0		0
	0		0		0		0		0
DECIMAL VALUES	2	XOR	5	=	7	AND	2	=	2

If you get stuck WAITing in an endless loop, press CTRL BREAK to exit the WAIT condition.

Each value listed in the WAIT statement must be between 0 and 255 (the range of values that can be held in an 8 bit memory cell).

VARPTR

While VARPTR (short for VARiable PoinTeR) is found in this Tandy BASIC, it's about as far from mainline BASIC as anything we have.

Take a Deep Breath

If a variable is *numeric*, VARPTR tells us the *location* of the **first byte** of the number stored in that variable.

If it's a *string* variable, VARPTR tells us where in memory the *index* to the variable is located. Read that last line carefully. We don't want anyone getting lost.

VARPTR doesn't have the common decency to point to the location of the *contents* of a *string* variable. Instead, it points to a three byte *index* to the variable. The three bytes contain:

1. The *length* of the string.

2. The least significant byte (LSB) of the *starting location* of the string.

3. The most significant byte (MSB) of the *starting location* of the string.

To actually find the *contents* of the string variable, we have to calculate the location using bytes 2 and 3 of the *index* to that variable. Sound complicated? Well, it is a bit tricky, but this example should clarify matters a bit.

Enter this NEW program:

```
10 REM  * STRING VARIABLE LOCATER *
15 DEF SEG
20 CLS
30 A$ = "12345"
40 X = VARPTR(A$)
50 PRINT "THE INDEX TO A$ IS AT";X
990 PRINT : LIST
```

...and RUN.

Line 40 uses VARPTR to store the address of the index to A$ in X. Line 50 PRINTs it.

We haven't found the *contents* of A$ yet, just the *index*. Hang in there. Add:

```
60 L = PEEK(X+1) + 256*PEEK(X+2)
70 PRINT "A$ IS HIDING AT LOCATION";L
```

...and RUN.

Line 60 uses some fancy footwork to convert bytes 2 (X+1) and 3 (X+2) of the *index* (X) into the actual *location* L of A$.

Line 70 PRINTs the *address* value.

How could we prove that we have found the correct *location?* Sure. PEEK at the contents of A$ and compare it with "12345." Add:

```
80 FOR I=L TO L+4
90  PRINT CHR$(PEEK(I)),
```

```
100 NEXT I
```

...and RUN.

Satisfied? The 5 digits in A$ are stored in 5 consecutive memory locations.

Now, knowing where a variable is located in memory may not seem too useful at first, but it has some surprising consequences. Once we have found the location of a string variable, we can modify its contents. Try this change:

```
100 READ N : POKE I,N
110 NEXT I : PRINT : PRINT A$ : PRINT
120 DATA 204,205,203,206,202
```

...and RUN. Then RUN again!

Surprise! We poked graphic codes into an unsuspecting "normal" string variable and transformed it into a pictorial masterpiece. Line 90 PRINTed the 5 "pieces," and Line 110 assembled the puzzle.

Type:

```
PRINT A$
```

to be sure we aren't just dreaming. Yes, we actually modified the contents of A$ by using VARPTR to **find** the string and then POKEing in new numbers. These computers can be downright fun once we get to know them.

Look at Line 30. Did we do that? I'm afraid so. A LISTing containing the actual graphics doesn't affect the program.

Leave with this thought. We packed a *dummy* string with only 5 graphic codes. A string variable **can** hold up to 255 characters (about one eighth of the video display). Just imagine what we could do with strings packed with up to 255 cursor control codes, graphic codes, and special character codes! If that doesn't push your imagination to overload, you might as well trade this computer in for a $4.95 calculator.

VARPTR$

VARPTR$ is similar to VARPTR except it gives us the character form of the address or location of a variable in memory. The address is printed as a three-byte string. Byte Ø indicates the type of variable, Byte 1 the first part of the address, and Byte 2 the last part of the address.

The VARPTR$ function is used mainly with PLAY and DRAW in programs you want to compile. The explanation for this is beyond the scope of this particular book.

Learned in Chapter 49

Statements	Functions
OUT	USR
INP	VARPTR
WAIT	VARPTR$
	CALL

PART 9

PROGRAM CONTROL

Chapter 50

Flowcharting

Most of the programs written for this book were simple; but they met simple, specific needs. Suppose we want to write a program to play chess or bridge, evaluate complicated investment alternatives, keep records for a bowling league or a small business, or do stress calculations for a new building? How would we approach writing such a complex program?

We break down a complex program into a series of smaller programs. This is called *modular programming*, and the individual programs are called *modules*. But how are the modules related -- and how do we write them, anyway?

Module is just a 75-cent word for "section" or "building block."

One way to plan a program is to make a picture displaying its logic. Remember, a picture is worth a thousand words. The picture that programmers use is called a *flowchart*.

Flowcharts are most helpful when kept simple. A cluttered flowchart is hard to read and usually isn't much more helpful than an ordinary program LISTing. A good flowchart is also helpful for "documentation" to give us (or others) a picture of how the program works -- for later on, when we've forgotten.

Flowcharts are so widely used that programmers have devised standard symbols. There are many specialized symbols in use, but we will examine only the most common ones.

TERMINAL BLOCK
(means Begin or End)

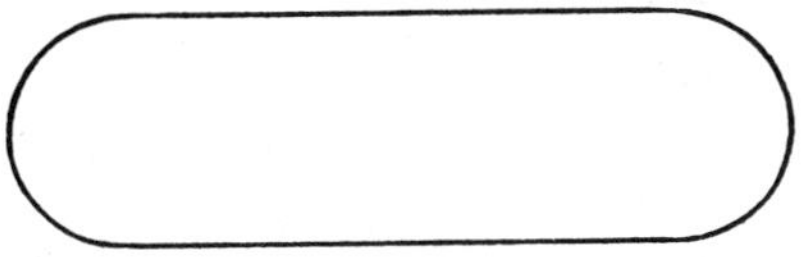

PROCESSING BLOCK
(something the Computer does without making any decisions)

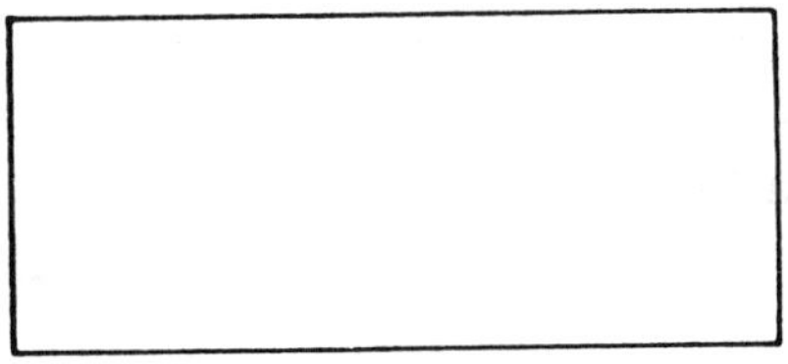

DECISION DIAMOND
(branches off in different directions depending on the decision it makes)

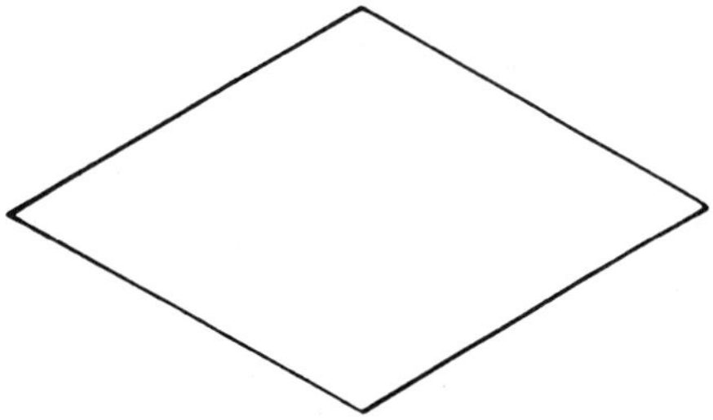

Each decision point asks a question such as *"Is A larger than B?"* or *"Have all the cards been dealt?"* The different branches are marked by YES or NO.

Other useful symbols are:

CONTINUATION
(contains a number which corresponds to a number on another page if the flowchart is too large for a single sheet)

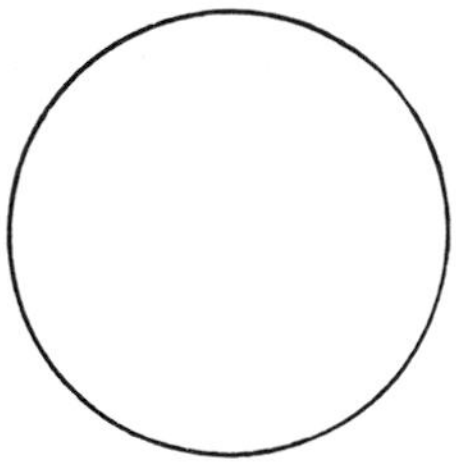

CONNECTOR ARROWS

(indicate the direction in which program execution proceeds)

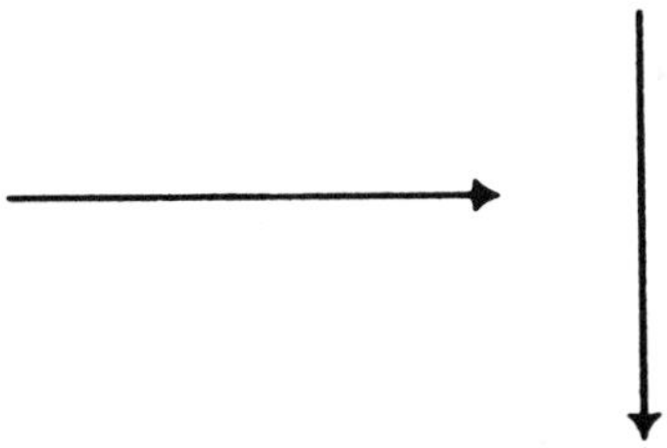

There are no hard-and-fast rules about what goes into a flowchart and what doesn't. A flowchart is supposed to help, not be more work than it's worth. It helps us plan the **logic** of a program. When it stops helping and makes us feel like we're back in arts and crafts designing mosaics, we've gone as far as the flowchart will take us (or more typically, it's passed its point of usefulness).

Suppose we want to grade a 5-question test by comparing each of the **students'** answers with the **correct** answer. We can put the correct answers in a DATA statement in the program, enter a student's answers through the keyboard, compare (grade) them, then PRINT the % of correct answers. This procedure can be repeated until all the students' papers are graded.

The flowchart might look like this:

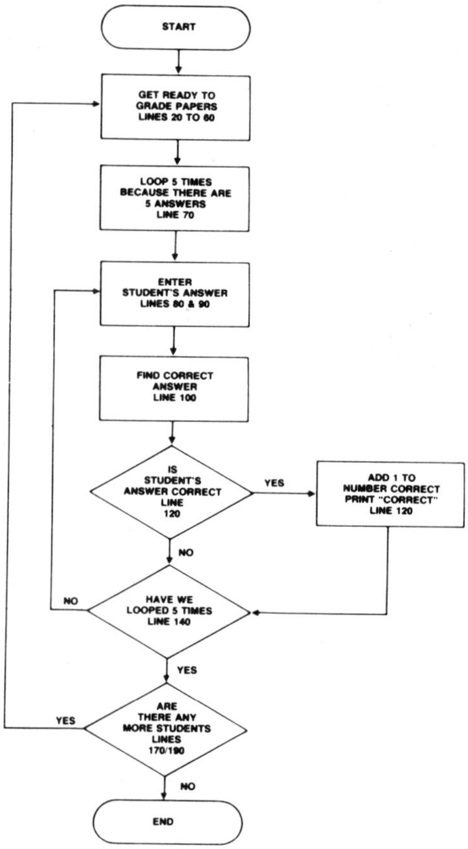

START
NO
READY?
YES
END
WELL, IT COULD USE A LITTLE FLESHING OUT.

This flowchart has three decision diamonds. In the first, the Computer determines if an answer is correct. In the second, the Computer determines if all the questions in a single student's paper have been graded. The third terminates execution when all tests have been graded.

> **EXERCISE 50-1:** Using the flowchart on the previous page as a guide, write a program that grades a test having five questions.

For more complicated problems, we may subdivide the flowchart into larger modules. A *master flowchart* will show the relationship among the flowcharts of individual programs.

For example, let's say we want to write a program that calculates the return on various investments. The options might be:

1 - CERTIFICATE OF DEPOSIT

2 - BANK SAVINGS ACCOUNT

3 - CREDIT UNION

4 - MORTGAGE LOAN

The main (or control) program will select one of these 4 options using an INPUT question, execute the correct sub-program, and PRINT the answer. Its flowchart might be as shown on the next page.

We can now flowchart each of the individual programs in the blocks separately. The Certificate of Deposit program would, for example, have to contain the rate of return, size of deposit, and maturity. The order in which that program INPUTs data and performs the calculations would be specified in its own flowchart.

> **EXERCISE 50-2:** Write the master program as flowcharted with a branch to a program to calculate the return on a Bank Savings Account paying simple interest.

> **EXERCISE 50-3:** Choose a program from an early Chapter and design your own flowchart.

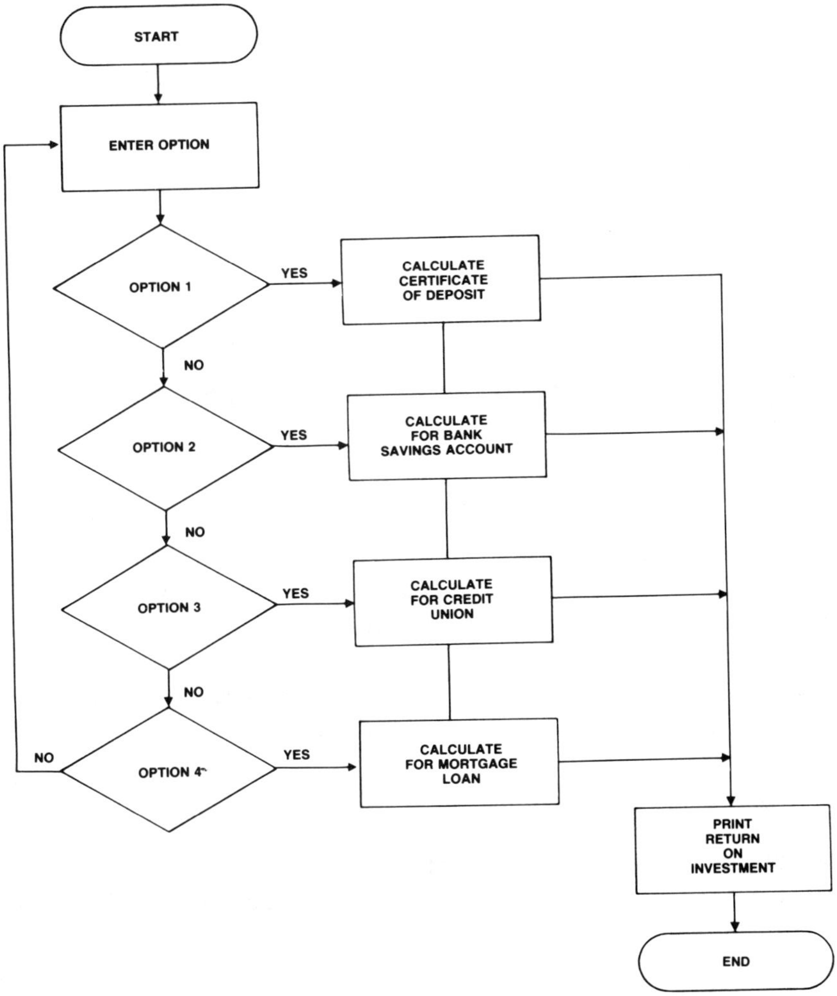

Learned in Chapter 50

Miscellaneous

Modular programming
Flowcharting

Chapter 51

Debugging Programs

Quick -- The Raid!

The Computer has given us plenty of nasty messages. We know something's wrong, but it isn't always obvious exactly where or why.

How do we find it? The answer is simple -- *be very systematic. Even experienced programmers make lots of silly mistakes ... but experience teaches how to locate mistakes quickly.*

Hardware, Cockpit or Software?

The first step in the *debugging* process is to isolate the problem as being either:

1. a hardware problem,
2. an operator problem, or
3. a software problem.

Is It Further to Ft. Worth or by Bus?

Starting with the least likely possibility -- is the Computer itself malfunctioning? Chances are very high that the Computer is working perfectly. There are several very fast ways to find out.

A. Warm Up

Our Tandy Computers perform an initial memory test before doing anything else. If there is the slightest possibility of an error in memory or of some other problem, the computer will tell you so.

If it does, take your computer down to the repair center for a quick checkup. Most of the time only one tiny memory chip will be the trouble, and you'll be back happily computing in no time.

Golly! These machines are smart!

B. BASIC Problems

Once the computer's checked itself out, you might still notice problems while programming in BASIC. If for some reason things just aren't working right, type:

```
PRINT FRE(Ø)
```

If there is no program loaded into memory, the answer should be somewhere around:

```
61109
```

Please note that this value will change with different releases of BASIC or machines with more than 256K of memory.

---

or the correct value previously noted for your system. If there is a program loaded, the answer should be some lesser value.

If the answer is too large (assuming, of course, you have not added more memory), there may be trouble. Or it's possible that the answer is a **negative** number. Trouble.

Possible Solution

In either of the above cases, shut the Computer OFF. (Or, as they say in the big time, "Take it all the way down.") Let it sit for a full minute before turning it on.

Yes, any program in memory will be lost, but at this point it's probably shot anyway. You could **try** to SAVE it before turning OFF the machine if it makes you feel any better.

Turn the machine back ON, and try the PRINT FRE(Ø) test again. If the results are the same, there is probably a chip failure that will require professional troubleshooting and replacement.

Video Monitor Problems?

The Video Monitor is very similar to its counterpart in a television set. It has adjustments for brightness and contrast on the front of the monitor.

Idiot Here -- What's Your Excuse?

Of course, **you** don't make silly mistakes!

Now that's settled,

1. Is everything plugged in? Correctly? Firmly?
2. Are the drive doors closed?
3. Is the printer turned ON and ON-Line?
4. Are you using "legal" commands?

If so go walk the dog, then check it all over again.

If...Then

If the trouble was not found in the cockpit or with the hardware, there is probably something wrong with the program. Dump out the troublesome program. LOAD in one that is known to work, and RUN it as a final hardware and operator check.

Common Errors

Here are some of the common sources of "computer-detected errors."

1. Assume the error is in a PRINT or INPUT statement.

   Did you:

   a. Forget one of the needed pair of quotation marks?
      EXAMPLE:

      ```
      10 PRINT "ANSWER IS, X : GOTO 5
      ```

      ERROR: No ending quotation mark after IS

Yes, I know it's Ok if the missing quote is the last character in the Line.

---

   b. Use an illegal variable name?
      EXAMPLE:

      ```
      10 INPUT 6G
      ```

      ERROR: Variable names must begin with a letter.

   c. Forget the Line number, accidentally mix a letter in with the number, or use a Line number larger than 65529?
      EXAMPLE:

      ```
      72B3 PRINT "BAD LINE NUMBER."
      ```

      ERROR (pointing to the B in 72B3)

   d. Accidentally have a double quotation mark in the text?
      EXAMPLE:

      ```
      10 PRINT "HE SAID "HELLO THERE."
      ```

   e. Type a Line more than 255 characters long?

   f. Misspell PRINT or INPUT **(It happens!).**

   g. Accidentally type a stray character in the Line especially an extra comma or semicolon?

QUIT GIVING ME THAT "TO ERR IS HUMAN" LINE OR I'LL PUNCH YOUR LIGHTS OUT!
TOUCHY, TOUCHY.

2. If the error is in a READ statement, almost all the previous possibilities apply, plus:

   a. Is there really a DATA statement for the Computer to read? Remember, it will only read a piece of DATA once unless it is RESTOREd.
   EXAMPLE:

   ```
   10 READ X,Y,Z

   20 DATA 2,5
   ```

   ERROR: There are only two numbers for the Computer to read. If we mean for Z to be zero, we must say so:

   ```
   20 DATA 2,5,0
   ```

   b. Does the DATA statement contain strings when READ expects numbers or vice versa?
   EXAMPLE:

   ```
   10 READ X,Y

   20 DATA "JAN","FEB"
   ```

   ERROR: X and Y are numeric variables, and the data are strings. If we want to READ strings, string variables are needed:

   ```
   10 READ X$,Y$
   ```

3. If the bad area is a FOR-NEXT loop, most of the previous possibilities apply, plus:

   a. Is there a NEXT statement to match the FOR?
   EXAMPLE:

   ```
   10 FOR A=1 TO N
   ```

   ERROR: Where's the NEXT A?

Some of these FOR-NEXT loop errors won't trigger actual error messages; the program may just wind up in an endless loop.

   b. Do you have all the requirements for a loop -- a starting point, an ending point, a variable name, and a STEP size if it's not 1?
   EXAMPLE:

   ```
   10 A=1 TO N
   ```

   ERROR: Must have a FOR and a NEXT.

c. Did you accidentally nest 2 loops using the same variable in both loops?
EXAMPLE:

```
10 FOR X=1 TO 5
20  FOR X=1 TO 3
30   PRINT X
40  NEXT X
50 NEXT X
```

ERROR: The nested loops must have different variables.

d. Does a variable in a loop have the same letter as the loop counter?
EXAMPLE:

```
10 A=22
20 FOR R=1 TO 5
30  R=18
40  Y=R*A
50  PRINT Y
60 NEXT R
```

ERROR: The value of R was changed by another R inside the loop, and NEXT R was overRUN since 18 is larger than 5.

e. Are the loops nested incorrectly with one not completely inside the other?
EXAMPLE:

```
10 FOR X=1 TO 6
20  FOR Y=1 TO 8
30   PRINT X,Y
40  NEXT X
50 NEXT Y
```

ERROR: NEXT Y must come before NEXT X.

4. If the goofed-up statement is an IF-THEN or GOTO, does the Line number specified by the THEN or GOTO really exist? Be

especially careful of this error when eliminating a Line in the process of "improving" or "cleaning up" a program.

5. The error comes back as "Out of memory," but PRINT FRE(0) indicates there is room left. If you are using an array and get an error, remember, **extra room (up to hundreds of bytes) has to be left for processing**. You have probably overrun the amount of *available memory*.

6. The ERROR comes back as "Subscript out of range." Did you forget to DIMension an array containing more than eleven elements?

7. The ERROR comes back as "Illegal function call." Did you exceed the limits of one of the built-in functions?

8. Did one of the *values* on the Line exceed the maximum or minimum size for numbers?

To find out whether you did any of these things, PRINT the values for all the variables used in the offending Line. If you still don't see the error, try carrying out the operations indicated on the Line. For example, the error may occur during a multiplication of two very large numbers.

PRINT the operation in calculator mode (no Line number).

These certainly aren't all the possible errors one can make, but at least they give some idea where to look first. Since we can't completely avoid silly errors, it's necessary to be able to recover from them as quickly as possible.

By the way ... a one-semester course in beginning typing can do wonders for your programming speed and typing accuracy.

From the Ridiculous to the Sublime:

All the Computer can tell us is that we have (or have not) followed all of its rules. Assuming we have, the Computer will not protest even if we're asking it to do something that's quite silly and not at all what we intended. It will dutifully put out garbage all day long if we feed it garbage -- even though we follow its rules. Remember GIGO?

GIGO stands for Garbage In, Garbage Out.

If the program has no obvious errors, what might be the matter?

Typical "unreported" errors are:

1. Accidentally reinitializing a variable -- particularly easy when using loops.
   EXAMPLE:

```
1Ø FOR N=1 TO 3
2Ø  READ A
3Ø  PRINT A
4Ø  RESTORE
5Ø NEXT N
6Ø DATA 1,2,3
```

2. Reversing conditions, i.e. using "=" when we mean "<>," or ">" when we mean "<."

3. Accidentally including "=," as in "≤," when we really mean only "<."

4. Confusing similarly named variables particularly the numeric variable A, the string variable A$, and the array variable A(X). **They are not at all related**.

5. Forgetting the order of program execution -- from left to right on each Line, but multiplications and divisions always have priority before additions and subtractions. Intrinsic functions (INT, RND, ABS, etc.) have priority over everything else.

6. Counting incorrectly in loops. `FOR I=Ø TO 7` causes the loop to be executed **eight**, not seven, times.

7. Using the same variable accidentally in two different places. This is okay if we don't need the old variable any more, but disastrous if we do. Be especially careful when combining programs or using the special subroutines.

But how do we spot these errors if the Computer doesn't point them out? Use common sense and let the Computer help. The rules are:

1. Isolate the error. Insert temporary "flags." Add STOP, END, and extra PRINT statements until you narrow the error down to one or two Lines.

   EXAMPLES OF USEFUL FLAGS:

   ```
   299 PRINT ,"LINE #299"
   399 IF X<0 THEN PRINT "X OUT OF RANGE AT
        #399" : STOP
   ```

   Line 299 checks whether the Line immediately following Line 299 is executed. Line 399 might be used to locate the point where X goes out of range.

   Although the details are different in every program, these techniques can be easily applied.

2. Make "tests" as simple as possible. Don't add "enhancements" until you've found the problem.

3. Check simple cases by hand to test the logic, but let the Computer do the hard work. Don't try to wade through complex calculations with pencil and paper. You'll introduce more new mistakes than you'll find. Use the calculator mode or a separate hand calculator for that work.

4. Remember that we can force the Computer to start a program at any Line number. Just type:

   `GOTO` (line number)

   This is a useful tool for working back through a program. Give the variables acceptable values using calculator-mode statements, then GOTO some point midway through the program. If the answers are what were expected, then the error is **before** the "test point." Otherwise, the error is after the test point.

5. Remember that it's not necessary to LIST the entire program just to look at the one section. Type:

`LIST` (line number)-(line number)

6. Practice *defensive programming*. Just because a program "runs okay," don't assume it's dependable. Programs that accept INPUT data and process it can be especially deceptive. Make a point of checking a new program at all the critical places.

   EXAMPLES: A square root program should be checked for INPUTs less than or equal to zero. Math functions should be checked at points where the function is undefined, such as TAN(90°).

Beware of Creeping Elegance

Programs grow more elegant with the ego reinforcement of the programmer. This "creeping elegance" increases the chance of silly errors. It's fun to let the mind wander and add some more program here and some more there, but it's also easy to lose sight of the program's purpose. It is at times like this when the flowchart is ignored, and the trouble begins. Nuff said.

Learned in Chapter 51

Miscellaneous

Defensive programming
Computer-detected errors
Flags
Hardware checkout procedures

Chasing Bugs

We have seen that the EDITor is a powerful aid in changing programs once we find out what is wrong. In this and the next Chapter we will learn how to use built-in diagnostic tools to help hunt down the errors.

TRON/TROFF

The simplicity and power of TRON/TROFF is awesome. Enter this NEW program:

```
10 FOR N = 1 TO 5
20  PRINT "SEE TRON RUN"
30 NEXT N
99 END
```

...and RUN to be sure it's OK.

Now, type:

`TRON` **ENTER** or just press **F7**

(which stands for TRacer ON), then RUN. The screen says:

```
[10][20]SEE TRON RUN
```

ME TRON/TROFF! YOU CALL, MASTER?
W-W-WELL, YES, YOU S-S-SEE THERE'S THIS B-B-BUG...

```
[30][20]SEE TRON RUN
[30][20]SEE TRON RUN
[30][20]SEE TRON RUN
[30][20]SEE TRON RUN
[30][99]
```

What Does It Mean?

The numbers between the [ ] are the program Line numbers. TRON traces the sequence of program execution and PRINTs each Line number as it is "hit." How's that for powerful?

Now type:

TROFF **ENTER** or just press **F8**

(for TRacer OFF) and RUN.

The tracing has stopped, and it's business as usual. TRON is the very essence of simplicity.

Since TRON and TROFF can be imbedded as program *statements* as well as used as BASIC *commands*, the possibilities for troubleshooting *program logic* are endless. Our little demonstration program can be enhanced by adding the following Lines and RUNning.

```
5 TRON
35 TROFF
```

Imagine its value in a program with dozens or even hundreds of program Lines all tangled up with IF-THEN's, ON-GOTO's, etc. The errors that drive us wild are those we can't see.

Learned in Chapter 52

Commands/Statements

TRON
TROFF

Chapter 53

Chasing the ERRORs

Tandy BASIC provides 53 different ERROR messages numbered 1-30 for the Elementary and Intermediate BASIC we have learned, and some between 50-77 for Disk BASIC. There are so many we need a separate Chapter plus an Appendix just to understand what they mean.

Let's quietly tiptoe into the hall of ERRORs by typing this NEW little test program:

```
10 REM * TESTING ERROR CODES *
20 INPUT"CHECK WHICH ERROR CODE";N
30 ERROR N
```

RUN the program a number of times (entering numbers between 1 and 77) forcing the Computer to PRINT out the message for various types of ERRORs. Don't waste time trying to understand them now. You can study them in detail in Appendix C.

The only new BASIC word is in Line 30. ERROR has little use in life except as above, PRINTing the Error Code from its code number.

ERROR Trapping

The ON ERROR GOTO statement is of more value. It is used when we think we're on the trail of a specific type of ERROR, but are not sure.

ERROR CODES

Code	Error
1	NEXT without FOR
2	Syntax error
3	RETURN without GOSUB
4	Out of DATA
5	Illegal function call
6	Overflow
7	Out of memory
8	Undefined line number
9	Subscript out of range
10	Duplicate Definition
11	Division by zero
12	Illegal direct
13	Type mismatch
14	Out of string space
15	String too long
16	String formula too complex
17	Can't continue
18	Undefined user function
19	No RESUME
20	RESUME without error
21	Unprintable error
22	Missing operand
23	Line buffer overflow
24	Device Timeout
25	Device Fault
26	FOR without NEXT
27	Out of Paper
29	WHILE without WEND
30	WEND without WHILE
	DISK ERRORS
50	FIELD overflow
51	Internal error
52	Bad file number
53	File not found
54	Bad file mode
55	File already open
57	Device I/O Error
58	File already exists
61	Disk full

Code	Error
62	Input past end
63	Bad record number
64	Bad file name
66	Direct statement in file
67	Too many files
68	Device Unavailable
69	Communication buffer overflow
70	Permission Denied/Disk write protected
71	Disk not Ready
72	Disk media error
73	Advanced Feature
74	Rename across disks
75	Path/File Access Error
76	Path not found
77	Deadlock

Suppose we suspect that someplace in the program there is an accidental square rooting of a negative number, and it's goofing up the results. Type in this NEW test program:

```
10 CLS : ON ERROR GOTO 70
20 PRINT
30 INPUT "FIND THE SQUARE ROOT OF";N
40 A = SQR(N)
50 PRINT "SQUARE ROOT OF";N;"=";A
60 GOTO 30
70 BEEP
80 PRINT "SQR ROOT OF NEGATIVE IS ILLEGAL!"
99 END
```

...and RUN.

21?, 21??
THAT'S AN UNPRINT-
ABLE ERROR!! I'LL
HAVE YOU REMEMBER,
SIR, THIS IS A G-RATED
BOOK!

Try positive values and 0, then try a negative value.

ON ERROR GOTO is acting much as our old friend ON X GOTO did, so there are no big surprises here.

Change Line 10 to a REM Line and try assorted values ending with a negative number. Again, no big surprise. An ERROR message was delivered pinpointing both the nature and location of the ERROR, and execution was terminated. Lines 70 and 80 were **not** executed, however.

Change Line 10 back to:

```
10 CLS : ON ERROR GOTO 70
```

and add:

```
90 RESUME 20
```

...and RUN with various values including negative ones.

Although the Computer was forced to operate with an ERROR (negative square root), execution did not terminate. The ERROR message was delivered, but the Computer kept on going, thanks to RESUME. This is the essence of good ERROR trapping -- identifying the ERROR without "crashing" the program. There may be several interrelated ERRORs that can be found easily only by continuing the RUN.

Change Line 90 to:

```
90 RESUME NEXT
```

...and RUN.

Although the results are similar to those obtained with:

```
RESUME 20
```

there is a subtle difference.

RESUME NEXT causes execution to RESUME at the NEXT Line immediately following the Line which made the ERROR. Thus Line 50 is PRINTed even though (in this case) it gives a wrong answer. RESUME 20 directed execution to a very specific Line. With a little head-scratching, we can quickly see how both of these features are useful in difficult debugging situations.

Next, change Line 90 to:

```
90 RESUME
```

...and RUN.

As we see and hear, RESUME by itself (or RESUME 0) sends execution back to the Line in which the ERROR is being made. The Computer keeps trying to take the square root of the same negative number. (If you are having difficulty visualizing what is taking place in any of these examples, turn on TRON, and read the road map.)

ERL

Change Line 90 back to:

```
90 RESUME 20
```

and add:

```
85 PRINT "ERROR IS IN LINE #";ERL
```

...and RUN.

The program now informs us that the

```
ERROR IS IN LINE # 40
```

ERL is a *reserved word* that PRINTs the **Line number** in which the ERROR occurs. For my money, this little jewel in combination with ON ERROR GOTO to snag 'em and RESUME NEXT (or RESUME Line number) to keep the program from crashing makes this whole hassle worthwhile.

ERR

A final esoteric touch may be obtained by adding the ERR (not ERL) statement. ERR produces the ERROR code number.

We've gone almost full cycle. Add Line 87:

```
87 PRINT "AND ERROR CODE IS";ERR
```

...and RUN.

More Variations on the Theme

BASIC allows us to assign our own Error Codes. These could be used to stop the user from doing something that the Computer would normally allow. Try this program:

```
10 REM THIS DEMONSTRATES HOW TO DEFINE ERROR CODES
20 ON ERROR GOTO 100
30 FOR I = 1 TO 20
40  IF I = 3 THEN ERROR 120
50  REM SET ERROR CODE TO 120 IF I = 3
55  PRIMT
60 NEXT I
100 REM THIS IS THE ERROR HANDLING ROUTINE.
110 IF ERR = 120 THEN PRINT
120 IF ERR <> 120 THEN PRINT "ERROR"; ERR; "PLEASE FIX"
130 RESUME NEXT
```

This program assigns the Error Code 120, which we chose, to the condition I=3. When we assign the error code, the ON ERROR traps it, and our error handling routine is executed. The Syntax Error in Line 55 is also caught by the ON ERROR test, and the other line in our Error Routine is executed.

A very useful application of ERROR traps allows the program to automatically LIST the program if there is an ERROR. It requires the addition of 2 temporary program Lines using all 3 ERROR statements.

From Appendix C (which covers the Error messages) comes an example of what happens when there is an ERROR in a FOR-NEXT loop. Type in:

```
NEW
10 FOR A = 1 TO 5
20  PRINT "THERE IS NO 'NEXT A'"
30 NEXT Z
```

...and RUN.

The Computer responds with:

```
NEXT without FOR in 30
```

There is a FOR-NEXT error in Line 30. Add the following Lines to approximate the same result, plus cause an automatic program LISTing:

```
5 ON ERROR GOTO 100          (to 'set' the ERROR trap)
99 END                       (to END execution if all is well)
100 PRINT ERL,ERR : LIST
```

Line 100 PRINTs the Line number of the ERROR and the ERROR code (found in Appendix C) and LISTs the program (or LIST (line number)-(line number)).

Try this "trapping and reporting" routine. If all is well in the program, nothing will be different. If there is an ERROR, it will be trapped and reported on the screen. Can you think of ways to make the "reporting" more elegant?

EXERCISE 53-1: Enter the following NEW program:

```
20 CLS
30 FOR I=1 TO 10
40  X = RND(21) : F = X-10/X
50  PRINT I,"X=" X,"F(X)= "F;
```

(continued)

```
60  IF F<0 THEN PUNT ELSE PRINT
70  IF X = 20 THEN READ A
80 NEXT I
90 INPUT "PRESS ENTER TO CONTINUE";Z : GOTO 20
```

Write an ERROR trapping routine that recovers from both ERRORs and PRINTs:

```
OUT OF DATA ERROR IN LINE NUMBER
SYNTAX ERROR IN LINE NUMBER
```
or as appropriate.

HINT -- Syntax error is code 2, and Out of DATA is code 4.

Learned in Chapter 53

Statements	Functions	Miscellaneous
ERROR	ERL	Error codes
ON ERROR GOTO	ERR	
RESUME		

SECTION B

ANSWERS TO EXERCISES

SAMPLE ANSWER FOR EXERCISE 4-1:

EDIT 10 ENTER	
Tap ⇨ 4 times	Move four spaces right
R	new character
Hold CTRL & tap ⇨ 3 times	Move to beginning of third word over
Tap DELETE 7 times	DELETE next 7 characters (including one space)
Hold CTRL & tap ⇨ 1 time	Move to beginning of next word
Tap DELETE 4 times	DELETE next 3 characters and 1 space
Tap ⇨ 2 times	Move two spaces right
MPUT	new characters
Hold CTRL & tap ⇨ 1 time	Move to beginning of next word
Tap ⇨ 5 times	Move 5 spaces right
AM	new characters
ENTER	Save the changes & leave EDITor mode
LIST	LIST edited line for inspection

SAMPLE ANSWER FOR EXERCISE 7-1:

```
50 PRINT D
```

SAMPLE RUN FOR EXERCISE 7-1:

```
6000
```

Note: You may have used a different Line number in your answer, but the way to get the answer PRINTed on the screen is by using the PRINT statement. If you didn't get it right the first time, don't be discouraged. Type in Line 50 above and RUN the program. Then return to Chapter 7 and continue.

SAMPLE ANSWER FOR EXERCISE 7-2:

```
10 REM * TIME SOLUTION KNOWING DISTANCE AND RATE *
20 D = 6000
30 R = 500
40 T = D / R
50 PRINT "THE TIME REQUIRED IS";T;"HOURS."
```

Note: Remember to ENTER each Line.

SAMPLE RUN FOR EXERCISE 7-2:

```
THE TIME REQUIRED IS 12 HOURS.
```

Note: In order to arrive at the formula in Line 40, it is necessary to transpose D = R * T and express in terms of T.

SAMPLE ANSWER FOR EXERCISE 7-3:

```
10 REM * CIRCUMFERENCE SOLUTION *
20 P = 3.14
30 D = 35
40 C = P * D
50 PRINT "THE CIRCLE'S CIRCUMFERENCE IS";C;"FEET."
```

SAMPLE RUN FOR EXERCISE 7-3:

```
THE CIRCLE'S CIRCUMFERENCE IS 109.9 FEET.
```

Note: Since pi is not included in our BASIC, we have to set a variable (in this case P was used) equal to the value pi (3.14).

SAMPLE ANSWER FOR EXERCISE 7-4:

```
10 REM * CIRCULAR AREA SOLUTION *
20 P = 3.14
30 R = 5
40 A = P * R * R
50 PRINT "THE CIRCLE'S AREA IS";A;"SQUARE INCHES."
```

SAMPLE RUN FOR EXERCISE 7-4:

```
THE CIRCLE'S AREA IS 78.5 SQUARE INCHES.
```

Note: Some BASICs do not have a function which means "raise to the power" to handle R^2 (our BASIC does). In easy cases like this one, we can simply use R times R (R*R). You'll learn how to use the simple EXPONENTIATION function as we proceed.

SAMPLE ANSWER FOR EXERCISE 7-5:

```
10 B = 225
20 C = 17 + 35 + 225
30 D = 40 + 200
40 N = B - C + D
50 PRINT "YOUR NEW BALANCE IS $";N
```

SAMPLE RUN FOR EXERCISE 7-5:

```
YOUR NEW BALANCE IS $ 188
```

SAMPLE ANSWER FOR EXERCISE 8-1:

```
10 REM * CAR MILES SOLUTION PROGRAM *
20 N = 1000000
30 D = 10000
40 T = N * D
50 PRINT "THE TOTAL NUMBER OF MILES DRIVEN IS";T
```

SAMPLE RUN FOR EXERCISE 8-1:

```
THE TOTAL NUMBER OF MILES DRIVEN IS 1E+10
```

Note: As discussed earlier, the answer is the number 1 followed by ten zeros, 10,000,000,000, Ten Billion. The Computer will not store a number in a variable over 9,999,999 without converting it to exponential notation.

SAMPLE ANSWER FOR EXERCISE 9-1:

```
10 REM * FAHRENHEIT TO CELSIUS CONVERSION *
20 F = 65
30 C = (F-32) * (5/9)
40 PRINT F;"DEGREES FAHRENHEIT =";C;"DEGREES CELSIUS."
```

SAMPLE RUN FOR EXERCISE 9-1:

```
65 DEGREES FAHRENHEIT = 18.33333 DEGREES CELSIUS.
```

Observe carefully how the parentheses were placed. As a general rule, when in doubt -- use parentheses. The worst they can do is slow down calculating the answer by a few millionths of a second.

SAMPLE ANSWER FOR EXERCISE 9-2:

```
30 C = F - 32 * (5 / 9)
```

SAMPLE RUN FOR EXERCISE 9-2:

```
65 DEGREES FAHRENHEIT = 47.22222 DEGREES CELSIUS.
```

Note how silently and dutifully the Computer came up with the wrong answer. It has done as we directed, and we directed it wrong. A common phrase in computer circles is GIGO (pronounced "gee-goe"). It stands for "Garbage In - Garbage Out." We have given the Computer garbage, and it gave it back to us by way of a wrong answer. Phrased another way, "Never in the history of mankind has there been a machine capable of making so many mistakes so rapidly and confidently." A computer is worthless unless it is programmed correctly.

SAMPLE ANSWER FOR EXERCISE 9-3:

```
30 C = (F - 32) * 5 / 9
```

SAMPLE RUN FOR EXERCISE 9-3:

```
65 DEGREES FAHRENHEIT = 18.33333 DEGREES CELSIUS.
```

SAMPLE ANSWER FOR EXERCISE 9-4:

Two possible answers:

```
30 - (9 - 8) - (7 - 6) = 28
30 - (9 - (8 - (7 - 6))) = 28
```

Sample programs:

```
10 A = 30 - (9 - (8 - (7 - 6)))
20 PRINT A
```

Or Line 10 might be

```
10 A = 30 - (9 - 8) - (7 - 6)
```

Try a few on your own.

SAMPLE ANSWER FOR EXERCISE 10-1:

```
10 A = 5
20 IF A <> 5 THEN 50
30 PRINT "A EQUALS 5."
40 END
50 PRINT "A DOES NOT EQUAL 5."
```

SAMPLE RUN FOR EXERCISE 10-1:

```
A EQUALS 5.
```

SAMPLE ANSWER FOR EXERCISE 10-2:

```
10 A = 6
20 IF A <> 5 THEN 50
30 PRINT "A EQUALS 5."
40 END
50 PRINT "A DOES NOT EQUAL 5."
60 IF A < 5 THEN 90
70 PRINT "A IS LARGER THAN 5."
80 END
90 PRINT "A IS SMALLER THAN 5."
```

SAMPLE RUN FOR EXERCISE 10-2:

```
A DOES NOT EQUAL 5.
A IS LARGER THAN 5.
```

Note: We had to put in another END statement (Line 80) to keep the program from running on to Line 90 after PRINTing Line 70.

SAMPLE ANSWER FOR EXERCISE 15-1:

```
1 CLS
2 INPUT "HOW MANY SECONDS DELAY DO YOU WISH";S
3 P = 680
4 D = S * P
5 FOR X = 1 TO D
6 NEXT X
7 PRINT "DELAY IS OVER.  TOOK";S;"SECONDS."
```

Change the value of P in Line 3 according to your computer:

1000 SX	P = 820
2000	P = 2000
3000s	P = 2800

Explanation:

Line 2	used the INPUT statement to obtain desired delay, S, in seconds.
Line 3	defined P, the number of passes required to for a one second delay. Check it against your watch for accuracy.
Line 4	multiplied the delay for one second times the number of seconds desired and called that product D.
Line 5	began the FOR-NEXT loop from 1 to whatever is required.
Line 6	is the other half of the loop.
Line 7	reported the end of the delay and printed S, the number of seconds. Obviously, S is only as accurate as the program itself since it merely copies the value of S you entered in Line 2.

SAMPLE ANSWER FOR EXERCISE 15-2:

```
60 PRINT "RATE", "TIME"
65 PRINT "(MPH)","(HOURS)"
```

If you honestly had trouble with this one, better go back and start all over because you've missed the real basics.

SAMPLE ANSWER FOR EXERCISE 15-3:

```
5 CLS
10 PRINT "   ***   S A L A R Y   R A T E   C H A R T   ***"
20 PRINT
30 PRINT "YEAR","MONTH","WEEK","DAY"
```

```
40 PRINT
50 FOR Y = 5000 TO 25000 STEP 1000
55  REM * CONVERT YEARLY INCOME INTO MONTHLY *
60  M = Y / 12
65  REM * CONVERT YEARLY INCOME INTO WEEKLY *
70  W = Y / 52
75  REM * CONVERT WEEKLY INCOME INTO DAILY *
80  D = W / 5
100  PRINT Y,M,W,D
110 NEXT Y
```

SAMPLE RUN FOR EXERCISE 15-3:

```
   ***   S A L A R Y   R A T E   C H A R T   ***

YEAR          MONTH          WEEK          DAY

 5000          416.6667       96.15384      19.23077
 6000          500            115.3846      23.07692
 7000          583.3333       134.6154      26.92308
 8000          666.6667       153.8462      30.76923
etc.
```

SAMPLE ANSWER FOR EXERCISE 15-4:

```
10 R = .01
20 D = 1
30 T = .01
35 CLS
40 PRINT "DAY","DAILY","TOTAL"
50 PRINT " #","RATE","EARNED"
60 PRINT
70 PRINT D,R,T
80 IF R > 1000000! THEN END
90 R = R * 2
100 D = D + 1
110 T = T + R
120 GOTO 70
```

SAMPLE RUN FOR EXERCISE 15-4:

```
DAY         DAILY        TOTAL
 #          RATE         EARNED

 1           .01          .01
 2           .02          .03
 3           .04          .07
 4           .08          .15
 5           .16          .31
 6           .32          .63
```
etc.

SAMPLE ANSWER FOR EXERCISE 15-5:

```
5 CLS
10 PRINT "WIRE FENCE","LENGTH","WIDTH","AREA"
20 PRINT " (FEET)","(FEET)","(FEET)","(SQ. FEET)"
30 F = 1000
40 FOR L = 0 TO 500 STEP 50
50  W = (F - 2 * L ) / 2
60  A = L * W
70  PRINT F,L,W,A
80 NEXT L
```

SAMPLE RUN FOR EXERCISE 15-5:

```
WIRE FENCE     LENGTH         WIDTH          AREA
 (FEET)        (FEET)         (FEET)         (SQ. FEET)
 1000           0              500            0
 1000           50             450            22500
 1000           100            400            40000
 1000           150            350            52500
 1000           200            300            60000
```
etc.

ADDENDUM TO EXERCISE 15-5:

Here's a program that lets the Computer do the comparing:

```
5 CLS
9 REM * SET MAXIMUM AREA AT ZERO *
10 M = 0
14 REM * SET DESIRED LENGTH AT ZERO *
15 N = 0
19 REM * F IS TOTAL FEET OF FENCE AVAILABLE *
20 F = 1000
24 REM * L IS LENGTH OF ONE SIDE OF RECTANGLE *
25 FOR L = 0 TO 500 STEP 50
29  REM * W IS WIDTH OF ONE SIDE OF RECTANGLE *
30  W = (F - 2 * L) / 2
35  A = W * L
39  REM * COMPARE WITH A CURRENT MAXIMUM, REPLACE IF NECESSARY *
40  IF A <= M THEN GOTO 55
45  M = A
49  REM * ALSO UPDATE CURRENT DESIRED LENGTH *
50  N = L
55 NEXT L
60 PRINT "FOR LARGEST AREA USE THESE DIMENSIONS:"
65 PRINT N;"FT. BY";500-N;"FT. FOR TOTAL AREA OF";M;"SQ. FT."
```

SAMPLE ANSWER FOR OPTIONAL EXERCISE 15-6:

```
10 REM * FINDS OPTIMUM LOAD TO SOURCE MATCH *
20 CLS
30 PRINT "LOAD","CIRCUIT","SOURCE","LOAD"
40 PRINT "RESISTANCE","POWER","POWER","POWER"
50 PRINT "(OHMS)","(WATTS)","(WATTS)","(WATTS)"
60 PRINT
70 FOR R = 1 TO 20
80  I = 120 / (10 + R)
90  C = I * I * (10 + R)
100  S = I * I * 10
110  L = I * I * R
120  PRINT R,C,S,L
130 NEXT R
```

SAMPLE RUN FOR OPTIONAL EXERCISE 15-6:

LOAD RESISTANCE (OHMS)	CIRCUIT POWER (WATTS)	SOURCE POWER (WATTS)	LOAD POWER (WATTS)
1	1309.091	1190.083	119.0083
2	1200	1000	200
3	1107.692	852.071	255.6213
4	1028.571	734.6939	293.8775
5	960	640	320
6	900	562.5	337.5
7	847.0588	498.2699	348.7889
8	800	444.4445	355.5556
9	757.8947	398.892	359.0028
10	720	360	360
11	685.7143	326.5306	359.1837

etc.

SAMPLE ANSWER FOR EXERCISE 16-1:

```
10 PRINT "THE              TOTAL            SPENT"
20 PRINT "BUDGET","YEAR'S","THIS"
30 PRINT "CATEGORY";TAB(15);"BUDGET";TAB(29);"MONTH"
```

SAMPLE ANSWER FOR EXERCISE 16-2:

```
30 PRINT " YEAR";TAB(18);"MONTH";TAB(32);"WEEK";
40 PRINT TAB(47);"DAY";TAB(60);"HOUR"
85 REM * CONVERT WEEKLY INCOME INTO HOURLY *
90 H = W / 40
100 PRINT Y,M,W,D,H
```

SAMPLE RUN FOR EXERCISE 16-2:

```
      ***   S A L A R Y   R A T E   C H A R T   ***
```

YEAR	MONTH	WEEK	DAY	HOUR
5000	416.6667	96.15384	19.23077	2.403846
6000	500	115.3846	23.07692	2.884616
7000	583.3333	134.6154	26.92308	3.365385
8000	666.6667	153.8462	30.76923	3.846154
9000	750	173.0769	34.61538	4.326923
10000	833.3333	192.3077	38.46154	4.807693
11000	916.6667	211.5385	42.3077	5.288462
12000	1000	230.7692	46.15385	5.769231
13000	1083.333	250	50	6.25

etc.

SAMPLE ANSWER FOR EXERCISE 16-3:

```
30 PRINT "INTER";TAB(10);"LOAD";TAB(21);"CIRCUIT";
35 PRINT TAB(36);"SOURCE";TAB(51);"LOAD"
40 PRINT "RESIST";TAB(10);"RESIST";TAB(21);"POWER";
45 PRINT TAB(36);"POWER";TAB(51);"POWER"
50 PRINT "(OHMS)";TAB(10);"(OHMS)";TAB(21);"(WATTS)";
55 PRINT TAB(36);"(WATTS)";TAB(51);"(WATTS)"
120 PRINT "  10";TAB(11);R;TAB(20);C;TAB(35);S;TAB(50);L
```

SAMPLE RUN FOR EXERCISE 16-3:

INTER RESIST (OHMS)	LOAD RESIST (OHMS)	CIRCUIT POWER (WATTS)	SOURCE POWER (WATTS)	LOAD POWER (WATTS)
10	1	1309.091	1190.083	119.0083
10	2	1200	1000	200
10	3	1107.692	852.071	255.6213
10	4	1028.571	734.6939	293.8775
10	5	960	640	320
10	6	900	562.5	337.5
10	7	847.0588	498.2699	348.7889
10	8	800	444.4445	355.5556

etc.

SAMPLE ANSWER FOR EXERCISE 17-1:

```
10 FOR A = 1 TO 3
20  PRINT "A LOOP"
30   FOR B = 1 TO 2
40    PRINT ,"B LOOP"
42     FOR C = 1 TO 4
44      PRINT ,,"C LOOP"
48     NEXT C
50   NEXT B
60 NEXT A
```

SAMPLE ANSWER FOR EXERCISE 17-2:

The program will be the same as the answer to Exercise 17-1 with the following additions:

```
45          FOR D = 1 TO 5
46           PRINT ,,,"D LOOP"
47          NEXT
```

Note: To get the full impact of this "4-deep" nesting, stop the RUN frequently to examine the nesting relationships between each of the loops.

SAMPLE ANSWER FOR EXERCISE 18-1:

Addition of the following single Line gives a nice clean PRINTout with all the values "rounded" to their integer value:

```
55  A = INT(A)
```

Worth all the effort to learn it, wasn't it?

SAMPLE ANSWER FOR EXERCISE 18-2:

```
55  A = INT(10 * A ) / 10
```

When 3.14159 was multiplied times 10, it became 31.4159. The INTeger value of 31.4159 is 31. 31 divided by 10 is 3.1, etc.

SAMPLE ANSWER FOR EXERCISE 18-3:

This was almost too easy.

```
55  A = INT(100 * A) / 100
```

SAMPLE ANSWER FOR EXERCISE 19-1:

```
10 INPUT "TYPE ANY NUMBER";X
20 T = SGN(X)
30 ON T+2 GOTO 50,70,90
40 END
50 PRINT "THE NUMBER IS NEGATIVE."
60 END
70 PRINT "THE NUMBER IS ZERO."
80 END
90 PRINT "THE NUMBER IS POSITIVE."
```

SAMPLE ANSWER FOR EXERCISE 20-2:

Make this change to Line 30 in the Craps program and add the following subroutine:

```
30 CLS : COSUB 10010
10000 REM * RANDOMIZER ROUTINE *
10010 RANDOMIZE VAL(RIGHT$(TIME$,2))
10020 RETURN
```

SAMPLE ANSWER FOR EXERCISE 23-1:

```
10 PRINT CHR$(84);CHR$(65);CHR$(78);CHR$(68);CHR$(89)
```

SAMPLE ANSWER FOR EXERCISE 23-2:

```
10 INPUT "ENTER A NUMBER";A$
20 A = ASC(A$)
30 IF A<48 THEN 10
40 IF A>57 THEN 10
50 PRINT "ASCII VALUE OF ";A$;" IS";A
```

SAMPLE ANSWER FOR EXERCISE 24-1:

```
10 CLS
20 INPUT "FIRST STRING";A$
30 INPUT "SECOND STRING";B$
40 PRINT : PRINT "ALPHABETICAL ORDER:"
50 IF A$<B$ THEN PRINT A$,B$ : END
60 PRINT B$,A$
```

SAMPLE ANSWER FOR EXERCISE 25-1:

```
10 CLS
20 INPUT "INPUT STRING";A$
30 IF LEN(A$)>10 THEN PRINT "THE 10 CHARACTER
   LIMIT WAS EXCEEDED."
```

SAMPLE ANSWER FOR EXERCISE 25-2:

```
10 CLS
20 INPUT "ENTER PASSWORD";A$
30 FOR X=1 TO 11
40  READ N
50  P$ = P$ + CHR$(N)
60 NEXT X
70 IF A$ = P$ THEN 100
80 PRINT "WRONG PASSWORD, TRY AGAIN!"
90 GOTO 20
100 PRINT "CORRECT PASSWORD, YOU MAY ENTER"
110 DATA 79,80,69,78,32,83,69,83,65,77,69
```

SAMPLE ANSWER FOR EXERCISE 26-1:

```
10 CLS
20 INPUT "INPUT YOUR STREET ADDRESS";A$
30 A = VAL(A$)
40 PRINT: PRINT "YOUR NEIGHBOR'S STREET NUMBER IS ";A+4
50 PRINT : LIST
```

SAMPLE ANSWER FOR EXERCISE 26-2:

```
10 CLS
20 FOR X = 101 TO 120
30  A$ = STR$(X)
40  PRINT A$+"WT",
50 NEXT X
60 PRINT : LIST
```

SAMPLE RUN FOR EXERCISE 26-2:

```
101WT      102WT      103WT      104WT      105WT
106WT      107WT      108WT      109WT      110WT
111WT      112WT      113WT      114WT      115WT
116WT      117WT      118WT      119WT      120WT
```

SAMPLE ANSWER FOR EXERCISE 27-1:

```
10 CLS
20 INPUT "ISN'T THIS A SMART COMPUTER";A$
30 B$ = LEFT$(A$,1)
40 IF B$ = "Y" THEN PRINT "AFFIRMATIVE":END
50 IF B$ = "N" THEN PRINT "NEGATIVE":END
60 PRINT "THIS IS A YES OR NO QUESTION"
70 GOTO 20
```

SAMPLE ANSWER FOR EXERCISE 27-2:

```
10 CLS : MAX$ = ""
20 FOR I = 1 TO 3
30  READ A$
40  N$ = MID$(A$,2,3)
50  IF N$>MAX$ THEN MAX$ = N$: P$ = A$
60 NEXT I
70 PRINT "THE PART NUMBER WITH THE LARGEST NUMERIC
PORTION IS ";P$
80 PRINT : LIST
90 DATA N106WT,A208FM,Z154DX
```

SAMPLE ANSWER FOR EXERCISE 27-3:

Choice C. P-

SAMPLE ANSWER FOR EXERCISE 27-4:

```
1 CLS
10 A$ = STRING$(30,42)
20 PRINT TAB(40-LEN(A$)/2);A$
30 PRINT : LIST
```

SAMPLE ANSWER FOR EXERCISE 28-1:

```
10 CLS
20 PRINT "DATE: ";DATE$,;
30 PRINT "TIME: ";TIME$
40 GOTO 10
```

SAMPLE ANSWER FOR EXERCISE 30-1:

```
10 CLS
20 A = 5 : B = 12
30 C = SQR(A^2 + B^2)
40 PRINT "THE SQUARE ROOT OF";A;
50 PRINT "SQUARED PLUS";B;"SQUARED IS";C
60 PRINT : LIST
```

SAMPLE ANSWER FOR EXERCISE 30-2:

```
10 INPUT "ENTER A NUMBER";N
20 PRINT "LOG (EXP (";N;") ) =";LOG(EXP(N))
30 PRINT "EXP (LOG (";N;") ) =";EXP(LOG(N))
40 PRINT
50 GOTO 10
```

SAMPLE ANSWER FOR EXERCISE 35-1:

```
A) 50 U$ = "####,##     "
B) 50 U$ = "$#####,##    "
C) 50 U$ = "$$####,##    "
D) 50 U$ = "$$,###,##    "
E) 50 U$ = "**$,###,##   "
```

SAMPLE ANSWER FOR EXERCISE 35-2:

```
10 CLS : PRINT TAB(26)"CREDITS    TAX     TOTAL"
20 FOR I = 1 TO 3
30  READ A$,X,Y,Z
39  REM    12345678901234567890123456789012345678901
40  U$ = "\        17        \   7   ##.##   5   .##   5
    ##.##"
50  PRINT USING U$; A$,X,Y,Z
60 NEXT I
70 READ A$,N
79 REM    1234567
80 V$ = "\ 2 \  4   ###.##"
90 PRINT TAB(36);:PRINT USING V$;A$,N
100 DATA ASTRAL COMPUTER, 18.30, .70, 19.00
110 DATA BIOFEEDBACK ADAPTER, 1.80,  00, 1.80
120 DATA PERSONALITY MODULE, 7.20, .30, 7.50
130 DATA "DUE:", 28.30
```

SAMPLE ANSWER FOR EXERCISE 36-1:

```
10 CLS
20 A$ = "REVENUES" : B$ = "EXPENSES" : C$ = "ASSETS"
30 U$ = "   6   \     10     \   7    \    7    \       12        \
       4       \"
40 PRINT USING U$; A$,B$,C$
50 A# = 1203104.22# : B# = 560143.8# : C = 0
60 V$ = "######,###.## 8 spaces ####,###.##   8 spaces
         #####,###.##-"
70 PRINT USING V$; A#,C,A#
80 PRINT USING V$; C,B#,-B#
90 PRINT : LIST
```

SAMPLE ANSWER FOR EXERCISE 39-1:

Add or change the following Lines:

```
10 DIM A(210) : CLS
20 INPUT "WHICH CAR TO EXAMINE ";W
30 FOR L = 1 TO 10
40  READ A(L)
50 NEXT L
60 FOR S = 101 TO 110
```

```
70  READ A(S)
80 NEXT S
90 FOR B = 201 TO 210
100  READ A(B)
110 NEXT B
130 PRINT
140 PRINT "CAR#","ENG. SIZE","COLOR","BODY STYLE"
150 PRINT W,A(W),A(W+100),A(W+200)
200 DATA 300,200,500,300,200
210 DATA 300,400,400,300,500
220 DATA 3,1,4,3,2,4,3,2,1,3
230 DATA 20,20,10,20,30,20,30,10,20,20
```

SAMPLE ANSWER FOR EXERCISE 39-2:

Delete Lines 500 - 540, and change Line 30 to:

```
30 FOR C=1 TO 52 : A(C)=C : NEXT C
```

SAMPLE ANSWER FOR EXERCISE 40-1:

Change Line 50 to:

```
50 IF A$(F) >= A$(S) THEN 90 'TEST FOR LARGER ASCII #
```

Another approach is to reverse the order of printing:

```
110 FOR D=N TO 1 STEP-1 : PRINT A$(D), : NEXT D
```

but that's not what we had in mind.

SAMPLE ANSWER FOR EXERCISE 41-1:

```
10 CLS
20 FOR E=1 TO 4
30  FOR D=1 TO 3
40  REM ENTRY DATA: NAME, NUMBER, $$$$
50  READ R$(E,D)
60  PRINT R$(E,D),
70  NEXT D : PRINT
80 NEXT E : PRINT
1000 REM * DATA FILE *
```

```
1010 DATA "JONES, C.", 10439, 100.00
1020 DATA "ROTH, J.", 10023, 87.24
1030 DATA "BAKER, H.", 12936, 398.34
1040 DATA "HARMON, D.", 10422, 23.17
```

SAMPLE ANSWER FOR EXERCISE 41-2:

Add:

```
100 REM *** SORT ***
110 FOR F=1 TO 3
120  FOR S=F+1 TO 4
130   IF R$(F,1) <= R$(S,1) THEN 190
140    FOR J =1 TO 3
150     T$ = R$(F,J)
160     R$(F,J) = R$(S,J)
170     R$(S,J) = T$
180    NEXT J
190  NEXT S
200 NEXT F
210 PRINT : PRINT "ALPHA SORT" : PRINT
220 FOR E=1 TO 4
230   FOR D=1 TO 3
240    PRINT R$(E,D),
250   NEXT D : PRINT
260 NEXT E : PRINT
```

Or using SWAP, replace Lines 150, 160, and 170 in the above program with:

```
160 SWAP R$(F,J),R$(S,J)
```

SAMPLE ANSWER FOR EXERCISE 41-3:

Change these lines:

```
130  IF VAL(R$(F,3)) <= VAL(R$(S,3)) THEN 190
210 PRINT : PRINT "NUMERIC SORT": PRINT
```

SAMPLE ANSWER FOR EXERCISE 45-1:

```
10 OPEN "SHOPPING" FOR OUTPUT AS 1
20 FOR X = 1 TO 5
30  PRINT "ENTER ITEM #";X;
40  INPUT A$
```

```
50  PRINT #1,A$
60 NEXT X
70CLOSE
```

SAMPLE ANSWER FOR EXERCISE 45-2:

```
80 OPEN "SHOPPING" FOR INPUT AS 1
90 FOR X = 1 TO 5
100  INPUT #1,A$
110  PRINT "ITEM #";X;"IS ";A$
120 NEXT X
130 CLOSE
```

SAMPLE ANSWER FOR EXERCISE 45-3:

```
10 OPEN "NAMEAGE" FOR OUTPUT AS 1
20 INPUT "ENTER A NAME OR 'DONE' TO END";N$
30 IF N$ = "DONE" THEN 80
40 PRINT #1,N$
50 INPUT "HOW OLD IS HE/SHE";A
60 PRINT #1,A
70 GOTO 20
80 CLOSE 1
90 OPEN "NAMEAGE" FOR INPUT AS 1
100 IF EOF(1) THEN 140
110 INPUT #1,N$,A
120 PRINT N$," IS";A;"YEARS OLD"
130 GOTO 100
140 CLOSE
```

SAMPLE ANSWER FOR EXERCISE 48-1:

```
10 INPUT "IS GATE 'X' OPEN";A$
20 INPUT "IS GATE 'Y' OPEN";B$
30 INPUT "IS GATE 'Z' OPEN";C$
40 PRINT
50 IF A$="Y" OR B$="Y" OR C$="Y" THEN 80
60 PRINT "OLD BESSIE IS SECURE IN PASTURE #1"
70 END
80 PRINT "A GATE IS OPEN. OLD BESSIE IS FREE TO ROAM."
```

SAMPLE ANSWER FOR EXERCISE 50-1:

```
10 REM * TEST GRADER *
20 CLS
30 PRINT "THIS IS A TEST GRADING PROGRAM"
40 PRINT "ENTER THE STUDENT'S FIVE ANSWERS AS REQUESTED"
50 RESTORE
60 N = 0
70 FOR I=1 TO 5
80  PRINT "ANSWER NUMBER";I;
90  INPUT A
100  READ B
110  PRINT A,B,
120  IF A=B THEN PRINT "CORRECT": N=N+1 ELSE PRINT ,"WRONG"
130  PRINT
140 NEXT I
150 PRINT N;"RIGHT OUT OF 5 WHICH IS";
160 PRINT INT(N/5 * 100);"%"
170 PRINT "ANY MORE TESTS TO GRADE";
180 INPUT "--1=YES, 2=NO";Z
190 IF Z=1 THEN CLS: GOTO 50
200 DATA 65,23,17,56,39
```

SAMPLE ANSWER FOR EXERCISE 50-2:

```
100 CLS
110 PRINT : PRINT
120 PRINT "ENTER THE NUMBER OF THE INVESTMENT"
130 PRINT
140 PRINT "   1 - CERTIFICATE OF DEPOSIT"
150 PRINT "   2 - BANK SAVINGS ACCOUNT"
160 PRINT "   3 - CREDIT UNION"
170 PRINT "   4 - MORTGAGE LOAN"
180 PRINT : INPUT "INVESTMENT";F
190 ON F GOTO 1000, 2000, 3000, 4000
200 GOTO 100
1000 REM * CERTIFICATE OF DEPOSIT PROGRAM GOES HERE *
1010 PRINT "THE C.D. PROGRAM HAS YET TO BE WRITTEN."
1020 GOSUB 10000 : GOTO 100
2000 REM * BANK SAVINGS ACCOUNT PROGRAM *
2010 CLS : PRINT "THE ROUTINE CALCULATES SIMPLE
INTEREST"
```

```
2020 PRINT "ON DEPOSITS HELD FOR A SPECIFIED PERIOD"
2030 PRINT "WITH A SPECIFIED PERCENTAGE OF INTEREST." : PRINT
2040 PRINT : INPUT "HOW LARGE IS THE DEPOSIT (IN DOLLARS)";P
2050 INPUT "HOW LONG WILL YOU LEAVE IT IN (IN DAYS)";D
2060 INPUT "WHAT INTEREST RATE DO YOU EXPECT (IN %)";R
2070 CLS : PRINT : PRINT
2080 PRINT "A STARTING PRINCIPAL OF $";P;"AT A RATE"
2090 PRINT "OF";R;"% FOR";D;"DAYS YIELDS INTEREST OF"
2100 REM INTEREST = (%/YR)/(DAYS/YR) * DAYS * PRINCIPAL
2200 U$ = "$$####.##"
2210 I = R / 100 / 365 * D * P
2300 PRINT : PRINT TAB(17) : PRINT USING U$;I
2400 END
3000 REM * CREDIT UNION PROGRAM GOES HERE *
3010 PRINT "THE C.U. PROGRAM HAS YET TO BE WRITTEN."
3020 GOSUB 10000 : GOTO 100
4000 REM * MORTGAGE LOAN PROGRAM GOES HERE *
4010 PRINT "THE M.L. PROGRAM HAS YET TO BE WRITTEN."
4020 GOSUB 10000 : GOTO 100
10000 FOR I = 1 TO 1000 : NEXT I : RETURN
```

SAMPLE ANSWER FOR EXERCISE 53-1:

```
10 ON ERROR GOTO 100
20 CLS
30 FOR I = 1 TO 10
40  X = INT(RND*21) : F = X - 10/X
50  PRINT I, "X=";X,"F(X)=";F;
60  IF F<0 THEN PUNT ELSE PRINT
70  IF X=20 THEN READ A
80 NEXT I
90 INPUT "PRESS ENTER TO CONTINUE ",Z : GOTO 20
100 IF ERR=2 THEN 140
110 IF ERR=4 THEN 130
120 PRINT "ERROR" : END
130 PRINT "OUT OF DATA ERROR IN LINE ";ERL: RESUME NEXT
140 PRINT : PRINT "SYNTAX ERROR IN LINE ";ERL: RESUME NEXT
```

SECTION C

PREPARED USER PROGRAMS

12-Hour Clock

```
1 REM * COPYRIGHT (C) 1986 BY COMPUSOFT. ALL RIGHTS RESERVED. *
3 REM *                <<<<< 12-HOUR CLOCK >>>>>              *
10 INPUT "THE HOUR IS"; E
20 F = INT(E/10) : E = E - (F*10)
30 INPUT "THE MINUTES ARE"; C
40 D = INT(C/10) : C = C - (D*10)
50 INPUT "THE SECONDS ARE"; A
60 CLS
70 B = INT(A/10) : A = A - (B*10)
80 FOR N=1 TO 680 : NEXT N
90 A = A + 1
100 IF A>9 THEN 120
110 GOTO 310
120 A = 0
130 B = B + 1
140 IF B>5 THEN 160
150 GOTO 310
160 B = 0
170 C = C + 1
180 IF C>9 THEN 200
190 GOTO 310
200 C = 0
210 D = D + 1
220 IF D>5 THEN 240
230 GOTO 310
240 D = 0
250 E = E + 1
260 IF E>9 THEN 280
270 GOTO 300
280 E = 0
290 F = F + 1
300 IF (F=1) AND (E=3) THEN A=0 : B=0 : C=0 : D=0 :
    E=1 : F=0
310 LOCATE 11,29 : PRINT F;E;":";D;C;":"B;A;
320 GOTO 80
```

Change the 2nd value of the FOR-NEXT loop in Line 80 according to the Computer you're using:

1000 SX, use 820
2000, use 2000
3000s, use 2800

Checksum for Business

For those responsible for inventory numbers or check clearing and balancing in business, a checksum is a most useful testing "code." This simple program calculates error-free checksums almost instantly. It is designed for 6-digit numbers and so can be used for stock number verification or other applications.

```
1 REM * COPYRIGHT (C) 1986 BY COMPUSOFT.  ALL RIGHTS RESERVED *
3 REM *       <<<<< CHECKSUM FOR BUSINESS >>>>>               *
10 PRINT
20 INPUT "THE FIRST DIGIT IS";A
30 INPUT "THE SECOND DIGIT IS";B
40 INPUT "THE THIRD DIGIT IS";C
50 INPUT "THE FOURTH DIGIT IS";D
60 INPUT "THE FIFTH DIGIT IS";E
70 INPUT "THE SIXTH DIGIT IS";F
80 PRINT
90 PRINT "THE NUMBER IS";A;B;C;D;E;F
100 S = A+2*B+C+2*D+E+2*F
110 T = INT(S/10)
120 U = S - T * 10
130 S = T + U
140 IF S>9 THEN 110
150 PRINT "   THE CHECKDIGIT IS"; S
```

Dow-Jones Industrial Average Forecaster

There is no guarantee that this program will make you instantly wealthy, but it is an example of converting a financial magazine article into a usable computer program. The article describing the market premises on which this program is built appeared in Forbes Magazine.

```
1 REM * COPYRIGHT (C) 1986 BY COMPUSOFT. ALL RIGHTS RESERVED. *
3 REM *   <<<<< DOW-JONES AVERAGE FORECASTER >>>>>          *
10 CLS
20 PRINT "*** PROJECTS TARGET DOW-JONES INDUSTRIAL AVERAGE
   AS A "
30 PRINT "FUNCTION OF YEARS JDI EARNINGS AND INFLATION RATE ***"
40 PRINT
50 REM * K = COST OF MONEY. ASSUME 3% *
60 K = .03
70 REM * P = RISK PREMIUM OF STOCK OVER BONDS. ASSUME 1% *
80 P = .01
90 PRINT "DO YOU KNOW YEARS PROJECTED EARNINGS OF 30 DJI (Y/N)";
100 INPUT A$
110 IF A$="Y" THEN 290
120 PRINT
130 PRINT "THIS METHOD WILL GIVE EARNINGS APPROXIMATIONS USING
    THE NEWSPAPER PRICES AND"
140 PRINT "P/E RATIOS.  BETTER FORECASTS OF EACH COMPANY'S
    EARNINGS MAY GIVE AN IMPROVED"
150 PRINT "OVERALL FORECAST"
160 PRINT
170 D=0
180 FOR N= 1 TO 30
190   READ A$
200   PRINT "WHAT IS THE CURRENT PRICE OF >--> ";A$;" <--<;
210   INPUT P
220   PRINT "THE CURRENT P/E RATIO: ";
230   INPUT R
240   E=P/R
250   D=E+D
260 NEXT N
270 PRINT
280 GOTO 330
290 PRINT "WHAT IS THE TOTAL PROJECTED EARNINGS FOR 1 SHARE OF
    EACH";
300 INPUT D
310 REM * I = ESTIMATED INFLATION RATE *
```

```
320 PRINT "WHAT IS THE INFLATION RATE";
330 INPUT I
340 T=D/(K+P+I*.01)
350 R=T/D
360 PRINT
370 PRINT "INFL. RATE","DJI EARN.","PROJ DJ AVE.","AVE./EARN.
    RATIO"
380 PRINT
390 PRINT I,D,T,R
400 DATA ALLIED CHEM., ALCOA, AMER. BRANDS, AMER. CAN, AMER. BELL
410 DATA BETH. STEEL, CHRYSLER, DUPONT, E. KODAK, ESMARK, EXXON
420 DATA GEN. ELECT., GEN. FOODS, GEN. MOTORS, GOODYEAR, INCO
430 DATA INT. HARV., INT. PAPER, JOHNS-MAN, MINN. MM.,
    OWENS-ILLS.
440 DATA PROCTOR & GAM., SEARS, STD. OIL CAL., TEXACO, UNION
    CARBIDE
450 DATA U.S. STEEL, UNITED TECHNOL., WESTINGHOUSE, WOOLWORTH
```

Craps

The game is as old as history -- testimonial to the intelligence and ingenuity of our ancient ancestors and an excellent way to demonstrate the running of twin Random Number Generators.

You don't need to know how to play the game -- the Computer will quickly teach you. (...There's one born every minute...)

```
1 REM * COPYRIGHT (C) 1986 BY COMPUSOFT. ALL RIGHTS RESERVED. *
3 REM *              <<<<<  CRAPS  >>>>>               *
10 CLS
20 INPUT "PRESS <ENTER> TO CONTINUE"; A$
30 CLS
40 GOSUB 250
50 PNT = ROLL
60 PRINT
70 PRINT "YOU ROLLED "; ROLL,,
80 ON ROLL GOSUB 100,140,140,170,170,170,110,170,170,170,110,140
90 GOTO 20
100 REM USED FOR THE ON STATEMENT IF ROLL=1 (WHICH IT CAN'T)
110 PRINT "YOU WIN!"
120 PRINT
130 RETURN
140 PRINT "YOU LOSE!"
```

```
150 PRINT
160 RETURN
170 PRINT "YOUR POINT IS "; PNT
180 PRINT
190 GOSUB 250
200 MARK = ROLL
210 PRINT "YOU ROLLED ";MARK
220 IF PNT = MARK THEN 110
230 IF MARK = 7 THEN 140
240 GOTO 190
250 DIE1 = INT(RND*6+1)
260 DIE2 = INT(RND*6+1)
270 ROLL = DIE1 + DIE2
280 RETURN
```

Sorry

SORRY is a popular board game by Parker Brothers. This program demonstrates how to load a deck of cards into a numerical array, draw them out in a random fashion, "reshuffle" the deck after the last card is drawn, and continue drawing. The program will pause between each drawing of the cards, allowing as much time as desired to actually move the pieces on your own SORRY board. Have fun!

```
1 REM * COPYRIGHT (C) 1986 BY COMPUSOFT. ALL RIGHTS RESERVED. *
3 REM *              <<<<< SORRY >>>>>                        *
10 RANDOMIZE : CLS : DIM A(45)
20 PRINT "STAND BY FOR THE SHUFFLING OF THE DECK OF CARDS"
30 PRINT : PRINT : PRINT
40 FOR N = 1 TO 45 : READ A(N) : NEXT N
50 PRINT : PRINT : PRINT
60 Y=1
70 PRINT "SHUFFLING COMPLETED . . . . GAME BEGINS!" : PRINT
80 R = INT(RND*45+1)
90 M = A(R)
100 IF M=0 THEN 80
110 A(R)=0 : T=0
120 FOR Z = 1 TO 45
130   T=A(Z) + T
140 NEXT Z
150 PRINT TAB(34);"PRESS ENTER ";:INPUT A$
160 IF T=0 THEN 180
```

```
170 GOTO 210
180 PRINT "END OF THE DECK.  THE CARDS ARE BEING RESHUFFLED"
190 RESTORE
200 GOTO 30
210 IF Y<0 THEN 240
220 PRINT TAB(10); "RED"
230 GOTO 250
240 PRINT TAB(60);"GREEN"
250 IF M=13 THEN 270
260 PRINT TAB(B+10); M
270 ON M GOTO 290,310,540,360,540,540,380,540,540,410,430,540,450
280 GOTO 520
290 PRINT TAB(B);"MAY MOVE A PIECE OUT"
300 GOTO 540
310 PRINT TAB(B);"MAY MOVE A NEW PIECE OUT"
320 PRINT : PRINT
330 PRINT TAB(B+5);"DRAW AGAIN . . ."
340 PRINT
350 GOTO 580
360 PRINT TAB(B);"MUST BACK UP 4 SPACES"
370 GOTO 540
380 PRINT TAB(B);"MAY SPLIT THE 7 BETWEEN"
390 PRINT TAB(B+3);" 2 PIECES"
400 GOTO 540
410 PRINT TAB(B);"MAY MOVE BACKWARDS 1 SPACE"
420 GOTO 540
430 PRINT TAB(B);"CAN SWAP A PIECE WITH OPPONENT"
440 GOTO 540
450 PRINT : PRINT
460 IF B=0 THEN 510
470 PRINT "     GOTCHA             <<<====<<<     <<<====<<<";
480 PRINT TAB(60);"S O R R Y !"
490 PRINT : PRINT
500 GOTO 540
510 PRINT "S O R R Y !        >>>====>>>     >>>====>>>";
520 PRINT TAB(70);"GOTCHA !"
530 PRINT TAB(40);"*"
540 FOR T=1 TO 1000 : NEXT T : FOR X=1 TO 4
550 PRINT TAB(40);"*"
560 NEXT X
570 Y = Y * (-1)
580 IF Y>0 THEN B=0 ELSE B=51
```

```
590 GOTO 80
600 DATA 1,1,1,1,1,2,2,2,2,3,3,3,3,4,4,4,4,5,5,5,5,7,7,7,7,8,8
610 DATA 8,8,10,10,10,10,11,11,11,11,12,12,12,12,13,13,13,13
```

Slowpoke

The kiddies will enjoy this one. It tests reaction time. When the Computer says "GO," you press the CTRL BREAK key to stop it. Then it's the next player's turn to RUN it. The player who stops it on the smallest number wins. Any player who gets a "SLOWPOKE" has to take the dog for a walk.

With a little easy rework of the PRINT statements, it can be converted into a "drunkometer" reaction time tester.

To change the speed of the printing, you can add a short FOR-NEXT loop between Lines 110 and 120.

```
1 REM * COPYRIGHT (C) 1986 BY COMPUSOFT. ALL RIGHTS RESERVED. *
3 REM *                  <<<<< SLOWPOKE >>>>>                    *
10 PRINT "   GET READY . . . . . . . . . . ."
20 FOR B=1 TO 500 : NEXT B
30 PRINT : PRINT : PRINT
40 PRINT TAB(30), "GET SET . . . . . . . . ."
50 X = RND(1500)
60 FOR N=1 TO X : NEXT N
70 CLS
80 PRINT : PRINT : PRINT : PRINT : PRINT
90 PRINT TAB(30), "G   O   !   !   !"
100 FOR Z=1 TO 50
110  PRINT Z
120 NEXT Z
130 PRINT : PRINT : PRINT
140 PRINT "    S  L  O  W    P  O  K  E"
150 FOR N=1 TO 1000 : NEXT N
```

Test Grader Program

```
1 REM * COPYRIGHT (C) 1986 BY COMPUSOFT. ALL RIGHTS RESERVED. *
3 REM *             <<<<< TEST GRADER PROGRAM >>>>>            *
10 CLS : N = 10
20 PRINT "WOULD YOU LIKE TO INPUT THE ANSWER"
30 PRINT "ONE AT A TIME OR 5 AT A TIME (ENTER 1 OR 5)" :
   INPUT T
40 IF (T=1) OR (T=5) THEN 60
50 GOTO 30
60 INPUT "ENTER THE STUDENT'S NAME (LAST NAME, FIRST NAME)" ;
   A$ , B$
70 CLS : PRINT "TEST FOR " ; B$ ; "  " ; A$
80 RESTORE
90 R = 0
100 FOR I=1 TO N STEP T
110  PRINT "ENTER ANSWER"; : IF T=5 THEN PRINT "S";I;"THROUGH ";
120  PRINT I + T - 1;
130  IF T=5 THEN INPUT A$(I),A$(I+1),A$(I+2),A$(I+3),A$(I+4) :
     GOTO 150
140  INPUT A$(I)
150 NEXT I
160 CLS
170 PRINT "RESULTS ON TEST FROM "; B$; " "; A$;  ":"
180 FOR I = 1 TO N
190  PRINT A$(I),
200  READ Z$ : PRINT Z$,
210  IF A$(I) = Z$ THEN PRINT "CORRECT"; : R=R+1
220  PRINT
230 NEXT I
240 PRINT "PERCENTAGE CORRECT:"; INT(R / N * 100 + .5)
250 PRINT : GOTO 60
260 DATA 5,3,A,D,C,E,T,T,F,T
```

Wheel of Fortune
(Or ... Never Give a Sucker an Even Break.)

Modeled after the large wheels of fortune found at carnivals and other such gatherings, this graphics program accurately replicates its odds. The numbers are read from a DATA bank and "rotated" through "windows" as the wheel is "spun".

As commonly played, a $1 bet on any number, 1, 2, 5, 10, 20 or 40 (the joker and Tandy) returns those amounts -- if that number comes up. If not -- it's a cheap education.

Step right up, stranger. Try your luck at the wheel of fortune.

```
1 REM * COPYRIGHT (C) 1986 BY COMPUSOFT. ALL RIGHTS RESERVED. *
3 REM *                 <<<<< THE WHEEL OF FORTUNE >>>>>       *
10 RANDOMIZE TIMER
20 DEFINT A-Z
30 DIM A(60),X(13),Y(13)
40 FOR I = 1 TO 60 : READ A(I) : NEXT I
50 FOR I = 0 TO 13 : READ Y(I),X(I) : NEXT I
60 REM *** FIRST SCREEN ***
70 CLS : KEY OFF
80 PRINT "STEP RIGHT UP, STRANGER.  TRY YOUR HAND AT THE " :
   PRINT : PRINT
90 PRINT TAB(6);"W H E E L  O F  F O R T U N E" : PRINT : PRINT
100 PRINT "PAYOFFS IN DOLLARS FOR A $1 BET ARE 1, 2, 5, 10, 20." :
    PRINT
110 PRINT "SPECIALS ARE THE JOKER (13) AND THE TANDY MICRO (99),
    EACH PAYING $40!" : PRINT
120 INPUT "ENTER YOUR CHOICE AS A 1, 2, 5, 10, 13, 20, OR 99";B
130 IF B=1 OR B=2 OR B=5 OR B=10 OR B=13 OR B=20 OR B=99 THEN 150
    ELSE 120
140 REM *** DRAW THE WHEEL ***
150 CLS
160 P = INT(RND*54 + 1)  :REM STARTING POSITION IN ARRAY
170 COLOR 31,0 : PRINT TAB(32)"WHEEL OF FORTUNE" : COLOR 7,0
180 LOCATE 3,36 : PRINT ">>----<<"
190 REM *** DRAW THE SQUARES ***
200 FOR C=7 TO 13
210  LOCATE Y(C),X(C)
220  PRINT STRING$(8,220);
230  FOR TOP=1 TO 3
240   LOCATE Y(C)+TOP,X(C)
```

```
250    PRINT CHR$(221)STRING$(6,32)CHR$(222);
260   NEXT TOP
270   LOCATE Y(C)+TOP,X(C)
280   PRINT STRING$(8,223);
290 NEXT C
300 LOCATE 17,32 : PRINT "ROUND AND ROUND IT GOES..."; 
310 LOCATE 2Ø,34 : PRINT "JOKER (13) &"
320 PRINT TAB(32);"TANDY MICRO (99)"
330 PRINT TAB(32);"BOTH PAY 4Ø TO 1";
340 REM *** SPINNING LOOP ***
350 FOR S = 1 TO 1ØØ + INT(RND*2 + 1)
360  FOR I = Ø TO 6
370   LOCATE Y(I),X(I)
380   PRINT A(P+I);
390  NEXT I
400  IF S < 65 THEN 46Ø
410  R = (S-65)^2
420  LOCATE 17,32
430  IF S > 98 THEN PRINT "PAYOFFS GO TO THE        "; ELSE  PRINT "ALMOST THERE . . . .          ";
440  IF S >= 1Ø2 THEN 46Ø
450   FOR DELAY = 1 TO R : NEXT DELAY
460  P = P - 1
470  IF P = Ø THEN P = 54
480 NEXT S
490 Q = A(P+4)
500 PRINT TAB(39);
510 GOSUB 65Ø
520 X = Ø
530 LOCATE 2Ø,3Ø : PRINT "YOUR CHOICE WAS";
540 Q = B
550 GOSUB 65Ø
560 LOCATE 21,28 : PRINT SPACE$(22)
570 LOCATE 22,32 : PRINT SPACE$(2Ø);
580 IF B <> A(P+4) THEN LOCATE 22,32 : PRINT "YOU LOSE." :  GOTO 6ØØ
590 LOCATE 21,3Ø : PRINT "YOU WIN AT"; ODDS;"TO 1 "
600 LOCATE 23,27 : PRINT "PRESS <";
610 COLOR 31,Ø : PRINT "ENTER"; : COLOR 7,Ø
620 INPUT "> TO CONTINUE";A$
630 GOTO 7Ø
640 REM *** CALCULATE CHOICE ***
650 ODDS = Q
```

```
660 IF (Q<>13) AND (Q<>99) THEN PRINT Q : RETURN
670 ODDS = 40
680 IF Q = 99 THEN PRINT " TANDY MICRO" ELSE PRINT " JOKER"
690 RETURN
700 REM *** NUMBERS FOR THE WHEEL ***
710 DATA 1,2,99,1,5,1,2,1,10,1,2,1,5,1,2,1,5,1,2,1,20,1,2,10
720 DATA 1,2,1,5,1,2,1,5,1,2,13,1,2,1,10,1,2,1,2
730 DATA 1,20,1,2,5,1,2,10,1,2,5,1,2,99,1,5,1
740 REM *** LOCATIONS FOR BOXES, VALUES IN BOXES ***
750 DATA 12,3,9,14,7,26,6,38,7,50,9,62,12,74
760 DATA 10,1,7,12,5,24,4,36,5,48,7,60,10,72
```

Alexander's Ragtime Band

This utilizes the SOUND statement to reproduce the old Dixieland favorite.

```
1 REM * COPYRIGHT (C) 1986 BY COMPUSOFT. ALL RIGHTS RESERVED. *
3 REM           <<<<< ALEXANDER'S RAGTIME BAND >>>>>          *
10 CLS
20 DEFINT A
30 REM *** CALCULATE CHECKSUM ON DATA ***
40 FOR X = 1 TO 194
50  READ A
60  B = B + A
70 NEXT X
80 IF B <> 660329! THEN PRINT "CHECKSUM ERROR" : STOP
90 RESTORE
100 REM *** CLOCK TICKS 18.2 TIMES PER SECOND ***
110 FOR X = 1 TO 26
120  READ A,L
130  SOUND A,L*18.2
140 NEXT X
150 RESTORE
160 FOR X = 1 TO 26
170  READ A,L
180  IF A=32767 THEN A=32767/1.3348
190  SOUND A*1.3348,L*18.2
200 NEXT X
210 WHILE A <> 784
220  READ A,L
230  SOUND A,L*18.2
240 WEND
250 END
```

```
260 REM *** DATA IS NOTE (IN HZ CONCERT PITCH), LENGTH (IN
    SECONDS) ***
270 DATA 262,1,440,1,349,1
280 DATA 466,.125,494,.375,466,.125,494,1,32767,.375
290 DATA 466,.125,494,.375,587,.125,494,1,32767,.375
300 DATA 466,.125,494,.375,587,.125,466,.375,440,.125,392,.375,
    330,.125
310 DATA 466,.25,440,.25,32767,.25,392,1,440, .25,32767,.375
320 DATA 494,.125,523,.375,554,.125,587,.25,32767,.25
330 DATA 659,.375,494,.125,587,.25,659,.5,494,.25
340 DATA 587,.325,32767,.05,587,.125,659,.375,494,.125,587,
    .5,32767,.5
350 DATA 392,.5,493,.375,294,.125,392,.375,466,.125,392,.375,
    294,.125
360 DATA 392,.375,466,.125,494,.25,587,.5,32767,1.25
370 DATA 440,.125,32767,.05,440,.45,32767,.05,440,.45,494,.5
380 DATA 554,.25,440,.375,32767,.125,440,.25,494,.325,32767,
    .05,494,.125
390 DATA 554,.375,32767,.125,587,1.5,32767,1.875
400 DATA 466,.125,494,.375,466,.125,494,1,32767,.375
410 DATA 466,.125,494,.375,587,.125,494,1,32767,.375
420 DATA 466,.125,494,.375,587,.125,466,.375,440,.125,392,.375,
    330,.125
430 DATA 466,.25,440,.25,32767,.25,392,.75,32767,.05,587,.5,
    32767,.05,784,1
```

SECTION D

APPENDICES

Appendix A

The ASCII Chart

ASCII value	Character
000	(null)
001	☺
002	☻
003	♥
004	♦
005	♣
006	♠
007	(beep)
008	◘
009	(tab)
010	(line feed)
011	(home)
012	(form feed)
013	(carriage return)
014	♫
015	☼
016	►
017	◄
018	↕
019	‼
020	¶
021	§
022	▬
023	↨
024	↑
025	↓
026	→
027	←
028	(cursor right)
029	(cursor left)
030	(cursor up)
031	(cursor down)
032	(space)
033	!
034	"
035	#
036	$
037	%
038	&
039	'
040	(
041	)
042	*
043	+
044	,
045	-
046	.
047	/
048	0
049	1
050	2
051	3
052	4
053	5
054	6
055	7
056	8
057	9
058	:
059	;
060	<
061	=
062	>
063	?

ASCII value	Character	ASCII value	Character
064	@	095	—
065	A	096	`
066	B	097	a
067	C	098	b
068	D	099	c
069	E	100	d
070	F	101	e
071	G	102	f
072	H	103	g
073	I	104	h
074	J	105	i
075	K	106	j
076	L	107	k
077	M	108	l
078	N	109	m
079	O	110	n
080	P	111	o
081	Q	112	p
082	R	113	q
083	S	114	r
084	T	115	s
085	U	116	t
086	V	117	u
087	W	118	v
088	X	119	w
089	Y	120	x
090	Z	121	y
091	[	122	z
092	\	123	{
093	]	124	¦
094	∧	125	}

ASCII value	Character
126	~
127	⌂
128	Ç
129	ü
130	é
131	â
132	ä
133	à
134	å
135	ç
136	ê
137	ë
138	è
139	ï
140	î
141	ì
142	Ä
143	Å
144	E
145	æ
146	Æ
147	ô
148	ö
149	ò
150	û
151	ù
152	ÿ
153	Ö
154	Ü
155	¢
156	£
157	¥
158	Pt
159	ƒ
160	á
161	í
162	ó
163	ú
164	ñ
165	Ñ
166	ª
167	º
168	¿
169	⌐
170	¬
171	½
172	¼
173	¡
174	«
175	»
176	░
177	▒
178	▓
179	│
180	┤
181	╡
182	╢
183	╖
184	╕
185	╣
186	║
187	╗
188	╝
189	╜
190	╛
191	┐

ASCII value	Character
192	└
193	┴
194	┬
195	├
196	─
197	┼
198	╞
199	╟
200	╚
201	╔
202	╩
203	╦
204	╠
205	═
206	╬
207	╧
208	╨
209	╤
210	╥
211	╙
212	╘
213	╒
214	╓
215	╫
216	╪
217	┘
218	┌
219	█
220	▄
221	▌
222	▐
223	▀
224	α
225	β
226	Γ
227	π
228	Σ
229	σ
230	μ
231	τ
232	Φ
233	θ
234	Ω
235	δ
236	∞
237	Ø
238	ϵ
239	∩
240	≡
241	±
242	≥
243	≤
244	⌠
245	⌡
246	÷
247	≈
248	°
249	•
250	·
251	√
252	^{n}
253	^{2}
254	■
255	(blank 'FF')

Appendix B

Reserved Words

Using these reserved words as variables will result in a syntax error.

ABS
AND
ASC
ATN
AUTO
BEEP
BLOAD
BSAVE
CALL
CDBL
CHAIN
CHDIR
CHR$
CINT
CIRCLE
CLEAR
CLOSE
CLS
COLOR
COM
COMMON
CONT
COS
CSNG
CSRLIN
CVD
CVI
CVS
DATA
DATE$
DEF
DEFDBL
DEFINT
DEFSNG
DEFSTR
DEF FN
DEF SEG
DEF USR
DELETE
DIM
DRAW
EDIT
ELSE
END
ENVIRON
ENVIRON$
EOF
EQV
ERASE
ERDEV
ERDEV$
ERL
ERR
ERROR
EXP
FIELD
FILES
FIX
FN
FOR
FRE
GET
GOSUB
GOTO
HEX$
IF
IMP
INKEY$
INP
INPUT
INPUT#
INPUT$

INSTR
INT
INTER$
IOCTL
IOCTL$
KEY
KEY$
KILL
LEFT$
LEN
LET
LINE
LIST
LLIST
LOAD
LOC
LOCATE
LOCK†
LOF
LOG
LPOS
LPRINT
LSET
MERGE
MID$
MKDIR
MKD$
MKI$
MKS$
MOD
MOTOR
NAME
NEW
NEXT
NOISE*
NOT
OCT$
OFF
ON
OPEN
OPTION BASE
OR
OUT
PAINT
PALETTE
PALETTE USING
PCOPY*
PEEK
PEN
PLAY
PMAP
POINT
POKE
POS
PRESET
PRINT
PRINT#
PSET
PUT
RANDOMIZE
READ
REM
RENUM
RESET
RESTORE
RESUME
RETURN
RIGHT$
RMDIR
RND
RSET
RUN
SAVE
SBN
SCREEN
SGN
SHELL
SIN
SOUND
SPACE$
SPC
SQR
STEP
STICK
STOP
STR$
STRIG
STRING$
SWAP
SYSTEM
TAB
TAN
TERM†
THEN
TIME$
TIMER
TO
TROFF
TRON
UNLOCK†
USING
USR
VAL
VARPTR
VARPTR$
VIEW
WAIT
WEND
WHILE
WIDTH
WINDOW
WRITE
WRITE#
XOR

* not on Tandy 2000
† Version 3.2 BASIC only

Error Messages

Code	Error
1	NEXT without FOR
2	Syntax error
3	RETURN without GOSUB
4	Out of DATA
5	Illegal function call
6	Overflow
7	Out of memory
8	Undefined line number
9	Subscript out of range
10	Duplicate Definition
11	Division by zero
12	Illegal direct
13	Type mismatch
14	Out of string space
15	String too long
16	String formula too complex
17	Can't continue
18	Undefined user function
19	No RESUME
20	RESUME without error
21	Unprintable error
22	Missing operand
23	Line buffer overflow
24	Device Timeout
25	Device Fault
26	FOR without NEXT
27	Out of Paper

Code	Error
29	WHILE without WEND
30	WEND without WHILE
	DISK ERRORS
50	FIELD overflow
51	Internal error
52	Bad file number
53	File not found
54	Bad file mode
55	File already open
57	Device I/O Error
58	File already exists
61	Disk full
62	Input past end
63	Bad record number
64	Bad file name
66	Direct statement in file
67	Too many files
68	Device Unavailable
69	Communication buffer overflow
70	Permission Denied*/Disk write protected
71	Disk not Ready
72	Disk Media error
73	Advanced Feature
74	Rename across disks
75	Path/File Access Error
76	Path not found
77	Deadlock

* 1000 SX and 3000 Series

Advanced Feature (73): the programs contain a function or statement used only in Advanced BASIC; it isn't available in this BASIC.

Bad file mode (54): PUT or GET is used with a sequential file or closed file, to MERGE a non-ASCII file, or to execute an OPEN with a file mode other than input, output, append, or random.

Bad file name (64): an invalid form is used for the filename with BLOAD, BSAVE, KILL, OPEN, NAME, or FILES (e.g., a filename starting with a period).

Bad file number (52): a statement references a file with a buffer number that isn't OPEN or is outside the range of buffer numbers specified at initialization; also displayed when device name in the file specification is too long or invalid or the filename is too long or invalid.

Bad record number (63): the record number in a PUT or GET statement is either greater than the allowable maximum or equal to zero.

Can't continue (17): the command CONT is typed and there no program to continue, the program had just been EDITed, a line has just been added or deleted, or an error stopped the program.

Communication buffer overflow (69): a communication input statement is executed, but the input buffer is already full. You should use an ON ERROR statement to retry the input when this condition occurs. Subsequent inputs will attempt to clear this faster than the program can process them.

Deadlock (77): (used with networking) two separate users attempt to OPEN a file at the same time.

Device Fault (25): an attempt is made to enter the wrong device designation.

Device I/O error (57): an error occurred on a device I/O operation. DOS can't recover from the error.

Device Timeout (24): BASIC was not given information from an input/output device within a preset amount of time.

Device Unavailable (68): an attempt is made to OPEN a file to a device which doesn't exist. Either you do not have the hardware to support the device (such as printer), or a device is disabled. (For example, you may have used /C:0 on the BASIC command to start Disk BASIC. That would disable communications devices.)

Direct statement in file (66): a direct statement (i.e., data in non-ASCII form) is encountered while LOADing or CHAINing to an ASCII format file. The LOAD or CHAIN is terminated. The ASCII file should consist only of statements preceded by line numbers. A line feed character in the input stream may cause this error.

Disk full (61): there is no more storage space on diskette. When this error occurs, files will be closed.

Disk media error (72): most likely, the diskette is damaged. You can SAVE your files by copying them on to a new diskette.

Disk not ready (71): either there is no diskette in the drive or the drive door is not closed.

Division by zero (11): the Computer is asked to divide a number by Ø.

Duplicate Definition (10): the Computer is told to DIMension a numeric or string Matrix after it has already been DIMensioned earlier in the same program.

FIELD overflow (50): the number of bytes specified for the record length of a random file in the OPEN statement is fewer than the number a FIELD statement is attempting to allocate; also displayed when the end of the FIELD buffer is encountered while doing sequential I/O (PRINT#, WRITE#, INPUT#, etc.) to a random file.

File already exists (58): a NAME statement has specified a filename that is identical to a filename already on the diskette.

File already open (55): an attempt is made to OPEN an already opened file for sequential output or append, or to KILL an open file.

File not found (53): the file referenced by LOAD, KILL, NAME, FILES, or OPEN does not exist on the specified drive.

FOR without NEXT (26): an attempt is made to RUN a program containing a FOR-NEXT loop, but the word "NEXT" is missing.

Illegal direct (12): while in the Immediate, or Direct mode, the Computer is asked to execute a statement which is not legal in that mode.

Illegal function call (5): illegal values are used with the built-in math functions or the Computer cannot figure out what to compute because of the values it received.

Input past end (62): this is an end of file error. An INPUT statement is executed for a null (empty) file, or after all the data in a sequential file was already input. Avoid by using EOF to detect the end of file. This error also occurs if you try to read from a file that was OPENed for output or append.

Internal error (51): there has occurred an internal malfunction in BASIC. The conditions under which the message appeared need to be reported to your Computer dealer.

Line buffer overflow (23): a line that has too many characters was entered.

Missing operand (22): the Computer is not given all the information required to carry out its directive.

NEXT without FOR (1): an attempt is made to RUN a program containing a FOR-NEXT loop, but the word "FOR" is missing.

No RESUME (19): an ON ERROR GOTO statement is used to branch to a specified program line, and the Computer does not encounter a RESUME statement before the program stops.

Out of DATA (4): the Computer is told to READ more items from the DATA statement than are available.

Out of memory (7): an attempt is made to store a program larger than the Computer's memory storage space; also displayed when a matrix variable is assigned more elements than there is space in memory to store it or when expressions used in a program are too complicated.

Out of Paper (27): the printer is either out of paper or it is not turned on. Insert paper if you need to, check to see the printer is properly connected, and the power is on. Continue with the program.

Out of string space (14): more letters or characters are assigned to a string variable than it is capable of storing.

Overflow (6): the Computer is unable to use a number because it is too large; can also be created by routine mathematical calculations at either the statement or command levels.

Path/File Access Error (75): an attempt is made to use an inaccessible file's filename when OPENing or reNAMEing a file or when MaKing, ReMoving, or CHanging a DIRectory.

Path not found (76): a nonexistent path is specified when OPENing a file or when MaKing, ReMoving, or CHanging a DIRectory.

Permission Denied*/Disk write protected (70): an attempt is made to write to a diskette with a write protect tab on it.

Renamed across disks (74): a new drive number was used when a file was being reNAMEd.

---

* 1000 SX and 3000 Series

RESUME without error (20): the Computer encounters a RESUME statement without first finding an ON ERROR GOTO statement.

RETURN without GOSUB (3): the Computer reads a RETURN statement and there is no corresponding GOSUB.

String formula too complex (16): string manipulation has become too complicated or too long for the Computer.

String too long (15): an attempt is made to store more than 255 letters or characters in a string variable.

Subscript out of range (9): the elements in a numeric or string matrix are beyond the range of values reserved in the DIM statement.

Syntax error (2): a command, statement or function is misspelled, an operator is omitted, or punctuation is incorrect.

Too many files (67): using SAVE or OPEN an attempt is made to create a new file when all directory entries on the diskette are full or the file specification is invalid.

Type mismatch (13): a numeric value is assigned to a string variable or a string is assigned to a numeric variable.

Undefined line number (8): a branching statement such as GOTO or GOSUB calls for a Line number that does not exist.

Undefined user function (18): a function is called before it was defined with a DEF FN statement.

WEND without WHILE (30): a WEND was found before a matching WHILE was executed.

WHILE without WEND (29): a WHILE statement does not have a matching WEND. A WHILE was executing when an END, STOP, or RETURN statement was found.

Appendix D

Sequential File Sample Program

The following program demonstrates how a data file can be used to create a list of data items, process and update it. Study it carefully and think how similar programs might handle inventories or any sequential lists.

```
10 REM  * TEMPERATURE AND HUMIDITY RECORDING PROGRAM *
20 REM  * DATA STORAGE MUST START ON THE FIRST DAY OF
   THE MONTH *
30 CLS
40 INPUT "WHAT DAY OF THE MONTH IS IT"; DAY
50 INPUT "WHAT IS TODAY'S TEMPERATURE"; TEMP
60 INPUT "WHAT IS TODAY'S HUMIDITY"; HUM
70 PRINT : PRINT
80 N = 1
90 IF DAY = 1 THEN 330
   'ON FIRST DAY NO PRIOR DATA
100 REM  * INPUTTING DATA STORED ON DISK DRIVE *
110 PRINT "WE MUST LOAD PRIOR DAYS TEMP & HUMIDITY FROM
    THE DISK"
120 PRINT : PRINT
130 INPUT "PRESS 'ENTER' WHEN YOU ARE READY TO GO";A$
```

```
140 CLS : PRINT "DATA IS NOW BEING READ FROM THE DISK."
150 PRINT : PRINT : PRINT "DATE","TEMP","HUMIDITY" : PRINT
160 OPEN "TEMPDATA" FOR INPUT AS 1
170 D = 1
180 IF EOF(1) THEN 230
190 INPUT #1, D,T,H
200 PRINT D,T,H
210 TTOT = TTOT + T : HTOT = HTOT + H : N = N + 1
220 GOTO 180
230 CLOSE 1
240 REM  * MONTH'S AVERAGES TO DATE *
250 AVGT = (TTOT+TEMP)/N : AVGH = (HTOT+HUM)/N
    'COMPUTES THE AVERAGES
260 PRINT DAY, TEMP, HUM
270 PRINT : PRINT "    **    THIS MONTH'S AVERAGES    **"
280 PRINT TAB(12);"TEMP";TAB(23);"HUMIDITY"
290 PRINT TAB(12);INT(AVGT);TAB(23);INT(AVGH)
300 REM  * STORING TODAY'S TEMP & HUMIDITY ON DISK *
310 PRINT : PRINT : INPUT "PRESS 'ENTER' WHEN READY
    TO CONTINUE";A$
320 CLS : PRINT : PRINT
330 PRINT "TODAY'S TEMPERATURE AND HUMIDITY WILL
    NOW BE SAVED"
340 PRINT "TO DISK."
350 OPEN "TEMPDATA" FOR APPEND AS 1
360 PRINT #1, DAY,TEMP,HUM
370 CLOSE 1
380 PRINT "TODAY'S NUMBERS HAVE BEEN ADDED TO THE FILE."
```

Lines 10 to 90 are the initialization.

Lines 40 to 60 ask for the current day, temperature and humidity. These values are assigned to variables DAT, TEMP, and HUM.

Line 90 tests to see if this is the first set of data in the file. If so, execution branches to Line 330. If not, program execution flows to Line 100.

Lines 100 to 230 read in any previous data from the disk file.

Line 160 OPENs the file TEMPDATA for INPUT through file buffer number 1. The number of data items being read into variable D (equivalent to the number of days already recorded in the month) are set to 1 in Line 170.

Line 180 tests for the EOF, or End Of File. If the last data item has been read in, EOF is true and program execution branches to Line 230. Otherwise the next pair of data is read in by the INPUT# statement in Line 190.

The data is displayed by the PRINT statement in Line 200, and the month's totals are calculated in Line 210.

Line 220 continues the INPUT# loop. Line 230 CLOSEs the file.

Lines 240 to 290 calculate and display the current month's average temperature and humidity.

Line 250 determines the current month's average temperature and humidity by dividing the total (from Line 210) by the number of days currently read.

Lines 260 to 290 display the data to the screen.

Lines 300 to 380 store the data for the current day's temperature and humidity to the disk.

Line 350 OPENs the file TEMPDATA for an APPEND through file buffer number 1. Because this is an APPEND, any data sent to disk will be stored at the end of the file. If there is no data in the file, as is the case the first time around, the file will be created by APPEND, and the data will be saved as the first element of the file.

Our data is sent to disk by the PRINT# statement in Line 360.

The file is CLOSED in Line 370.

For a sample run of the program, assume it is the first day of the month. Enter plausible temperature and humidity figures. Continue RUNning the program until you have a cumulative listing for several days. Getting the feel for data files?

Be sure to SAVE this program as TEMPHUMD since it's a valuable lesson.

SECTION E

INDEX